FOUNDATIONS OF PARALLEL PROGRAMMING

Cambridge International Series on Parallel Computation

Managing Editor W.F. McColl,
Programming Research Group, University of Oxford

Editorial Board

T.F. Chan, *Department of Mathematics, University of California at Los Angeles*
A. Gottlieb, *Courant Institute, New York University*
R.M. Karp, *Computer Science Division, University of California at Berkeley*
M. Rem, *Department of Mathematics and Computer Science, Eindhoven University*
L.G. Valiant, *Aiken Computation Laboratory, Harvard University*

Titles in the series

1. G. Tel *Topics in Distributed Algorithms*
2. P. Hilbers *Processor Networks and Aspects of the Mapping Problem*
3. Y-D. Lyuu *Information Dispersal and Parallel Computation*
4. A. Gibbons & P. Spirakis (eds) *Lectures on Parallel Computation*
5. K. van Berkel *Handshake Circuits*

Cambridge International Series on Parallel Computation: 6

Foundations of Parallel Programming

David Skillicorn
Queen's University, Kingston

CAMBRIDGE
UNIVERSITY PRESS

CAMBRIDGE UNIVERSITY PRESS
Cambridge, New York, Melbourne, Madrid, Cape Town, Singapore, São Paulo

Cambridge University Press
The Edinburgh Building, Cambridge CB2 2RU, UK

Published in the United States of America by Cambridge University Press, New York

www.cambridge.org
Information on this title: www.cambridge.org/9780521455114

© Cambridge University Press 1994

First published 1994
This digitally printed first paperback version 2005

A catalogue record for this publication is available from the British Library

ISBN-13 978-0-521-45511-4 hardback
ISBN-10 0-521-45511-1 hardback

ISBN-13 978-0-521-01856-2 paperback
ISBN-10 0-521-01856-0 paperback

Contents

Preface   xi

1   The Key Idea   1

2   Approaches to Parallel Software Development   3
   2.1   What's Good About Parallelism   4
   2.2   What's Bad About Parallelism   5
   2.3   The State of the Art in Parallel Computing   6
   2.4   Models and their Properties   8
   2.5   Categorical Data Types   11
   2.6   Outline   14

3   Architectural Background   15
   3.1   Parallel Architectures   15
   3.2   The Standard Model   18
   3.3   Emulating Parallel Computations   20
      3.3.1   Emulating on Shared-Memory MIMD Architectures   21
      3.3.2   Emulating on Distributed-Memory MIMD Architectures   22
      3.3.3   Emulating on Constant-Valence MIMD Architectures   23
      3.3.4   Emulating on SIMD Architectures   24
   3.4   Implications for Models   25

4   Models and Their Properties   27
   4.1   Overview of Models   28
      4.1.1   Arbitrary Computation Structure Models   29
      4.1.2   Restricted Computation Structure Models   39
   4.2   Implications for Model Design   45

5   The Categorical Data Type of Lists   49
   5.1   Categorical Preliminaries   49
   5.2   Data Type Construction   50
   5.3   T-Algebras   52
   5.4   Polymorphism   57
   5.5   Summary of Data Type Construction   58
   5.6   Practical Implications   59

5.7   CDTs and Model Properties   61
5.8   Other List Languages   64
5.9   Connections to Crystal   65

6   Software Development Using Lists   67
6.1   An Integrated Software Development Methodology   67
6.2   Examples of Development by Transformation   70
6.3   Almost-Homomorphisms   72

7   Other Operations on Lists   75
7.1   Computing Recurrences   75
7.2   Permutations   79
7.3   Examples of CLO Programs   81
       7.3.1   List Reversal and FFT   81
       7.3.2   Shuffle and Reverse Shuffle   82
       7.3.3   Even-Odd and Odd-Even Split   83
7.4   CLO Properties   83
7.5   Sorting   85
       7.5.1   The Strategy and Initial CLO Program   85
       7.5.2   The Improved Version   87

8   A Cost Calculus for Lists   89
8.1   Cost Systems and Their Properties   89
8.2   A Strategy for a Parallel Cost Calculus   91
8.3   Implementations for Basic Operations   94
8.4   More Complex Operations   98
8.5   Using Costs with Equations   105
8.6   Handling Sizes Explicitly   112

9   Building Categorical Data Types   115
9.1   Categorical Data Type Construction   115
9.2   Type Functors   117
9.3   T-Algebras and Constructors   118
9.4   Polymorphism   122
9.5   Factorisation   125
9.6   Relationships between T-Algebras   126

10 Lists, Bags, and Finite Sets   129
10.1   Lists   129
10.2   Bags   131
10.3   Finite Sets   133

11 Trees   135
11.1   Building Trees   135
11.2   Accumulations   137
11.3   Computing Tree Catamorphisms   141

11.4 Modelling Structured Text by Trees 143
    11.4.1 Global Properties of Documents 144
    11.4.2 Search Problems 146
    11.4.3 Accumulations and Information Transfer 148
    11.4.4 Queries on Structured Text 148

12 Arrays   **151**
  12.1 Overview of Arrays 152
  12.2 Sequences and Their Properties 153
  12.3 Flat Array Construction 155
  12.4 Evaluation of Flat Array Catamorphisms 157
  12.5 Nested Arrays 158
  12.6 Evaluation of Nested Array Catamorphisms 161

13 Graphs   **163**
  13.1 Building Graphs 163
  13.2 Evaluation of Graph Catamorphisms 166
  13.3 More Complex Catamorphisms 167
  13.4 Construction of Other Graphs 168
  13.5 Molecules 169

14 Conclusions   **171**

A C++ Library for Lists   **173**

B Historical Background   **177**

Index   **194**

List of Figures

2.1   Role of a Model of Parallel Computation   8

3.1   A Shared-Memory MIMD Architecture   16
3.2   A Distributed-Memory MIMD Architecture   17
3.3   A Distributed-Memory MIMD Architecture   17
3.4   An SIMD Architecture   18
3.5   The Trace of a Parallel Computation   20
3.6   Power and Scalability of Architecture Classes   25

4.1   Summary of Properties – Arbitrary Computation Models   46
4.2   Summary of Properties – Restricted Computation Models   47

5.1   Homomorphism between T_A-Algebras   52
5.2   Homomorphism from an Initial T_A-Algebra   53
5.3   Evaluating a Catamorphism   54
5.4   Length expressed as a Catamorphism   55
5.5   Defining Prefix   61

6.1   An Integrated Scheme for Parallel Software Development   68
6.2   Basic Identities for Lists   70

7.1   Parallel Algorithm for Computing x_4   78
7.2   Parallel Algorithm for Computing $[x_0, x_1, x_2, x_3, x_4]$ 79
7.3   CLO with $n = 8$, $w = 1$ and $h = 0$ 80
7.4   CLO with $n = 8$, $w = 0$ and $h = 1$ 80
7.5   CLO with $n = 8$, $w = 1$ and $h = 1$ 81
7.6   Pairing Pattern Sequence for Reversal   82
7.7   Sequence for Shuffle and Reverse Shuffle   83
7.8   Sequence for Even-Odd and Odd-Even Split   84
7.9   Sequence for Merging using Alternated Reversal   86
7.10 Order-Reverse Alternate Group Sequence   87
7.11 Sequence After Collapsing Ordering and Reversal   88

8.1   Critical Paths that may Overlap in Time   92
8.2   Data Flow for Prefix   101
8.3   Data Flow for Concatenation Prefix   103
8.4   Summary of Operation Costs   106
8.5   Summary of Cost-Reducing Directions   110

9.1   T-Algebras and a T-Algebra Homomorphism   120
9.2   Relationship of a Data Type to its Components   121

9.3   General Computation of a Catamorphism 122
9.4   Promotion 123
9.5   Building a Generalised Map 124
9.6   Building a Generalised Reduction 124
9.7   Factoring Catamorphisms 125
9.8   Relationships between T-Algebra Categories 127
9.9   Catamorphism Relationships 128

10.1 Map for Lists 130
10.2 Reduction for Lists 131
10.3 Factorisation for Lists 131

11.1 Map for Trees 137
11.2 Reduction for Trees 138
11.3 Factoring Tree Catamorphisms 138
11.4 Evaluating a Tree Catamorphism 138
11.5 An Upwards Accumulation 139
11.6 A Downwards Accumulation 140
11.7 A Single Tree Contraction Step 142
11.8 A Simple Finite State Automaton 146

12.1 A Flat Array Catamorphism 158
12.2 Recursive Schema for Flat Array Catamorphisms 158
12.3 A Nested Array Catamorphism 161

13.1 Evaluating a Graph Catamorphism 166
13.2 A Graph Catamorphism Using an Array Catamorphism 167

Preface

This book is about ways of developing software that can be executed by parallel computers. Software is one of the most complex and difficult artefacts that humans build. Parallelism increases this complexity significantly. At the moment, parallel software is designed for specific kinds of architectures, and can only be moved from architecture to architecture by large-scale rewriting. This is so expensive that very few applications have been discovered for which the effort is worth it. These are mostly numeric and scientific.

I am convinced that the only way to move beyond this state of affairs and use parallelism in a wide variety of applications is to break the tight connection between software and hardware. When this is done, software can be moved with greater ease from architecture to architecture as new ones are developed or become affordable. One of the main claims of this book is that it is possible to do this while still delivering good performance on all architectures, although not perhaps the optimal wall-clock performance that obsesses the present generation of parallel programmers.

The approach presented in this book is a generalisation of abstract data types, which introduced modularity into software design. It is based on categorical data types, which encapsulate control flow as well as data representation. The semantics of powerful operations on a data type are decoupled from their implementation. This allows a variety of implementations, including parallel ones, without altering software. Categorical data types also face up to the issue of software construction: how can complex parallel software be developed, and developed in a way that addresses performance and correctness issues?

Although this book reports on research, much of it still very much in progress, many of the ideas can be applied immediately in limited ways. A major benefit of the categorical data type approach is that it provides both a structured way to search for algorithms, and structured programs when they are found. These structured programs are parameterised by component functions, and can be implemented by libraries in many existing languages. Small-scale parallel implementations can be built using mechanisms such as process forking. For application domains that warrant it, massive parallelism is also possible.

We use categorical data types as a *model* of parallel computation, that is an abstract machine that decouples the software level from the hardware levels. From the software perspective a model should be abstract enough to hide those details that programmers need not know – there are many such details in a parallel setting. A model should also make it possible to use all of the good software engineering techniques that have been discovered over the past few decades – reasoning about programs, stepwise refinement, modularity, and cost measures. From the hardware perspective, a model should be easy to implement, so that its performance is acceptable on different architectures, some of which might not even have been thought of yet. The difficult part is to satisfy these two kinds of requirements which are often in conflict.

The approach presented in this book integrates issues in software development, transformation, implementation, as well as architecture. It uses a construction that depends on category theory. For most readers, parts of the book may require supplemental reading. I have tried to point out suitable sources when they exist.

A book like this does not spring from a single mind. I am very grateful to the people at Oxford who introduced me to the Bird–Meertens formalism, from which this work grew, and who got me thinking about how to use new architectures effectively: Jeff Sanders, Richard Miller, Bill McColl, Geraint Jones and Richard Bird. Grant Malcolm's thesis introduced me to the construction of categorical data types. My colleagues and students have also been of great help in showing me how to understand and apply these ideas: Pawan Singh, Susanna Pelagatti, Ian Macleod, K.G. Kumar, Kuruvila Johnson, Mike Jenkins, Jeremy Gibbons, Darrell Conklin, Murray Cole, Wentong Cai, Françoise Baude, David Barnard, and Colin Banger. The C++ code in Appendix A was written by Amro Younes.

A large number of people read drafts of the book and made helpful comments which have improved it enormously. They include: Susanna Pelagatti, Gaétan Hains, Murray Cole, Wentong Cai, Françoise Baude, and David Barnard.

Chapter 1

The Key Idea

Homomorphisms are functions that respect the structure of their arguments. For structured types, this means that homomorphisms respect the way in which objects of the type are built. If a and b are objects of a structured type, and $\bowtie$ is an operation that builds them into a larger object of the structured type (a *constructor*), then h is a homomorphism if there exists a $\circledast$ such that

$$h(a \bowtie b) = h(a) \circledast h(b)$$

Intuitively this means that the value of h applied to the large object $a \bowtie b$ depends in a particular way (using $\circledast$) on the values of h applied to the pieces a and b. Of course, a and b may themselves be built from simpler objects, so that the decomposition implied by the equation can be repeated until base objects are reached.

This simple equation has two important implications.

1. The computation of h on a complex object is equivalent to a computation involving h applied to base objects of the structured type and applications of the operation $\circledast$. Structured types are often complex and finding useful homomorphisms can be difficult. Operations such as $\circledast$ exist within simpler algebraic structures and are often easier to find.

2. The computations of $h(a)$ and $h(b)$ are independent and so can be carried out in parallel. Because of the recursion, the amount of parallelism generated in this simple way is often substantial. It is well-structured, regular parallelism which is easy to exploit.

The first point is the foundation for software development because it makes it possible to look for and build programs on complex structures by finding simpler algebraic structures. The second point is the foundation for effective computation of homomorphisms on parallel architectures; and computation that is often both architecture-independent and efficient. These two properties make computation of homomorphisms on structured types an ideal model for general-purpose parallel computation.

Restricting programs to the computation of homomorphisms might seem at first to be very limiting. In fact, many interesting computations can be expressed as homomorphisms, and a great many others as almost-homomorphisms for which the same benefits apply.

The implications of these ideas are far-reaching. The rest of the book develops them for practical parallel programming. Unlike many other approaches to parallel programming, we are concerned with efficiency in the software development process far more than efficiency of execution; and we seek to apply parallelism to all areas of computation, not just the numeric and scientific. Even computations that appear ill-structured and irregular often show considerable regularity from the perspective of an appropriate type.

Chapter 2

Approaches to Parallel Software Development

Parallel computation has been a physical reality for about two decades, and a major topic for research for at least half that time. However, given the whole spectrum of applications of computers, almost nothing is actually computed in parallel. In this chapter we suggest reasons why there is a great gap between the promise of parallel computing and the delivery of real parallel computations, and what can be done to close the gap.

The basic problem in parallel computation, we suggest, is the mismatch between the requirements of parallel software and the properties of the parallel computers on which it is executed. The gap between parallel software and hardware is a rapidly changing one because the lifespans of parallel architectures are measured in years, while a desirable lifespan for parallel software is measured in decades. The current standard way of dealing with this mismatch is to reengineer software every few years as each new parallel computer comes along. This is expensive, and as a result parallelism has only been heavily used in applications where other considerations outweigh the expense. This is mostly why the existing parallel processing community is so heavily oriented towards scientific and numerical applications – they are either funded by research institutions and are pushing the limits of what can be computed in finite time and space, or they are working on applications where performance is the only significant goal.

We will be concerned with bridging the gap between software and hardware by decoupling the semantics of programs from their potentially parallel implementations. The role of a bridge is played by a *model of parallel computation*. A model provides a single parallel abstract machine to the programmer, while allowing different implementations on different underlying architectures. Finding such a model is difficult, but progress is now being made. This book is about one kind of model, based on *categorical data types*, with an object-based flavour.

We begin then by examining what is good about parallelism, and the problems that have prevented it from becoming a mainstream technology. These problems, together with results from the theory of parallel computation, suggest properties that a model of parallel computation should possess. We show that a model based on categorical data types possesses these properties.

2.1   What's Good About Parallelism

Why should we be concerned about parallelism? Some take the view that the failure of parallelism to penetrate mainstream computing is a sign that it isn't really essential, that it's an interesting research area with little applicability to real computing. The needs of real computing, they say, will be met by new generations of uniprocessors with ever-increasing clock rates and ever-denser circuitry.

There are, however, good reasons to be concerned with parallelism in computations. Some of these reasons indicate that, at least in the long run, there's little alternative but to face up to parallelism.

- Many computer programs represent or model some object or process that takes place in the real world. This is directly and obviously true of many scientific and numerical computations, but it is equally true of transaction processing, stock market future predictions, sales analysis for stores, air traffic control, transportation scheduling, data mining, and many other applications. If the problem domain is a parallel one, it is natural to conceive of, and implement, the solution in a parallel way. (Arguably, the requirement to sequentialise solutions to problems of this kind is one reason why they seem so difficult.)

- Parallel computations handle faults in a graceful way, because there is a trade-off between working hardware and performance. Failures are handled by continuing with the computation, but more slowly.

- There is no inherent limit to the expansion, and therefore computational power, of parallel architectures. Therefore, parallelism is the only long-term growth path for powerful computation. Uniprocessor performance growth has been, and continues to be, impressive. However, there are signs of diminishing returns from smaller and faster devices, as they begin to struggle with getting power into, and heat out of, smaller and smaller volumes. Costs of the development process are also growing faster than performance so that each new generation of processors costs more to build than the last, and offers smaller performance improvements. And eventually the speed of light is an upper limit on single device performance, although we are some way from that particular limitation.

- Parallelism is a cost-effective way to compute because of the economics of processor development. The development costs of each new uniprocessor must be recouped in the first few years of its sales (before it is supplanted by an even faster processor). Once it ceases to be leading-edge, its price drops rapidly, much faster than linearly. An example based on some artificial numbers shows how this works. If a generation $i + 1$ uniprocessor is ten times faster than a generation i processor, a multiprocessor built from generation i processors outperforms the new uniprocessor with only a hundred processors. Furthermore, the price of generation i processors is probably so low that the multiprocessor is only small multiples of the price of the leading-edge uniprocessor. Of course, this depends on two things: the multiprocessor must use standard uniprocessors as its component processors, and it must be possible to replace the component processors as each generation is developed to help amortise the cost of the multiprocessor infrastructure (interconnection network, cabinets, power supply, and so on).

The extent to which parallel computers are cost-effective has been largely obscured by the difficulties with programming them, and hence of getting their rated performance from them; and also by the lack of economies of scale in the tiny parallel computing market.

Thus there are short-term reasons to use parallelism, based on its theoretical ability to deliver cost-effective performance, and longer-term necessity, based on the limit of the speed of light, and heat and power dissipation limits. Why haven't these reasons been compelling?

2.2 What's Bad About Parallelism

There are three reasons not to use parallelism:

- It introduces many more degrees of freedom into the space of programs, and into the space of architectures and machines. When we consider ways of executing a program on a machine from a particular architecture class, the number of possibilities is enormous. It is correspondingly difficult to find an optimal, or even an acceptable, solution within these spaces. It is also much more difficult to predict the detailed behaviour and performance of programs running on machines.

- Human consciousness appears to be basically sequential (although the human brain, of course, is not). Thus humans have difficulties reasoning about and constructing models of parallel computation. The challenge is to provide suitable abstractions that either match our sequential style of thinking, or make use of other parts of our brain which are parallel. For example, the activity lights on the front panels of several commercial multiprocessors allow us to capture the behaviour of the running system using the parallelism of the human object recognition system.

- The basic work of understanding how to represent parallel computation in ways that humans can understand and parallel computers can implement has not been done. As a result, the whole area is littered with competing solutions, whose good and bad points are not easy to understand.

Since the use of parallelism seems unavoidable in the long term, these reasons not to use parallelism should be regarded as challenges or opportunities. None is a fundamental flaw, although they do present real difficulties. The reason for the failure of parallel computation so far is much more pragmatic – its roots lie in the differences between the characteristics of parallel hardware and parallel software. To explore this problem, we turn to considering the state of parallel computation today.

2.3   The State of the Art in Parallel Computing

The current state of parallelism can be summed up in these two statements: architecture-specific programming of parallel machines is rapidly maturing, and the tools used for it are becoming sophisticated; while architecture-independent programming of parallel machines is just beginning to develop as a plausible long-term direction.

Commercial parallel machines exist in all of the architecture classes suggested by Flynn [77], SISD (Single Instruction, Single Data, that is uniprocessors), SIMD (Single Instruction, Multiple Data), and MIMD (Multiple Instruction, Multiple Data). MIMD machines are commonly divided into two subclasses, depending on the relationship of memory and processors. Shared-memory, or tightly-coupled, MIMD architectures allow any processor to access any memory module through a central switch. Distributed-memory, or loosely-coupled, MIMD architectures connect individual processors with their own memory modules, and implement access to remote memory by messages passed among processors. The differences between these classes are not fundamental, as we shall see in the next chapter. Shared-memory machines using a modest number of processors have been available for a decade, and the size of such machines is increasing, albeit slowly, as the difficulties of providing a coherent memory are gradually being overcome. Distributed-memory machines have also been readily available for a decade and are now commercially available with thousands of processors. More adventurous architectures are being developed in universities and a few companies. Dataflow machines have never been commercially successful, but their descendants, multithreaded machines, seem about to become a force in the commercial arena. Individual processors are becoming internally parallel as pipelining and superscalar instruction scheduling are pushed to their limits. Optical technology is beginning to make an impact on inter-chip communication and is used experimentally on-chip. Optical computation is also in its infancy. In summary, on the architectural front new ideas have appeared regularly, and many have eventually made their way into successful processor designs. For the next few decades, there seems to be no prospect of a shortage of new parallel architectures, of many different forms, with different characteristics, and with different degrees of parallelism.

Parallel software has been successfully developed for each of these architectures, but only in an architecture-specific way. Programming models were quickly developed for each different architecture class: lockstep execution for SIMD machines, test-and-set instructions for managing access in shared-memory machines, and message passing and channels for distributed-memory machines. Languages, algorithms, compiler technology, and in some cases whole application areas, have grown up around each architectural style. Proponents of each style can point to their success stories.

Second generation abstractions have also been developed for most architecture classes. Some examples are:

- The relaxation of the SIMD view of computation so that synchronisation does not occur on every instruction step, but only occasionally. The result is the SPMD (Single Program Multiple Data) style, which still executes on SIMD machines, but works well on other architectures too.

- The distributed-memory MIMD view of message passing has been enhanced to make it simpler and easier to build software for by adding concepts such as shared associative tuple spaces for communication, or memory-mapped communication so that sends and receives look the same as memory references.

- The dataflow approach has converged with lightweight process and message-based approaches to produce multithreaded systems in which processes are extremely lightweight and messages are active.

The tools available for using parallel machines have also become more sophisticated. They include

- Graphical user interfaces that build programs by connecting program pieces using a mouse, and display the program as a process graph on a screen [134, 191].

- Assistants for the process of parallelising code, either existing "dusty deck" code, or new code developed as if for a sequential target. Such tools include profilers that determine which parts of a program are executed together and how much work each does (and display the resulting data in effective graphical form) [42, 132].

- Debuggers that determine the state of a thread and its variables and allow programs to be interrupted at critical moments. Such tools are decreasing their intrusiveness so that behaviour is not disturbed by the debugging task itself [154].

- Visualisation tools that take the output of a program or a collection of programs and display the data in a maximally useful way for humans to understand [130, 164, 165].

Architecture-specific parallel computing is thus becoming quite sophisticated. If any architecture class were the clear performance winner and could be guaranteed to remain the performance winner as technologies develop, the current state of affairs in parallel computation would be satisfactory. However, this isn't the case – no architecture can be expected to hold a performance lead for more than a few years. In fact, there are theoretical reasons to expect no long-term hope for such an architecture (see Chapter 3). As a result, the progress made in architecture-specific computation is not enough to make parallel computation a mainstream approach. Potential users are concerned that committing to a particular architecture will leave them at a disadvantage as new architectures become important. There is a pent-up desire to exploit parallelism, matched by a wariness about how to do so in an open-ended way.

The problem lies in the differences between the styles of parallel software that have grown up around each kind of architecture. Such software is not, by any stretch of the imagination, portable across architectures. Sometimes it is not even portable onto larger versions of the same system. Thus software developed for one style of parallel machine can only be moved onto another style of parallel machine with an immense amount of work. Sometimes it is almost equivalent to developing the software from scratch on the new architecture.

The expected lifetimes of a piece of parallel software and the parallel machine platform on which it executes are very different. Because of rapid developments in architecture, the platform can be expected to change every few years; either by being made larger, by having its processors replaced, or by being replaced entirely. Often, the speed with which this happens is limited only by how fast the existing hardware can be depreciated. Software, on the other hand, is normally expected to be in use for decades. It might execute on four or five different architectures from different classes during its lifetime. Very few users can afford to pay the price of migration so frequently and, as a result, they are understandably reluctant to use parallelism at all. Many potential users are quite consciously waiting to see if this problem can be resolved. If it cannot, parallelism will remain the province of those who need performance and who can afford to pay for it. This kind of user is increasingly scarce, with obvious consequences for the parallel computing industry.

At the heart of the problem is the tight connection between programming style and target architecture. As long as software contains embedded assumptions about properties of architectures, it is difficult to migrate it. This tight connection also makes software development difficult for programmers, since using a different style of architecture means learning a whole new style of writing programs and a new collection of programming idioms.

The mismatch between parallel architectures and parallel software can be handled by the development of a model of parallel computation that is abstract enough to avoid this tight coupling. Such a model must conceal architectural details as they change, while remaining sufficiently concrete that program efficiency is maintained. In essence, such a model describes an abstract machine, to which software development can be targeted, and which can be efficiently emulated on parallel architectures. A model then acts as the boundary between rapidly-changing architectures and long-lived software, decoupling software design issues from implementation issues (Figure 2.1).

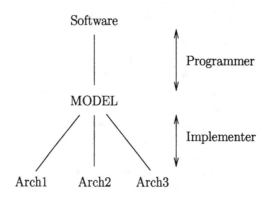

Figure 2.1: Role of a Model of Parallel Computation

2.4 Models and their Properties

A useful model for parallel computation must carefully balance the divergent needs, of software developers, implementers, and users. What properties should such a model possess?

A model for parallel computation should have the following properties:

- **Architecture Independence.** Program source must not need to change to run the program on different architectures. The model cannot encode any particular features of an architectural style, and any customising required to use a particular architecture must be hidden by the compiler. We are not yet requiring that the program be able to run efficiently on all architectures, although we rule out the trivial architecture independence that occurs because any (Turing-complete) architecture can simulate any other.

- **Intellectual Abstractness.** Software executing on a large parallel machine involves the simultaneous, or apparently simultaneous, execution of many thousands of threads or processes. The potential communication between these threads is quadratic in the number of threads. This kind of complexity cannot be managed directly by humans. Therefore a model must provide an abstraction from the details of parallelism, in particular,

  - an abstraction from *decomposition*, that is the way in which the computation is divided into subpieces that execute concurrently,

  - an abstraction from *mapping*, that is the way in which these pieces are allocated to particular physical processors,

  - an abstraction from *communication*, that is the particular actions taken to cause data to move, and the way in which source, destination, and route are specified, and

  - an abstraction from *synchronisation*, that is the points at which threads must synchronise, and how this is accomplished.

Decomposition and mapping are known to be of exponential complexity in general, and upper bounds for heuristics have been hard to find [193]. It is therefore unlikely that any model that relies on solving the decomposition and mapping problem in its full generality can provide this level of abstraction. The issue becomes choosing the best restriction of the problem to get the most effective model.

Communication and synchronisation are difficult when handled explicitly because each process must understand the global state of the computation to know whether some other process is ready to receive a possible communication, or to decide that a synchronisation action is necessary. Without a strong abstraction it will simply prove impossible to write software, let alone tune it or debug it.

- **Software Development Methodology.** Parallel software is extremely complex because of the extra degrees of freedom introduced by parallel execution. This complexity is enough to end the tradition of building software with only scant regard for its correctness. Parallel software must be correct because we owe it to those who use the software, but also for more pragmatic reasons – if it isn't correct it will probably fail completely rather than occasionally, and it will be impossible to debug. To be sure, parallel debuggers have already been developed and are in use, but they have primarily been applied to scientific applications which, although long running, are usually well-structured and relatively simple. Parallel debugging as part of normal software construction seems impractical.

A model for parallel computation must address the problem of developing correct software and must do so in an integrated way, rather than as an afterthought. One approach to developing correct sequential software is verification, that is the demonstration that a constructed program satisfies its specification. This approach does not seem, on the face of it, to scale well to the parallel case. The required proof has a structure that is determined by the structure of the program, which can be awkward unless it was built with verification in mind. It is also not clear how a large parallel program can be built without structuring the construction process itself in some way. If structure is necessary, let it be structure that is also conducive to building the software correctly.

A much better alternative is to adapt the derivational or calculational approach to program construction to the parallel case. Using this approach a program is constructed by starting from a specification, and repeatedly altering or refining it until an executable form is reached. Changes to the specification must be guaranteed to preserve properties of interest such as correctness. The refinement process can be continued to make the executable form more efficient, if required. There are several advantages to this approach:

- It structures the development process by making all the steps small and simple, so that big insights are not required.

- It exposes the decision points, forcing programmers to choose how each computation is to be done, rather than using the first method that occurs to them.

- It provides a record of each program's construction that serves as documentation.

- It preserves correctness throughout the process, by using only transformations that are known to be correctness-preserving; hence there is no remaining proof obligation when a program has been developed.

- Proofs of the correctness-preserving properties need only be done during the construction of the derivation system; hence it is not as important a drawback if these proofs are difficult, because they are done by specialists.

- **Cost Measures.** There must be a mechanism for determining the costs of a program (execution time, memory used, and so on) early in the development cycle and in a way that does not depend critically on target architecture. Such cost measures are the only way to decide, during development, the merits of using one algorithm rather than another. To be practical, such measures must be based on selecting a few key properties from both architectures and software. If a derivational software development methodology is used, there is an advantage in requiring a stronger property, namely that the cost measures form a cost calculus. Such a calculus allows the cost of a part of a program to be determined independently of the other parts, and enables transformations to be classified by their cost-altering properties.

- **No Preferred Scale of Granularity.** The amount of work that a single processing node of a parallel machine can most effectively execute depends on the kind of architecture it belongs to. The processors of large parallel machines will continue to increase in performance, as they adapt the best of uniprocessor technology. Thus a model of computation must allow for the pieces of computation that execute on each processing node of a parallel machine to be of any size. If the model imposes some bound on the size of work allocated to each processor (the grain size), then there will be programs that require many processors, but fail to utilise any of them well, or which can only use a few processors. Some architectures (for example, multithreaded ones) require small grains if they are to be effective at all, and models must be prepared to handle this as well.

Some modern architectures make use of parallelism at two different levels, across the machine and within each processor, for example. This again requires flexibility in the size of grains used, and the ability to aggregate work at several nested levels.

- **Efficiently Implementable.** Finally, a model of parallel computation must make it possible for computations to be implemented on a full range of existing and imaginable architectures with reasonable efficiency. This requirement need not be as strong as is assumed in existing high-performance computing – for the great majority of parallel applications, the cost of software development is much higher than any costs associated with execution time of the software when it is built. It is probably sufficient to ask that execution times on different parallel architectures be of the same order, and that the constants not be too large. It is even conceivable that logarithmic differences in performance are acceptable in some application domains.

Much is now known about the relative power of architectures to execute arbitrary computations. Architectures are classified by power as follows:

- Shared-memory multiprocessors, and distributed-memory multiprocessors whose interconnect capacity grows as $p \log p$ (where p is the number of processors), emulate arbitrary computations with no loss of efficiency.

- Distributed-memory multiprocessors whose interconnect capacity grows as p emulate arbitrary computations with inefficiency of order $\log p$.

- SIMD architectures emulate arbitrary computations with inefficiency of order p.

These results immediately limit the form of a model for parallel computation if it is to be efficient over these last two architecture classes. This issue is explored further in Chapter 3.

These desirable properties of a model of parallel computation are to some extent mutually exclusive, and finding the best balance among them is not easy (and is an active topic for research). We will examine a wide range of existing models and languages for parallel computation in Chapter 4, and see how they measure up to these requirements.

2.5 Categorical Data Types

This book is about a class of models for parallel computation based on *categorical data types*. Categorical data types (CDTs) are a generalisation of abstract data types. They come equipped with parallel operations that are used to program in a data-parallel or skeleton style. Because they are built using category theory, they have a sufficiently deep foundation to satisfy the requirements associated with software development. This foundation also pays off in practical ways.

An abstract data type is defined by giving a set of operations that are applied to the data type and a set of equations that these operations must satisfy. To build a new type, a set of operations which operate on objects of the type must be chosen. These may be of three kinds: constructors, which build objects of the new type, destructors, which take apart objects of the new type, and others. There is no organised way to choose this set of operations which will guarantee that all the useful functions are present. Also, there is no general way to construct the set of equations and be sure that:

- the set contains all of the equations needed to describe the type; and

- there are no redundant equations.

Mistakes in the set of equations are common errors in defining abstract data types.

The categorical data type construction avoids these deficiencies of abstract data types. A categorical data type depends only on the choice of operations that build the type, the constructors. The construction then produces the following "for free":

- a polymorphic data type, that is an instance of the constructed data type for each existing type;

- a single way of evaluating all homomorphisms on a type – a way that is often parallel, that can be implemented using predictable patterns of computation and communication, and that reveals the connections between superficially different second-order operations;

- an equational structure, involving the new operations and the constructors, that is used for program transformation;

- a guarantee of the completeness of the set of equations in the sense that any formulation of a homomorphism on the type can be transformed into any other formulation by equational substitution;

- a reference or communication pattern for homomorphisms on the constructed type that depends on the constructors.

A categorical data type can be regarded as a generalisation of an object which encapsulates data representation and also the control flow involved in evaluating homomorphisms. Such an object contains a single method, the argument to which is an object representing the algebraic structure which is the homomorphism's codomain. Abstraction from control flow is exactly the right kind of abstraction for eventual parallel execution, since the actual control flow can then depend on the target architecture, without being visible at the software level. We describe the construction in more detail in Chapters 5 and 9.

The construction has been used to build a categorical data type, and hence a parallel programming model, for lists [138, 189], bags, trees [83], arrays [23], molecules [181], and graphs [175]. We illustrate these types and show how they are built in Chapters 5, 10, 11, 12, and 13.

Categorical data types satisfy most of the requirements for a parallel programming model because of the way they are built.

Architecture Independence. No assumptions about the target architecture are made in the model, so migrating to a new system does not require source alteration.

Intellectual Abstractness. Categorical data type programs are single-threaded with the parallelism internal to the structured operations. They are thus conceptually simple to understand and reason about. In particular, decomposition occurs only in the data, and communication and synchronisation are hidden within the new operations.

Software Development Methodology. The categorical data type approach views software development as the transformation of an initial, obvious solution into an efficient one. Many initial solutions have the form of comprehensions. It is straightforward to check that a particular comprehension satisfies a specification, but comprehensions are typically expensive computationally. Using equations, the comprehension form of a program can be transformed into one that is more efficient. Since transformation is equational, correctness is necessarily preserved. The completeness of the equational system guarantees that the optimal homomorphic solution is reachable, and that mistakes made during derivation are reversible. A program that computes a homomorphism has a normal form called a *catamorphism* into which it can always be translated.

Cost Measures. Implementation on distributed-memory MIMD architectures with only a fixed number of communication links connected to each processor is easier if all communication occurs between near neighbours. The locality of operations on categorical data types reflects the locality of the constructors of the data type, that is, the extent to which building an object of the type involves putting together pieces at a small number of points. For example, concatenation involves joining lists at a single point; a constructor that forms a cartesian product does not. For all the types we consider, locality does seem to be a natural property of constructors, so that the resulting CDT theories exhibit considerable locality.

Since local communication can be implemented in constant time, naive cost measures for CDT programs can be those of "free communication" models. Such cost measures only account for operations and their arrangement. These cost measures hold for implementations on a wide range of architectures, provided that CDT computations can be mapped onto their topologies while preserving near-neighbour adjacencies. This can certainly be done for lists, and there seems to be no fundamental impediment for other, more complex, types. For some types, better performance can be achieved by more subtle implementations.

No Preferred Scale of Granularity. Because categorical data types are polymorphic, components of data objects can themselves be arbitrarily complex data objects. Programs typically manipulate nested structures, and the level at which the parallelism is applied can be chosen at compile time to match the target architecture.

Efficiently Implementable. Categorical data type theories are not very demanding of architectures. Simple implementations require only a subgraph in the architecture's communication topology that matches the structure of the relevant datatype's constructors. All communication is local so the global communication structure is of little relevance. For more complex types, important questions of implementability are still open.

2.6   Outline

In the next few chapters, we examine the constraints on models imposed by technology-independent architectural properties, and rate existing models according to how well they meet the requirements for a model of parallel computation (Chapters 3 and 4).

Then we examine the categorical data type of join lists in some detail. Chapter 5 shows how to use the CDT construction to build the type of lists and shows how parallel operations can be built. Chapter 6 uses the constructed type in derivations to illustrate the software development methodology. Chapter 7 illustrates some more complex operations on lists. Chapter 8 develops a cost calculus for lists.

The remainder of the book covers the CDT construction in more generality (Chapter 9), and its use to build more complex types: sets and bags in Chapter 10, trees in Chapter 11, arrays in Chapter 12, and graphs in Chapter 13. While the construction of such types is well understood, relatively little is known about implementing parallel operations using them.

Chapter 3

Architectural Background

In this chapter, we explore the constraints imposed on models by the properties of parallel architectures. We are only concerned, of course, about theoretical properties, because we cannot predict technological properties very far into the future. Recent foundational results, particularly by Valiant [200], show that arbitrary parallel programs can be emulated efficiently on certain classes of parallel architectures, but that inefficiencies are unavoidable on others. Thus a model of parallel computation that expresses arbitrary computations cannot be efficiently implementable over the full range of parallel architecture classes. The difficulty lies primarily in the *volume* of communication that takes place during computations. Thus we are driven to choose between two quite different approaches to designing models: accepting some inefficiency, or restricting communication in some way.

3.1 Parallel Architectures

We consider four architecture classes:

- shared-memory MIMD architectures, consisting of processors executing independently, but communicating through a shared memory, visible to them all;

- distributed-memory MIMD architectures, consisting of processors executing independently, each with its own memory, and communicating using an interconnection network whose capacity grows as $p \log p$, where p is the number of processors;

- distributed-memory MIMD architectures, consisting of processors executing independently, each with its own memory, and communicating using an interconnection network whose capacity grows only linearly with the number of processors (that is, the number of communication links per processor is constant);

- SIMD architectures, consisting of a single instruction stream, broadcast to a set of data processors whose memory organisation is either shared or distributed.

A shared-memory MIMD architecture consists of a set of independent processors connected to a shared memory from which they fetch data and to which they write results (see Figure 3.1). Such architectures are limited by the time to transit the switch, which grows with the number of processors. The standard switch design [110] has depth proportional to $\log p$ and contains $p \log p$ basic switching elements. The time to access a memory location (the *memory latency*) is therefore proportional to the logarithm of the number of processors. Systems with a few processors may have smaller memory latency, by using a shared bus for

Processors

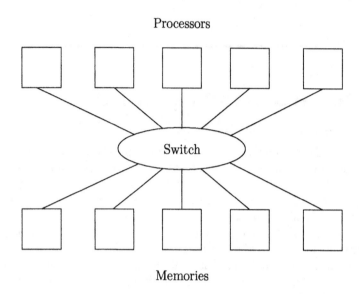

Memories

Figure 3.1: A Shared-Memory MIMD Architecture

example, but such systems do not scale. Even the advent of optical interconnects will not change the fundamental latency of shared interconnects, although the absolute reductions in latency may make it possible to ignore the issue for a while.

A distributed-memory MIMD architecture whose interconnection network capacity grows as $p \log p$ consists of a set of *processing elements*, that is a set of processors, each with its own local memory. The interconnect is usually implemented as a static interconnection network using a topology such as a hypercube. Data in the memories of other processors is manipulated indirectly, by sending a message to the processing element that owns the memory in which the data resides, asking for it to be read and returned, or stored. A simple example of such an architecture is shown in Figure 3.2.

The machine's topology determines its most important property, the interconnect diameter, that is the maximum number of links a message traverses between two processors. For any reasonable topology with this interconnect volume, the diameter will be bounded above by $\log p$.

These two architecture classes can be regarded as ends of a spectrum, with the whole spectrum possessing similar properties. A shared-memory MIMD machine is often enhanced by the addition of caches between the processors and the switch to shared memory. This has obvious advantages because of the long latency of the switch. If these caches are made large, and a cache consistency scheme is imposed on them, there eventually becomes no need for the memory modules at all, and the result is a distributed-memory machine. This similarity has real implications, and we shall soon consider these two classes as essentially the same.

A distributed-memory MIMD architecture with interconnect capacity linear in the number of processors has processing elements, as the previous architecture class did, but has a simpler

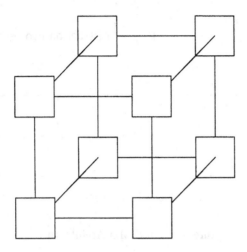

Figure 3.2: A Distributed-Memory MIMD Architecture (Using a Hypercube Interconnect)

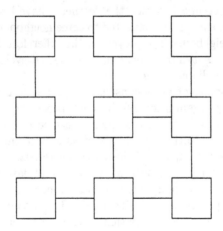

Figure 3.3: A Distributed-Memory MIMD Architecture (Using a Constant Number of Links per Processing Element)

interconnect. As the interconnect grows only linearly with the processors, it usually has a fixed number of communication links to each processing element. The diameter of such an interconnect can still be reasonably assumed to be bounded above by $\log p$, by a result of Bokhari and Raza [43]. They show that any topology can be enhanced by the addition of at most one communication link per processor so as to reduce its diameter to $\Theta(\log p)$. There are some special topologies with larger diameters which are of interest because of the ease

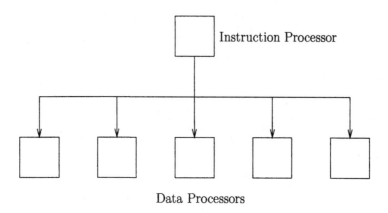

Figure 3.4: An SIMD Architecture

with which they can be embedded in space, for example the mesh.

One example of a topology with a constant number of links per processor, which will be useful later, is the *cube-connected-cycles* topology [159], because of its resemblance to the hypercube. Consider a hypercube in which the "corners" have been replaced by cycles of size d. Each processing element is now connected to three neighbours, one along the original hypercube edge and two neighbours in the cycle. It has therefore become a topology with linear interconnect capacity. A d-dimensional cube-connected-cycles topology connects $2^d d$ processing elements, and has diameter $3d$.

An SIMD architecture consists of a single instruction processor and a set of data processors (Figure 3.4). The memory organisation of the data processors can be either shared or distributed, although access to distributed memory must be in the form of a permutation, since there is no possibility of multi-link transfers of data on a single step.

SIMD machines have instruction sets of the same general size and complexity as MIMD machines. There is usually a mechanism to allow individual data processors to ignore the instruction being broadcast on a step; thus the data processors can collectively execute a small number of different operations on a single step. It is possible to provide translation tables in the memory of each data processor that enable the machine as a whole to function in an MIMD way by using the broadcast instruction as an index into these tables. Under these circumstances, it is probably better to treat the architecture as being in the appropriate MIMD class.

An overview of parallel architectures can be found in [177].

3.2   The Standard Model

The standard model for parallel computation is the PRAM, an abstract machine that takes into account factors such as degree of parallelism and dependencies in a parallel computation, but does not account for latencies in accessing memory or in communicating between concurrent computations. A PRAM consists of a set of p (abstract) processors and a large shared memory. In a single machine step, each processor executes a single operation from a fixed instruction set, or reads from, or writes to a memory location. In computing the total execution time of a computation, these steps are assumed to take unit time. A program in the PRAM model describes exactly what each processor does on each step and what memory references it makes. Computations are not allowed (at least in the simplest version of the PRAM) to reference the same memory location simultaneously from different processors. It is the responsibility of the programmer to make sure that this condition holds throughout the execution of each program (and it is an onerous responsibility).

The PRAM model has been used to design many parallel algorithms, partly because it is a direct model of what seemed a plausible parallel architecture, and partly because it provides a workable complexity theory [116]. The complexity of a computation is given by the maximal number of processors that are required to execute it (p), and by the number of global steps that the computation takes (which is a surrogate measure for execution time). The product of these two terms measures the *work* required for a computation and can reasonably be compared with the time complexity of a sequential algorithm. For example, the work of a parallel algorithm cannot in general be smaller than the time complexity of the best known sequential algorithm, for the parallel computation could be executed sequentially, a row at a time, to give a better sequential algorithm. The ratio of the work of a parallel computation to the time complexity of the best sequential algorithm measures a kind of inefficiency related fundamentally to execution in parallel [124]. We are interested in a different form of inefficiency in this chapter.

Whatever the form in which a PRAM algorithm is described, it is useful to imagine the trace of the executing computation. At each step, actions are performed in each of the p threads or virtual processors. There may be dependencies between the sequences of actions in threads, both sequentially within a single thread and between threads when they communicate. Communication occurs by having one thread place a value in a memory location that is subsequently read by another. If each thread is imagined as a vertical sequence of operations, then communication actions are imagined as arrows, joining threads together. These arrows cannot be horizontal, because each memory access takes at least one step. The entire trace forms a rectangle of actions whose width is p and whose height is the number of steps taken for the computation, say t. The area of this rectangle corresponds to the work of the computation. An example of a trace is shown in Figure 3.5.

The drawback of the PRAM model is that it does not account properly for the time it takes to access the shared memory. In the real world, such accesses require movement of data and this must take more than unit time. In fact, for any realistic scalable architecture, such accesses require time at least proportional to the logarithm of the number of processors, which is too large to discount. This discrepancy cannot be discounted by simply multiplying all time complexities for PRAM computations by an appropriate factor, preserving their *relative* complexities. The amount by which the execution time should be increased to account for communication depends on the precise arrangement of memory accesses within the computation. Hence algorithm A might seem to do less work than Algorithm B using the PRAM model, but Algorithm B actually does less work than Algorithm A when communication is accounted for (perhaps because Algorithm B uses global memory less).

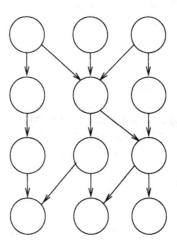

Figure 3.5: The Trace of a Parallel Computation

3.3   Emulating Parallel Computations

We now consider the effect of target architecture properties on the execution of an abstract computation, particularly the extent to which the amount of work changes when communication latency is taken into account.

We have described the form of a trace of a general parallel computation expressed in the PRAM model. Clearly, if we execute such a trace on an architecture from any of the four architecture classes, the computation will take longer than the number of steps in the trace suggests. Whenever there is a communication action in the trace (an arrow from one thread to another), there is a latency in actually moving the data from one place to another. The latency depends on the number of processors that are being used to execute the computation. We expect it to be at least $\log p$, probably much longer because of congestion in the interconnect. (Of course, emulating the computation on an SIMD architecture is more difficult because of the restriction on what happens on a single step – we will return to this.)

Suppose that the trace of the computation we wish to emulate has p threads and takes t steps. Since emulating computations in which many threads are idle on many steps might be easy for reasons unrelated to architecture, we assume that every thread is always active and that each thread does some communication on every step. This makes emulation as difficult as possible.

We cannot hope that the apparent time (in steps) of the trace will be the actual execution time on any of the real architectures, because of latency. The strongest property we can hope for is that the work, the product of processors and time, is preserved during real execution. If it is, we say that the implementation is *efficient*; if it is not, the amount by which they differ measures the inefficiency of the implementation.

$$\text{Inefficiency} = \frac{\text{Work when emulated on architecture}}{\text{Work on PRAM}}$$

This ratio certainly captures inefficiency due to communication. It is otherwise hard to justify the PRAM as the model against which comparisons are made, except that there is, at the moment, no reasonable alternative.

The emulation of an arbitrary parallel computation varies depending on the particular properties of the architecture on which the emulation takes place. We consider each of these in turn.

3.3.1   Emulating on Shared-Memory MIMD Architectures

If we emulate the trace directly on a shared-memory MIMD architecture, each step involves memory references and so takes time $\Omega(\log p)$. The time for the whole trace is $t\Omega(\log p)$ using p processors, for a total work of

$$\text{work} = \Omega(pt \log p)$$

This lower bound is based on the completion of memory references in time $\log p$, and this is highly unlikely if there are many simultaneous references. The actual work, and hence the inefficiency, could be much larger.

A technique called *memory hashing* is used to spread memory locations randomly among memory modules, reducing the chances of collisions in the switch to a constant number. The technique is due to Mehlhorn and Vishkin [145] and bounds the switch transit time in the presence of multiple memory references with high probability. The memory locations used to actually store variables are generated using a hash function that provably distributes them well across the available memory modules. So-called uniform hash functions guarantee, with high probability independent of p, that no more than a constant number of memory references are to the same module. This enables us to replace the lower bound given above by an exact bound. The work of the emulation becomes

$$\text{work} = \Theta(pt \log p)$$

This is not good news, because the inefficiency of the emulation is logarithmic in the number of threads in the computation. The more parallel our algorithm, the more inefficient it is to implement. Fortunately, there is a way to use excess parallelism (or fewer processors) to hide latency, an important idea that we will use repeatedly.

Instead of using a parallel machine where the number of processors matches the number of threads (that is, the parallelism of the algorithm), we emulate on a machine with fewer processors. Choose the number of processors of the emulating machine, p', such that

$$p' \log p' = p$$

Now we have p threads to emulate on fewer, p', processors. We do this by making each processor responsible for the execution of $\log p'$ threads. It executes these threads in a round-robin way to preserve the semantics of the trace. It executes the first operation of the first thread, then the first operation of the second thread, and so on, before continuing to the second operation of the first thread.

Between the execution of the first and second steps of any thread, time $\log p'$ has elapsed. On a machine with p' processors, this is long enough to have completed a memory reference. Thus the latency of the memory reference has been "hidden" by the sharing of the processor among multiple threads.

There are now many more outstanding messages to and from memory than there are in the direct emulation. At any moment, each processor has $\log p'$ outstanding memory requests for a total of

$$\text{memory requests} = p' \log p'$$

The switch connecting processors and memory has width p' and depth $\log p'$ and so has exactly enough capacity to store each of these outstanding requests. Fortunately, memory hashing distributes requests just evenly enough that congestion effects do not come into play and there are no hot spots in the switch (with high probability).

The emulation takes time $t \log p'$, because memory latency must still be counted for each step along every thread. However, we are only using p' processors, so the total work of the emulation is

$$\text{work} = \Theta(t \log p' p') = \Theta(tp)$$

so we have an efficient implementation.

There is a cost associated with this emulation, but it is an indirect one. The amount of parallelism in the algorithm (the *virtual* parallelism) must exceed the physical parallelism used by a logarithmic factor. This is called *parallel slackness*. The cost is that we cannot "throw hardware at the problem," that is, there comes a point when using more processors does not improve the performance of the computation. Note also the implication for parallel machines that they should be designed so as to allow many active threads at all times, and therefore that they should implement context switching as cheaply as possible.

Shared-memory MIMD architectures are powerful in the sense that they implement arbitrary computations efficiently. Unfortunately, as a class they are not attractive because they do not scale well. The need for a central switch causes bottlenecks when embedding in three-dimensional space is considered. The size and complexity of the switch, which grow faster than the number of processors, are also unattractive.

3.3.2   Emulating on Distributed-Memory MIMD Architectures

We might expect that the results for emulation on a distributed-memory MIMD architecture with large interconnect capacity would resemble those for shared-memory machines, and that turns out to be the case. A direct emulation, without parallel slackness, has exactly the same inefficiency as the direct emulation on a tightly-coupled architecture. However, parallel slackness is used to hide latency, much as before; and this is the origin of the requirement for interconnect capacity of $p \log p$.

As before, we use p' processors where $p' \log p' = p$. In a distributed-memory machine we no longer have long-latency memory accesses, but long-latency message passing instead. In the absence of congestion, it is reasonable to treat such transfers as taking time logarithmic in the number of processors of the machine because this is the likely diameter of the interconnection topology.

Congestion can, of course, occur. A combination of memory hashing and a randomised routing algorithm are used to reduce it. Two-phase randomised routing [200] is a routing algorithm in which data transfer from node A to node B is achieved by randomly selecting some other node of the system, say node C, using a deterministic routing algorithm to send the data from A to C, and then using a deterministic algorithm to send the data from C to B. For many useful practical networks, this spreads network traffic sufficiently that, with high probability, messages are delivered in time bounded by the diameter of the network.

When emulating the trace of an arbitrary computation, each request for data from another thread takes time $\Theta(\log p')$. Once again $\log p'$ threads are multiplexed on each processor, so that there is sufficient time between successive steps in any thread for its communications to have been completed.

As before, the total work of the emulation using parallel slackness is equivalent to that of the abstract computation, so an efficient emulation is possible:

$$\text{work} = \Theta(t \log p' p') = \Theta(tp)$$

The class of distributed-memory architectures with high-capacity interconnect suffers from some of the scalability problems of shared-memory architectures. Because of the scaling of interconnect capacity, the number of communication links to which a processor is connected depends on the size of machine in which it is used. Once a processor has been fabricated with a certain number of links, it can only be used in suitably small ensembles. Thus increasing the size of a machine may require using new processors. It is also difficult to embed these interconnects in three-dimensional space without running into space and heat dissipation problems.

3.3.3 Emulating on Constant-Valence MIMD Architectures

Now we consider emulating an arbitrary computation on distributed-memory MIMD architectures in which the interconnect capacity grows linearly with the number of processors. A direct emulation, using the same number of processors as threads, generates at least $\log p$ inefficiency as for the other architectures. On the other hand, using parallel slackness, as we have done with the previous two classes, depends on the interconnect supporting a superlinear number of outstanding messages at any time. The present class cannot handle that many outstanding messages, because they must all make progress on each step if they are to be delivered quickly enough, and there is not enough capacity to do so. If the interconnect capacity is of order p', then only p' messages make progress on each step; but the parallel slackness approach depends on $p' \log p'$ messages making progress on each step.

At most p' messages make progress, so communication capacity overruns can only be avoided by slowing the execution rate by a factor of $\log p'$. The total time to emulate the computation is then

$$\Theta(t \log p' \log p')$$

using p' processors for a total work of

$$\text{work} \;=\; \Theta(tp \log p')$$

The inefficiency is a term of size $\log p'$. This inefficiency is fundamental to the capacity of the system and cannot be further reduced by clever scheduling.

This class of architectures is the first we have considered that is truly scalable. Because of the fixed number of links per processors, the neighbourhood of each processor is the same no matter what size of machine it is embedded in. Thus nothing about the processor needs to be changed as the machine of which it is a part grows. Also interconnects that grow linearly with number of processors can be reasonably embedded in three-dimensional space without requiring the length of each point-to-point connection to grow with machine size.

3.3.4   Emulating on SIMD Architectures

The difficulty with emulating an arbitrary computation on an SIMD architecture lies in the variability of actions that take place on any step of the abstract computation rather than directly on communication. Clearly it is hard to deal with many simultaneous distinct actions on a machine that only executes a few different operations at a time. We show that efficient implementation is not possible, no matter how the information broadcast by the instruction processor is coded.

Suppose that there is a bounded bandwidth between the instruction processor and the data processors, say b. This bandwidth is sufficient to distinguish all of the instructions that the instruction processor understands. Thus the size of the instruction set of the instruction processor is no larger than 2^b.

Now suppose that the SIMD machine on which the abstract computation is emulated has p' data processors. We assume that $p' \leq p$ since otherwise some of the data processors are always idle. We emulate the abstract computation by executing the first p' threads from the first step, then the next p' and so on. Suppose that the instruction set of the abstract computation, that is the number of choices of what to do in each abstract processor in each step, is of size $2^{b'}$. Then $p'b'$ different bit patterns are required to distinguish the possible steps in the segment of p' threads we are emulating. The available bandwidth delivers b bits per unit time, so emulating this segment of steps takes time

$$\frac{b'p'}{b}$$

and emulating a single step of the abstract computation takes time

$$\frac{p}{p'} \frac{b'p'}{b} = \frac{pb'}{b}$$

Thus the time required for the emulation is

$$\Theta\!\left(tp\frac{b'}{b}\right)$$

Architecture	Inefficiency	Scalable?
Shared memory	1	No
Dist. memory, rich interconnect	1	No
Dist. memory, sparse interconnect	Logarithmic	Yes
SIMD	Linear	Yes

Figure 3.6: Power and Scalability of Architecture Classes

and the total work (since p' processors are used) is

$$\text{Work} = \Theta(tpp'\frac{b'}{b})$$

In the normal situation in which $b' = b$, that is the instruction set of the emulating processor is the same as that of the abstract processor, the inefficiency is p'. In the special case when p' equals 1, that is we emulate the computation on a single processor, there is of course no loss of efficiency. For real SIMD machines, the inefficiency grows linearly with the number of processors in the emulating machine.

The class of SIMD architectures is therefore the least powerful in terms of its ability to emulate arbitrary computations. SIMD architectures are relatively scalable, although there may eventually be difficulties with the skew in distribution of the signal from the instruction processor.

Of course, an SIMD architecture can emulate an MIMD architecture by loading the program threads into the data processor memories as data and then using the instruction broadcast as an index into this data. An SIMD machine with this capability might as well be considered as an MIMD machine, and the emulation results of previous sections apply, depending on the memory arrangement.

The results of the last few sections allow us to arrange architecture classes in order of power, measured by efficiency at emulating arbitrary computations, and of scalability (Figure 3.6). We see that there is no architecture class that is an obvious winner, since power and scalability are not simultaneously achievable.

3.4   Implications for Models

If we want models of parallel computation that can be implemented across all of these architectures, then the results of this chapter show that either such models must be restricted, or they must be inefficient. Arbitrary computations, if they are allowed in the model, automatically introduce inefficiencies in implementations on distributed-memory machines with sparse interconnects. What needs to be restricted in a model for efficiency is the *volume* of communication that the model requires of the architecture. There are three different ways to reduce the volume of communication: reduce the number of data transfers that are initiated, reduce the distance each data transfer travels, or both.

The first approach is the basis for *Bulk Synchronous Parallelism* [141]. If global communication or access to global memory is allowed to occur only at intervals, the total volume is reduced. The reduction in communication frequency is a function of the size of the target machine, so this constraint on the model is not architecture-independent. We will discuss this approach further in the next chapter.

The second approach is to restrict the distance that data transfers travel in the interconnect. This requires exploiting *locality*, and building a concept of locality that is as independent as possible of the precise topology of the target machine. This approach leads to models in which a set of predetermined, structured operations are used, with all of the communication taking place inside these operations. It is known as skeleton-based or data-parallel programming. We will see examples of it in the next chapter as well. Using locality means renouncing memory hashing and randomised routing, since these approaches prevent use of any information about location. Thus there does not seem to be middle ground in which these two approaches are blended to reduce the total communication load.

A third approach is to reduce both the frequency of communication, and the distance individual messages travel. This requires rather specialised interconnection topologies. We shall see it as the HPRAM in the next chapter.

Chapter 4

Models and Their Properties

In Chapter 2 we listed some of the requirements that a model for general-purpose parallel computation should satisfy: architecture independence, intellectual abstractness, having a software development methodology, having cost measures, having no preferred scale of granularity, and being efficiently implementable. In Chapter 3, we saw how results about emulation of arbitrary computations on architectures mean that efficient implementability can only be achieved by restricting the communication allowed in computations. In this chapter, we examine existing models and parallel programming languages and see how they measure up to these requirements.

Many of these models were not developed with such an ambitious set of requirements in mind, so it is not a criticism of them if they fail to meet some. Nevertheless, it provides a picture of the current situation. The absence of a popular or standard model, even in particular application domains, and the wide range of models that have been proposed, underline some of the difficulties of using parallelism in a general-purpose way that were discussed in Chapter 2. It is not possible to cover all proposed models for parallel computation, but a representative selection has been included.

There are several other good surveys of programming models from different perspectives. Crooks and Perrott [59] survey models for distributed-memory architectures, particularly those that provide abstractions for data partitioning and distribution. Turcotte [195] surveys models suitable for networks of workstations. Bal *et al.* [20] survey architecture-specific models.

The distinctions between models and programming languages are not easy to make. We regard a model as embodying an abstract machine. Therefore some of the models we discuss in this chapter are called "models" by their designers, while others are called programming languages. Nevertheless, they all provide some kind of interesting abstraction to the programmer. In our view, a model is a more fundamental concept than a programming language. It is possible in principle for more than one programming language to be built on top of a single model.

It is also possible to emulate more than one of the models we discuss using another model. Thus models cannot be compared in a single dimension, as if they were all at the same level of abstraction. Comparisons are complicated; while we have tried to provide a useful view of possible models, some complexities are unavoidable.

The properties we are assessing for models have very precise meanings. For example, when we say that a model is not efficiently implementable, we do not mean that implementations with useful speed-ups are not possible. We do mean that, asymptotically, they will exhibit some inefficiency on some architecture classes.

Arbitrary computation structure
Abstract
Higher-order functional
Interleaving
Rewriting
Partly abstract
Coordination languages
Process nets
Active messages
Low-level
Architecture-independent
Architecture-specific
PRAM
Restricted computation structure
Vertical tiling
Block tiling
Horizontal tiling
Algorithmic skeletons
Data-type-specific
Data-type-independent

Table 4.1: Classification of Models of Parallel Computation

4.1   Overview of Models

Table 4.1 shows a classification of models for parallel computation. The primary classification is based on whether or not the form of computations expressible in the model is restricted, in line with the observations in Chapter 3. Tables at the end of chapter rate the various models according to how well they satisfy the requirements for a model of parallel computation.

As we have seen, the most important determinant of whether it is possible to implement a program efficiently on the full range of architectures is the volume of communication that takes place. If the volume of communication is greater than linear in the number of emulating processors, the program is not efficiently implementable on a distributed-memory machine with a linear capacity interconnect. Thus we categorise models according to whether they allow arbitrary computations to be written, or whether they restrict the form of computations to limit communication volume.

4.1.1 Arbitrary Computation Structure Models

We begin by considering models that allow arbitrary computation structures. In these models, any program can be written directly in the form in which the programmer thinks of it. We further classify such models by how much intellectual abstraction they provide, that is how well they hide details of decomposition and communication. All of the models in this section are architecture-independent, and all fail to be efficiently implementable, asymptotically, because of the amount of communication they permit.

Abstract
Higher-order functional
Haskell
Interleaving
UNITY
Action systems
Concurrent rewriting
OBJ and relatives
Maude

Table 4.2: Abstract Models

Abstract Models. (Table 4.2) The first category are those models that do not explicitly require either the decomposition into threads, or the communication between threads to be given. In such models, a computation says what is to be done, but does not say how it is to be done, in what pieces, how the pieces are to interact, or where they are to execute. These details are inferred by the compiler. We consider such models under three headings: higher-order functional programming, interleaving languages, and rewriting systems.

Higher-order functional programming is the most popular declarative approach to parallel programs, close to the mathematical statement of computations to be performed. It is characterised by the absence of state. Programs are collections of mathematical functions, and the meaning of a program is a solution to these equations (usually a least fixed point). As a result, there is no obvious operational interpretation associated with individual equations, or the program as a whole. Several languages based on higher-order functional programming have been designed and implemented [66, 117, 157, 161] but most work is now concentrated on the language Haskell [107].

The most popular execution model for this programming model is graph reduction. A program is translated into a graph, which is then repeatedly rewritten using a set of canonical rewrite rules. Since there are often multiple places in the graph where rules apply, there are naturally opportunities for parallelism (although some exploitation of strictness is required to provide substantial parallelism). Graph reduction has been demonstrated quite successfully on shared-memory machines, but has been only a limited success on distributed-memory machines. Essentially the graph is a large shared data structure that is accessed in ways that are unpredictable statically. Attempts to divide the graph statically quickly lead to load imbalances. Dividing the graph dynamically is also difficult because the focus of activity can change faster than work can be migrated between processors. Quite small parts of the graph can generate large amounts of work very quickly, and it is difficult both to predict when this will happen, and to shed the extra work without saturating communication locally.

Higher-order functional programming does not require any description of how a computation is to be decomposed. The execution environment takes advantage of any opportunities that it finds to execute parts of the computation in parallel, but this is not specified as part of the program. Communication is not explicit in programs either – it occurs because the graph being reduced is a shared data structure. The result of one subcomputation is made available to others by replacing the subcomputation description in the graph by its value. Synchronisation occurs because tasks leave placeholders when they remove parts of the graph to work on. Other tasks needing the result of that part suspend until it becomes available. So the model abstracts well from the details of the parallel execution of the computation. Because so little operational strategy is specified in the program, the compiler (using abstract interpretation for strictness analysis, for example) and the run-time system have to work hard to find opportunities for parallelism. This makes performance difficult to achieve, especially when emulating a shared data structure in a distributed memory. Distributed garbage collection is also a difficult implementation problem.

The functions appearing in programs often satisfy equalities that can be used to transform them. Such transformations are usually directed at improving the performance of the program, but they can also be used as part of a calculational program derivation system [44]. Thus the model possesses a software development methodology.

Cost measures are not possible for higher-order functional programming, because of the number of free choices that the implementation system has about how to do its job. Approximations, such as the number of function calls or the number of cells in the graph, have been used, but they provide only lower bounds on execution time, since they do not (and cannot) account for communication [129]. Higher-order functional programming does not require any particular granularity of tasks, although such things may have significant effects on performance.

Interleaving approaches depend on a semantics for sequential computation in which different interleavings of operations are equivalent. Equivalent operations can be executed concurrently. These ideas go back to Dijkstra's guarded command language and CSP [105]. The logical view of a program's execution is as an infinite repetition of a step in which a set of guards is evaluated, one is selected from among those that evaluate to true, and the corresponding statement is executed. If the statements corresponding to true guards are independent they can be evaluated concurrently without altering the program's semantics. This idea lies behind UNITY [50], and an alternative that actively considers independence of statements, action systems [13–16].

Such models abstract from decomposition into subcomputations, in the sense that the programmer has no idea which guarded commands actually execute concurrently, although some division into guarded commands must be done. Communication and synchronisation are not visible at the program level.

Both models have a software development methodology based on refinement. The level of abstraction prevents useful cost measures. Any granularity of action is possible, although it is not possible to infer finer granularity than that specified by the guarded commands.

A third style of abstract programming model is based on *concurrent rewriting*. This includes OBJ [86, 88], a functional language with semantics based on equational logic (and its relatives FOOPS with an object oriented capability and Eqlog with a logic programming capability), and Maude [146].

These models abstract completely from decomposition, communication, and synchronisation. They have a software development methodology based on the logics that underlie them and the theory inheritance mechanism in OBJ. Any granularity is possible. Cost measures are not possible, again because of the level of abstraction.

All of these approaches to models have similar properties: they are all strong on the development aspects of software, but weak on the implementation properties. It is precisely the high level of abstraction that is responsible – on the one hand, it relieves programmers from considering details, but it makes it hard for compiler and run-time system to guarantee performance and predictability.

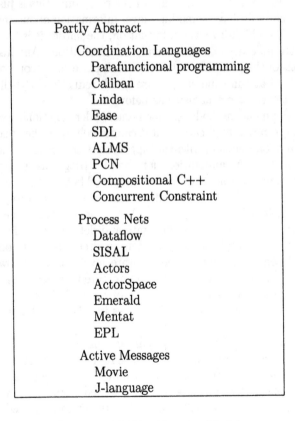

Partly Abstract

    Coordination Languages
       Parafunctional programming
       Caliban
       Linda
       Ease
       SDL
       ALMS
       PCN
       Compositional C++
       Concurrent Constraint

    Process Nets
       Dataflow
       SISAL
       Actors
       ActorSpace
       Emerald
       Mentat
       EPL

    Active Messages
       Movie
       J-language

Table 4.3: Partly Abstract Models

Partly Abstract Models. (Table 4.3) The second category of models are less abstract in the sense that programs say more about how decomposition or communication are done.

Again we distinguish several different approaches: coordination languages, process nets, and active messages.

Coordination languages make decomposition partly or completely explicit, but hide some of the details of communication. They are called coordination languages because they treat communication actions as dividing up the control flow in each thread into sections. The content of these sections is independent of communication, and can be treated by the communication languages as single step. Thus the control-and-computation language is independent of, and orthogonal to, the communication language. Coordination languages can, in principle, be added to any ordinary sequential programming language.

The first subclass of such models are those based on higher-order functional programming, but in which programs are annotated with information about partitioning structure and partial ordering of the subcomputations they contain. Examples are Parafunctional Programming [106] and Caliban [57, 117]. Such languages attempt to make the compiler's job easier and to increase the effectiveness of the compiler's decisions. They do so by requiring programmers to say more about the structure of the program – this is justified by the claim that programmers usually do have some high-level information about the likely progress of a computation. The more high-level the information, the harder it is for compilers to infer.

Such models partly hide decomposition and communication. Annotations are typically used for large sections of the program, but within each piece the decomposition and communication are determined at run-time as for pure graph reduction. Synchronisation remains hidden, since it uses the same mechanisms as before.

The software development methodology for higher-order functional programming (equational transformation) remains applicable, but it cannot help with the annotation step, which is more informal. An open question with this approach is the extent to which the programmer can actually provide useful annotations for complex programs. Certainly it is plausible that programmers understand something of the high-level behaviour of programs they write. However, it is less clear that they understand the interaction of the program behaviour with the implementation choices made at run-time. Annotations require that the programmer's view of the execution environment be an accurate and detailed one. This has two unpleasant side-effects: it limits the implementer's freedom to alter this execution environment; and it reveals target architecture details at the software level. So the knowledge required for effective annotation seems incompatible with architecture independence.

Cost measures cannot be constructed because of level of abstraction remains high, although in practice there are probably fewer surprises in this style than in the more abstract style.

Another subclass of coordination languages are languages that make decomposition fully explicit but provide abstractions for messaging. The best known example is Linda [6, 46–48], which decouples the send and receive parts of a communication by providing the abstraction of a tuple space. A tuple space is an associatively accessed storage area visible to all threads in a program. It is accessed by primitives that allow tuples to be placed in the tuple space, and that search the tuple space for tuples that "match" a given pattern. This means that two threads which communicate are not linked either spatially or temporally. The "sending" thread does not need to know the identity or even existence of the "receiving" thread. This abstraction is useful since it removes the need to match send and receive statements which may be widely separated in programs.

A model that improves Linda by adding to it some ideas from Occam is the language Ease [205–208]. Ease threads communicate by means of contexts, shared data areas that are hybrids of Occam channels and Linda tuple space. Threads read and write data to contexts in the Linda style, but may also use a second set of primitives that move data to a context and relinquish ownership of it, or retrieve data from a context and remove it from the context. Such operations can use pass-by-reference since they can guarantee that the data is only referenced by one thread at a time.

Both of these models require decomposition to be done explicitly, although Ease provides a process structuring mechanism to help with it. Both partly hide communication by providing abstractions designed to simplify it – associative addressing, and decoupled communication. Synchronisation is hidden in both. The combination of explicit decomposition and decoupled, but synchronised, communication is slightly dangerous. It is relatively easy to construct programs that deadlock because an attempt to find a tuple in tuple space blocks waiting for a tuple that is never added to tuple space. Finding the blocked attempt to match then provides no hint of where the missing insertion was supposed to be.

No software development methodology has been suggested for either. Cost measures do not appear possible because of the difficulty of implementing the communication abstractions with bounded delivery times. In fact, Linda implementations do not usually implement tuple space, but compile adds to and deletions from tuple space that will match at run time into point-to-point communication whenever possible. This approach is remarkably successful – most real programs can be compiled in this way. This suggests that a restriction of these languages that would guarantee such a property would be of interest, since it would have partly measurable costs. The restriction might also have implications for the construction of programs. Both Linda and Ease allow arbitrary granularity of threads.

SDL [166] is a generalisation of Linda that addresses several of its weaknesses. Programs share a common associatively-addressed data space, but operations larger than single adds and removes from the data space may be made atomic. This avoids some of Linda's potential for deadlock by adding the concept of scope. A mechanism called "views" allows a subset of the tuple space to be selected, acted upon by a collection of processes as if it were the whole tuple space, and then added back to the main tuple space. This gives the ability to program in a more abstract and structured way than in Linda.

SDL improves on Linda by allowing decomposition to be dealt with at a higher level, while providing the same kind of abstractions for communication. Synchronisation is again hidden from the programmer. Otherwise, it is similar to the previous two models.

Other related languages reduce the complexity of communication, for example by making it appear more like memory reference. ALMS [156] treats message passing as if it were memory-mapped. References to certain message variables in different threads behave like a message transfer from one to the others. Such models do not hide decomposition but provide a partial abstraction for communication and synchronisation.

PCN [79] and Compositional C++ [49] also hide communication by single-use variables. An attempt to read from one of these variables blocks the thread if a value has not already been placed in it by another thread. Since variables can only be used once, the effect of stream communication is achieved by recursively calling threads, so that each new context uses each variable once. Thus they hide synchronisation, but not decomposition or communication. PCN also uses a process structuring approach like Occam to help with the difficulty of decomposition.

These models do not hide decomposition, although they help to manage it by providing process structuring in the same way as Ease does. They provide partial abstractions for communication and synchronisation. While no full software development methodology has been developed, it is an important goal of the design of these languages, and reasoning about the composition of processes is possible. Cost measures are not possible. Any granularity is possible using process composition.

A related model is *concurrent constraint programming*, a model that generalises several logic programming languages [170]. There are several variants but, in the principal one, each storage location (roughly "variable") has an associated constraint (that is, predicate on the values it may take). There are two operations: the first, *ask*, determines whether a constraint associated with a storage location entails a constraint given as an argument, blocking if it does not. The other, *tell*, adds a constraint to a storage location. Both operations are idempotent. Programs compute by tightening the restrictions on the values of storage locations until no further progress can be made. The values can then be thought of as the result of the program.

Concurrent constraint programming partly abstracts from decomposition. Programmers are responsible for choosing variables, and for using the ask and tell operations (which play a communication role, although the parallel is not exact). Its logical foundations provide the basis for a software development methodology. Granularity is already at the level of single variables. Cost measures are not possible, since the model exploits non-deterministic execution.

The second major subapproach that is partly abstract is *process nets*, networks of more or less autonomous computations that communicate using message passing, usually asynchronous and one-directional. Message passing is more explicit than for coordination language models, and decomposition is still mostly the responsibility of the programmer.

The best known model of this kind is dataflow [100]. Dataflow graphs are directed graphs whose nodes denote operations and whose edges denote data dependencies between operations (and hence the flow of data resulting from computations to become arguments to further computations). Because dataflow graphs make data dependencies explicit, any two operations that are not directly connected are executable concurrently. Decomposition arises as a side-effect of describing the computation. The decomposition determined by data dependencies tends to be fine-grained, so most dataflow compilers aggregate operations to form larger threads. However, having the finest decomposition available from the start means that any granularity can be achieved by choosing the aggregation strategy. Configuration languages are sometimes used. Communication between operations is not done by explicit sends and receives but rather by the use of a variable name on the left hand side of an assignment in one place and on the right hand sides of statements in others. It is therefore visible, but not especially cumbersome to use.

Such models technically do not provide abstractions for decomposition, although it is hardly an issue since each expression is independent of all others unless they share a name. They partially abstract from communication (which is based on name matching rather than explicit actions). They also completely abstract from synchronisation, which is hidden in the *firing rule* for each language. Dataflow models do not provide a software development methodology (although they are often almost functional); nor are cost measures possible because of the extent to which scheduling is done dynamically at run-time subject to the availability of operands. Arbitrary granularity is possible, although some pragmatic difficulties have been encountered in ensuring that the critical path of computations is not unduly delayed by other enabled instructions. This is a direct result of the eager-evaluation style characteristic of dataflow.

Sisal [143, 176] is a single assignment language designed for scientific computation. Its origins are as a dataflow language but, although it can be executed in a dataflow style, the best implementations are on other kinds of architectures. Sisal programs contain syntactic loops, but each loop body is conceptually an independent entity with its own copies of variables. A keyword **old** is used to indicate that a reference is to the value in the previous iteration. These restrictions are sufficient to allow compilers to discover an unusual amount of information about the likely progress of a computation, and to optimise accordingly.

The Sisal model abstracts partly from decomposition by allowing for program structures that encapsulate parallelism, and abstracts partly from communication as dataflow does. Synchronisation is completely hidden. There is no complete software development methodology, although the single assignment style does allow reasoning about programs, and certain kinds of optimisations (for example, loop fusion) can be expressed formally. Cost measures are not possible. Any granularity is possible.

Another model based on process nets is actors [4, 27, 28, 115], and related models based on object-oriented ideas. Decomposition into threads is quite explicit, as in Linda. Communication emphasises the send step rather than the receive step, with actors willing to accept messages asynchronously from any other actor who knows their name. Actors is the "natural" model for distributed-memory MIMD architectures in the same sense that the PRAM model is the "natural" model for shared-memory MIMD architectures.

Actors require decomposition to be explicit, but provide partial abstractions for communication and synchronisation. They are not equipped with a software development methodology, nor can reasonable cost measures be developed (although bounds can be given in general [27]).

ActorSpace [5] is an extension of ideas from actors and from Linda. An actorspace holds actors, pattern-matching incoming messages on the basis of actor attributes. Messages contain both an actorspace name and a pattern, as well as the message contents. The actorspace delivers the message non-deterministically to any actor whose attributes match the pattern. ActorSpaces are sets of actors, and can contain and overlap with other actorspaces.

The actorspace idea removes some of the sequential bottlenecks that actor systems can exhibit, while providing a more open system based on interfaces. It does not abstract from decomposition, but does abstract from communication in the same way as a Linda tuple space. Synchronisation behaviour can be implemented in different ways in different actorspace systems – for example, a message that matches no actor might block until one comes into existence. Because they allow for arbitrarily nested abstractions, software development is probably easier than for plain actors. Actors can be of any size so any granularity is possible. Cost measures are not possible.

Many object-oriented models have been developed and it is difficult to separate ideas from syntax in deciding whether most have any new conceptual contribution from the perspective of models of parallel computation. Emerald [97, 114] is a distributed object-based language that emphasises mobility, and we will use it to represent this class of models. Both data and tasks in Emerald are objects. Communication between objects uses remote procedure calls, but transparent mobility of objects may turn a remote call into a local one. There are several ways to give hints to the compiler about how to place objects. It therefore shares some characteristics of actors and some of the active message approach discussed below.

These models do not provide abstractions for decomposition and communication, and only partial ones for synchronisation. No software development methodology has been constructed, and no cost measures are possible, given the dynamic behaviour of the system. Any granularity is possible.

Mentat [91, 92] is a related object-oriented model, built on C++. It uses objects whose methods may be implemented in parallel. Decomposition is left to the programmer, while communication, synchronisation, and scheduling are managed by the compiler and run-time system. Like other object-oriented approaches it does not have a software development methodology, although objects are obviously useful abstractions in software design. Cost measures are not possible because of the number of decisions postponed until compile-time or run-time. Granularity is partially variable, but might require rewriting outside a certain range.

EPL [192] is a language in which programs are mutually recursive equations. To limit the difficulties of dealing with general recursion, these equations define ragged multidimensional arrays of values. Programs are functional but can be connected together by ports which provide non-deterministic merging.

The EPL model does not abstract from decomposition, but does abstract from communication and synchronisation. There is no software development methodology, although equations are a natural way of expressing many scientific problems, so that this kind of software is easy to develop. Cost measures are not possible. Any granularity is possible by choosing the size of programs appropriately.

A third partly abstract approach is based on *active messages*. Here messages are not regarded as data objects passed between threads, but rather as active agents in their own right. A message is sent by a thread to another processor, where it transmutes into an active thread on that processor. This approach reduces the complexity of communication by removing the need for a receive operation altogether and because decomposition follows from the communication structure rather than requiring a separate set of decisions. It is embodied in the Movie system [74], and in the J-language [61, 153].

These models do not hide decomposition. They simplify message passing because a sender effects both ends of the data transfer by sending a handling process packaged as part of the message. Synchronisation is also simplified by this approach to messaging. No software development methodology is possible and neither are cost measures. Movie has no preferred granularity, but the J-language does not provide task abstractions, making large granularity difficult to work with.

These models are weaker than the very abstract approaches with respect to software development properties but stronger with respect to implementation. Indeed, they have often been motivated by the existence of very efficient implementations on one or two architecture classes. The lack of software development methodology, however, makes the development of large software problematic in most of these models.

```
┌─────────────────────────────────────────────────────┐
│   Low-level                                          │
│                                                       │
│       Architecture-Independent                       │
│          Pi, PMI                                     │
│          Orca                                         │
│          SR                                           │
│          PVM                                          │
│          p4                                           │
│          Express                                      │
│          Parmacs                                      │
│                                                       │
│       Architecture-Specific                          │
│          Occam                                        │
│          message passing Fortran and C               │
│          test&op language                            │
│          Message Passing Interface (MPI)             │
│          SDL                                          │
└─────────────────────────────────────────────────────┘
```

Table 4.4: Low-level Models

Low-Level Models. (Table 4.4) The third category of models are low-level models that do not hide decomposition and communication. Many of today's architecture-specific models are at this detailed level. We distinguish between those models that are architecture-independent, that is which try to provide enough facilities to use any architecture, and those that are tightly tied to a particular style of architecture.

Architecture-independent models are represented by system such as Pi and PMI [62, 201], that provide a rich set of primitives to allow any architecture to be programmed effectively without needing to worry about the specific mechanisms that each architecture uses. This can be seen as an attempt to pick out the basic ideas underlying a range of architectures and provide them in abstract, and hence architecture-independent, ways.

These models do not provide abstractions for decomposition, communication or synchronisation. In fact, they provide multiple ways of implementing all of these, giving programmers a lot of choice. There is no associated software development methodology or cost measures. Any granularity is possible but, like the J-language, working with complex tasks is difficult because of the lack of task abstractions.

Another set of models of the same general kind are the programming languages Orca [21] and SR [10, 11]. Several different mechanisms are provided to achieve each possible effect, but there is no specific attempt to make these languages simultaneously architecture-independent and efficient.

These models do not provide abstractions for decomposition, communication or synchronisation. There is no software development methodology, or cost measures. Any granularity is possible. They provide better ways of structuring computations than PMI.

A third set of models are those developed primarily to harness the unused power of networks of workstations. Since such networks are usually heterogeneous, these models are forced to be architecture-independent. They include systems such as PVM [29, 30], p4 [45],

Express [73, 76], and Parmacs [98, 99]. They are basically message passing systems with very-large-grain processes, and so suffer from the drawbacks of such systems. Networks of workstations are by far the most common parallel systems installed today, so these models have become popular.

These models do not provide abstractions for decomposition, communication or synchronisation. They do not have software development methodologies or cost measures. Any granularity is possible, although the systems are designed for architectures with long communication latencies, so fine-grained parallelism is expensive.

It is a commentary on the quality of tools for parallel software development that models with such weak properties have become the most popular way of developing software for large numeric computations. No doubt this is partly motivated by the availability of ensembles of workstations, but it is still an interesting phenomenon.

Architecture-specific low-level models cover all of the programming approaches that are specific to particular architecture styles. This includes most of the programming systems in production use today. A survey can be found in [20]. Some examples are Occam [105, 113], message passing extensions to Fortran and C, Test&Set extensions [90], and the Message Passing Interface (MPI) [70].

Occam has a sufficiently strong semantic foundation that reasoning about programs and transforming them is possible, so that some of the software development issues are addressed by the language. Nevertheless, the consensus seems to be that Occam's low-level treatment of process decomposition and communication is too awkward to make it practical for developing large software systems.

Many parallel languages have been built by adding message-passing operations to ordinary sequential imperative languages. These range from simple send and receive operations (blocking and non-blocking), to the full-blown complexity of the newly developed Message Passing Interface standard.

For shared-memory architectures, programmers must either carefully check that memory references do not collide or must use operations that enable them to gain exclusive access to a memory location for the duration of an access. Operating system concepts for critical sections were quickly added to sequential imperative languages for this purpose. Before making a reference to a shared location, each task must enter a critical section. This is often implemented by an atomic test&set instruction.

All of these models are closely tied to the architecture class for which they were designed. Those that are designed for distributed-memory architectures can be implemented on shared-memory architectures fairly easily, and so are architecture-independent to that extent. They do not provide any abstractions for decomposition, and the operations for communication and synchronisation are low-level and explicit in programs. Occam has an underlying theory (CSP [105]) that can be used to develop software, but the others have no support for software development.

Because of their close ties to architectures, cost measures are possible for these models, although the amount of detail required to compute them is so large that they are generally impractical. Any granularity is possible, because these models work at the lowest level with the smallest possible tasks which can be aggregated as necessary.

The PRAM Model. The final model that allows arbitrary computations to be written is the PRAM model [116]. The PRAM model is the most detailed of all of these models in the sense that the programmer is responsible for describing exactly how decomposition into threads is done, how the shared memory is managed so that two processors do not try to access the same memory location at the same time, and therefore how all of the communication is done. Writing PRAM programs is so complex that almost all published PRAM algorithms are in fact SIMD, with every processor executing the same action on each step. This is so much the case that the PRAM model is even sometimes regarded as an SIMD model.

The PRAM model does not provide any abstraction for decomposition, communication or synchronisation – all must be done by hand. There is no software development methodology, and the difficulty of development can be judged by the fact that papers are regularly published about the construction of a new program.

On the other hand, cost measures are possible, and form the basis of parallel complexity theory (although, as we have seen, it has deficiencies from a practical point of view because it does not account for communication).

A large number of PRAM extensions have been proposed in the literature, most intended to correct one or more of the deficiencies in the cost structure [2, 3, 8, 52, 94, 196].

4.1.2 Restricted Computation Structure Models

The second major subdivision of models are those that restrict the form of computations. Sometimes these restrictions are imposed to make programming in the models more abstract by providing higher-level abstractions and structures; sometimes the models have been designed with communication restriction and easier mapping in mind.

All of the models of this kind are architecture-independent, and almost all are efficiently implementable, at least in principle.

Since all of these models restrict the form of a computation, it is useful to think of them as requiring the trace of a computation to be made up from some set of tiles, templates, or dominoes. In some models, there is assumed to be a fixed set of such tiles, but this need not always be the case. Tiles are chosen to achieve the goals outlined above: to allow a new level of abstraction in thinking about the computation, and to restrict the amount of communication that occurs within each tile.

We classify models by the shape of tile that they use. There are three possible shapes: vertical tiles, describing the actions of a single processor (and thus equivalent to part of a thread), block tiles, describing the actions of a cluster of processors, and horizontal tiles, describing the actions of all the processors for some time period.

Vertical Tiling Models. (Table 4.5) Vertical tiling models have tiles that are restricted to one global communication action per tile. By requiring tiles to be of a certain size, they reduce the number of communication actions initiated by a computation, but do not limit the distance each message travels in the interconnect. Since the only requirement is to reduce the total volume, this approach is one way to prevent interconnect overload.

Valiant [198–200] defined the Bulk Synchronous Parallelism model [141], in which computations are divided into phases, alternating global communication and local computation.

Vertical tiling
Synchronised
Bulk Synchronous Parallelism
GPL
Unsynchronised
logP
Multithreading

Table 4.5: Vertical Tiling Models

Each phase begins with the issuing of global communication operations. Computation within each thread then proceeds using only local data references, while independently the interconnect satisfies the communication requests. At the end of each phase, called a superstep, all of the communication actions are guaranteed to have completed (which may require a barrier synchronisation) and the results of global memory references take effect locally. From a programmer's point of view, requests for data from a remote memory must be made in the superstep preceding the one in which they are used.

The size (that is the duration in time) of supersteps is determined by the delivery capability of the interconnect of the target machine. A programming language, GPL, implementing this approach has been designed [140, 142].

The BSP approach, because the emphasis is on what happens in each individual processor, still requires explicit decomposition into threads. Communication and synchronisation are still mostly explicit as well. In a sense communication is harder to manage because it is constrained to be well-spaced within each thread. Presumably some of this complexity could be hidden by a compiler, but no work in that direction has yet been attempted.

The other big handicap of the BSP approach is the lack of a software development methodology. The drawback of vertical tiling is that it is not a very structured abstraction – it structures in time but not in space. However, recent extensions to a Fortran compiler to provide BSP extensions suggest that it is a major advance over explicit message passing [147].

Cost measures are possible for BSP-based models; in fact, BSP can be viewed as a realistic cost system for the PRAM model. If a computation cannot be expressed using sufficiently large tiles for the intended target architecture, it is still possible to compute exactly how much communication overrun there will be, and so how the apparent performance will be degraded.

Any granularity can be used in programs, but not if efficiency is also required. Programs whose grains are too small for a particular target may require too frequent communication, which in turn destroys efficiency.

Another related approach is logP [60], in which similar vertical tiles are used, but there is no requirement to have all of the global communication occur in a synchronous way. Instead, each tile is permitted a single global communication action, and the size of tiles is determined by properties of the target architecture. Thus a machine with slow communication or little interconnect bandwidth must use large tiles. The properties of logP are almost exactly the same as BSP, as the models are similar.

Multithreading is, in a sense, a model in this class since it aims to conceal latency by overlapping the execution of many short threads. Multithreading does not yet suggest an obvious abstraction for use in a programming language and it seems unlikely that software will be written directly at its low level. Indeed, multithreading can be regarded as logP viewed from the more pragmatic perspective of machine designers. It hides synchronisation a little better because the compiler technology is more advanced, and lacks cost measures because it is less structured. The confluence of the three models discussed here could lead to interesting programming languages.

For both GPL and logP, it may happen that a particular algorithm cannot be expressed using tiles large enough to conceal all of the communication latency of a target machine. When this happens, efficient implementation is not possible. However, it is possible to determine exactly how inefficient the implementation will be. A similar property holds for the YPRAM [68].

Block tiling
HPRAM

Table 4.6: Block Tiling Models

Block Tiling Models. (Table 4.6) Block tiles decompose computations into tiles that cover multiple threads and multiple time steps. Communication must remain within each block, with the understanding that each block executes on a submachine of the target and hence encounters smaller latencies for intra-block communication. Global communication requires an occasional block that covers the full width of the machine. For example, in the hypercube, a block of size any power of two can be allocated as a submachine. Communication within such a submachine of size 2^x takes at most x steps.

The only model of this kind is the Hierarchical PRAM (HPRAM) developed by Heywood and Ranka [101–103]. This model does not abstract from decomposition, since the way the computation is divided into subcomputations is critical to the efficient implementation. It helps a little with communication and synchronisation because they take place within subcomputations, and therefore involve fewer threads. There is no methodology to assist with dividing computations and therefore no software development methodology or a way to use any granularity. However, cost measures are possible because the limited communication can be factored into costs directly.

Horizontal Tiling Models. (Table 4.7) Horizontal tiling uses the full width of the machine for each tile and may have an extent in time as well. The tile may be internally structured and contain significant internal communication and computation. It must restrict communication, either in frequency, or more commonly by reducing the distance travelled by each message. Because the implementer can choose how to organise the internal structure of the tile, subcomputations that need to communicate are placed in close processors. Unlike

```
Horizontal Tiling

    Algorithmic Skeletons
        Cole's Skeletons
        KIDS
        P³L
        Darlington's Skeletons
        Enterprise
        Parsec

    Data-Type-Specific

        Lists
            Scan
            Multiprefix
            Paralations
            Dataparallel C
            Scan Vector, NESL
            DPML
        Bags
            Parallel SETL
            Parallel Sets
            Match and Move
        Sets
            Gamma
        Arrays
            Array Theory, Nial
            Math. of Arrays
            Fortran D, 90, Vienna, HPF
            Pandore II
            C**
    Data-Type-Independent

        Crystal
        Categorical Data Types
```

Table 4.7: Horizontal Tiling Models

block tiling, however, the arrangement into submachines is done once for each tile by the implementer, rather than for each program by the programmer.

Horizontal tiling is a much more popular strategy for restricting computations than either of the previous two forms of tiling. We further subdivide such models according to how the tiles are chosen and what kind of operations they capture. Horizontal tiles are often called data-parallel operations in an imperative setting, and skeletons in a functional setting.

Some skeletons are based on popular algorithms or common program structures. We call them *algorithmic skeletons* since they are the parallel analogues of control structures and library routines. Some allow dynamic behaviour in the skeletons – this generally makes cost measures much harder to build and causes difficulties with efficient implementation.

The first algorithmic skeletons were designed by Cole in his thesis [54]. He chose four skeletons (fixed degree divide-and-conquer, iterative combination, clusters, and task queues) on the basis of their utility. He then worked out in detail how each should be implemented on a parameterised grid.

These skeletons abstract from decomposition, communication and synchronisation almost completely. Because the skeletons were defined in a functional style, it is possible to do some software development using equational reasoning. Cost measures for grid implementation were worked out. However, there is no nesting in the skeletons so granularity is restricted.

The KIDS system [182–185] contains a powerful software development tool that is capable of completely deriving a program given some knowledge of the application domain and information about what kind of algorithm is needed. Some of the algorithm styles that it can build are divide-and-conquer, greedy optimisation, and dynamic programming. The KIDS system has deep knowledge of such program templates, and is probably the most advanced program derivation system today.

The KIDS system is high level enough to hide almost all of decomposition, communication, and synchronisation. It provides a transformational software development methodology. However, it only provides partial cost measures and partial efficient implementation because of the possibility of dynamic computations, which in turn produces problems of task generation and migration at run-time.

The Pisa Parallel Programming Language (P^3L) [19, 63–65] uses a set of algorithmic skeletons that capture common parallel programming paradigms such as pipelines, worker farms, and reductions. It hides decomposition, communication, and synchronisation, has an equational software development methodology (some parts of it still under development), and a set of cost measures.

Similar work is also being done by a group at Imperial College, headed by Darlington [67, 155]. The skeletons used in this project hide decomposition, communication, and synchronisation, and the functional style makes transformational software development possible. No cost measures have yet been developed, but there is no reason in principle why they could not be, at least partly. Granularity is a problem because of the lack of nesting.

Another model based on program structures is Enterprise [134, 191]. Enterprise aims to allow existing sequential code to be used in a parallel setting by providing high-level graphical tools to connect code pieces together. The structuring of a parallel program is done by analogy with a business organisation: procedures are called assets and are connected together sequentially, or in a pool whose size can be fixed or dynamic. Assets are collected together in departments, each of which has a receptionist that acts as an interface to the rest of the program. Higher-level abstractions are also provided. The actual program construction uses a graphical user interface that abstracts from the names of communication points.

Parsec [75] is another system with a graphical interface. Processes and ports are manipulated on the screen rather than with a configuration annotation language. The power of Parsec comes from its group structure, which specifies a collection of processes to be part of a particular kind of skeleton. The internal connections are then made automatically.

These models provide no abstraction from decomposition (except for a structuring mechanism), but the graphical interface provides a partial software development methodology.

Cost measures are not possible. There is some flexibility in choosing granularity, and efficient implementation of some high-level structures is possible.

Other skeletons are based on operations that are *data-type-specific*. Most such models restrict themselves to a particular data type, so we classify them accordingly.

The construction of the Connection-Machine-2 provided a huge impetus to programming models based on lists, since this was the natural data type supported by the architecture. A wide variety of languages were soon developed whose basic operations were data-parallel list operations. These usually included a map operation, some form of reduction, perhaps using only a fixed set of operators, scans (parallel prefixes) and permutation operations. In approximately chronological order, these models are: scan [37], multiprefix [162], paralations [89, 167], Dataparallel C [95, 96, 160], and the scan-vector model and NESL [38–41].

All of these models abstract from decomposition, communication and synchronisation. The earlier ones do not have sufficiently strong semantic foundations for a software development methodology, but reasoning about some NESL operations is possible. All of the models allow cost measures to be built, although mapping strategies may make it difficult in some cases. The first four models are essentially flat, allowing a single level of data parallelism. NESL allows full nesting and hence has no problem with arbitrary granularity.

A related model is DPML [93], a functional language with an abstract machine structured as a one-dimensional array. DPML does not abstract from decomposition (in fact only one decomposition is possible) and only abstracts slightly from communication. It has stronger semantics than imperative list-based languages, so that software development and cost measures are possible. It is, however, a flat language so that arbitrary granularity is not possible.

Similar models have been developed based on sets and/or bags: parallel SETL [108, 109], parallel sets [118, 119], Match and Move [173, 174], and Gamma [22, 58, 152]. Parallel SETL and Gamma can be regarded as data-parallel languages on bags and sets respectively. Parallel sets is related to Parallel SETL but is an object-oriented language in which the data parallelism is encapsulated within objects.

These models all abstract from decomposition, communication, and synchronisation. All can be equipped with cost measures, although for set-based languages there are some difficulties. All allow for nested data-parallel operations, so that any granularity is possible. None has a strong enough semantic foundation to provide a software development methodology.

Match and Move is derived from data-parallel list languages. The match operation selects those elements of a bag that satisfy some property while move rearranges according to the property. The rearrangement step prevents cost measures being developed, since it can take arbitrary amounts of time, depending on the permutation being realised. The model is also flat, causing granularity problems.

There are also models based on the data type of arrays. This includes languages which derive from APL, such as Mathematics of Arrays (MOA) [151], and Nial and Array Theory [150]. Such languages are based on equational theories of array properties.

They abstract from decomposition, communication, and synchronisation, and have a transformational software development methodology based on their equational structure. Cost measures are possible, and nesting permits any granularity (except in MOA).

Further array-based models include languages developed from Fortran, such as Fortran-D [194], High Performance Fortran [104, 190], and Pandore II [9]. All these languages allow arrays to be partitioned and allocated to processor arrays using language annotations. As a result, they are only partial abstractions of decomposition, since programmers must decide data allocation, which drives the task allocation. Once decomposition has been specified, communication and synchronisation follow automatically. Cost measures can be derived from program structure, and nested allocation is possible. However, a software development methodology is not known.

The data-parallel language C** [128] is the array analogue of parallel sets, an object-oriented language in which objects contain arrays, whose elements are operated upon independently. Its properties are the same as the Fortran-based models, except that it does a better job of hiding decomposition.

It is also possible to take a data-type-independent approach to data-parallel programming. Crystal [51, 133, 202–204] is an approach to data parallelism that encompasses more than a single type, by using a generalised data type called an *index domain*. Index domains capture topological information about various data types. This information can be related by means of index domain morphisms that act as higher-order functions for combining data-parallel operations. Crystal satisfies all of the requirements for a model of parallel computation.

The other model that allows data-type independence is categorical data types. The independence here is different from Crystal's ability to combine data-type operations. Rather it is a generalised way to construct data-parallel languages for specific data types. It too satisfies all of the requirements for a model of parallel computation. These two models are quite closely connected. We explore this connection in Chapter 5.

The final model considered here is *systolic arrays*. These are a restricted form of computation originally used to model synchronous, limited interconnect computation in hardware. However, systolic arrays can be regarded as a model whose target domain is mesh-like architectures [131]. Thus they are not architecture-independent, nor do they provide abstractions for decomposition or communication. They do provide an abstraction for synchronisation, they do have a software development methodology [135, 171], they do possess cost measures, and they are efficiently implementable over their limited range of target architectures.

4.2 Implications for Model Design

Figure 4.1 and 4.2 summarise the properties of the models we have described. From this summary, we draw several conclusions.

From these Figures it is easy to see that models that best satisfy the requirements come from the extremes – on the one hand, models that are very abstract and on the other models based on horizontal tiles.

High-level models easily satisfy the requirements for architecture independence, for intellectual abstraction, and for a software development methodology. They cannot, however, be efficiently implemented without some restrictions, as we have seen in Chapter 3. More pragmatically, they are often difficult to implement even with the efficiency that the emulation results suggest. Some of the gap between abstract program mechanisms and architectures can be bridged by compilers, but enough remains that sophisticated run-time systems are needed – and the dynamic behaviour that results prevents useful cost measures from being possible.

Model	Arch. Independ.	Abstracts from Dec.,Comm.,Syn.			S/W Develop.	Cost Measures	Any Granul.	Effic. Implem.
Haskell	y	y	y	y	y	n	y	n
UNITY	y	y	y	y	y	n	p	n
Action systems	y	y	y	y	y	n	p	n
OBJ	y	y	y	y	y	n	y	n
Maude	y	y	y	y	y	n	y	n
Parafunctional	y	p	p	y	n	n	y	n
Caliban	y	p	p	y	n	n	y	n
Linda	y	n	p	y	n	n	y	n
Ease	y	n	p	y	n	n	y	n
SDL	y	p	p	y	n	n	y	n
ALMS	y	n	p	p	n	n	y	n
PCN	y	p	p	p	p	n	y	n
Compos. C++	y	p	p	p	p	n	y	n
cc	y	n	n	y	y	n	y	n
Dataflow	y	n	p	y	n	n	y	n
SISAL	y	p	p	y	n	n	y	n
Actors	y	n	p	p	n	n	y	n
ActorSpace	y	n	y	p	p	n	y	n
Emerald	y	n	n	p	n	n	y	n
Mentat	y	n	y	y	n	n	y	n
EPL	y	n	n	n	n	n	y	n
Movie	y	n	p	y	n	n	y	n
J-language	y	n	p	y	n	n	p	n
Pi, PMI	y	n	n	n	n	n	p	n
Orca	y	n	n	n	n	n	y	n
SR	y	n	n	n	n	n	y	n
PVM etc.	y	n	n	n	n	n	y	n
Occam	y	n	n	n	p	y	y	n
TestSet	n	n	n	n	n	y	y	n
Mess. Pass.	y	n	n	n	n	y	y	n
PRAM	y	n	n	n	n	y	y	n

Figure 4.1: Summary of Properties – Arbitrary Computation Models; p indicates *partial* support for the property

The interesting problems with abstract models are:

- Can they be implemented well enough so that only the logarithmic inefficiency occurs (in which case such models become interesting in any domain in which complexities are large enough that such overheads can be ignored)?

- What is the best restriction on abstractness to make reasonably efficient implemen-

Model	Arch. Independ.	Abstracts from Dec.,Comm.,Syn.			S/W Develop.	Cost Measures	Any Granul.	Effic. Implem.
BSP, GPL	y	n	n	p	n	y	p	y
logP	y	n	n	p	n	y	p	y
Multithreading	y	n	p	y	n	p	p	y
HPRAM	y	n	p	p	n	y	p	y
Cole skeletons	y	y	y	y	p	y	n	y
KIDS	y	y	y	y	y	p	n	p
P^3L	y	y	y	y	y	y	p	y
Darlington skels	y	y	y	y	y	p	p	p
Enterprise	y	n	p	p	p	n	p	p
Parsec	y	n	p	p	p	n	p	p
Scan	y	y	y	y	n	p	n	y
Multiprefix	y	y	y	y	n	p	n	y
Paralations	y	y	y	y	n	p	n	y
Dataparallel C	y	y	y	y	n	p	n	y
NESL	y	y	y	y	p	p	y	y
DPML	y	n	p	y	p	p	n	y
Parallel SETL	y	y	y	y	n	y	y	y
Parallel Sets	y	y	y	y	n	y	y	y
Match&Move	y	y	y	y	n	n	n	p
Gamma	y	y	y	y	n	y	y	y
AT	y	y	y	y	y	y	y	y
MOA	y	y	y	y	y	y	n	y
Fortran	y	p	y	y	n	y	y	y
Pandore II	y	p	y	y	n	y	y	y
C**	y	y	y	y	n	y	y	y
Crystal	y	p	y	y	y	y	y	y
CDTs	y	y	y	y	y	y	y	y
Systolic arrays	n	p	p	p	y	y	p	y

Figure 4.2: Summary of Properties – Restricted Computation Models; *p* indicates *partial* support for the property

tation possible, without sacrificing intellectual abstractness or software development methodology?

The other kinds of models that satisfy many of the requirements are those based on horizontal tiling. It is straightforward to choose tiles that can be efficiently implemented, by ensuring that communication is restricted. This also makes the development of cost measures possible. Such models even do well at providing intellectual abstractness since they usually allow programs to appear single-threaded.

Their weakness lies in the dependence of a software development methodology on the properties of the tiles in relation to one another. Choosing a set of tiles for pragmatic reasons such as their apparent applicability makes it hard to say anything strong about program transformation, for example. The best models of this kind select their tiles using some underlying algebraic setting. This allows for rigorous software development and, as a side-effect, seems to increase the expressiveness of the resulting language as well.

We take the view that efficient implementation is the hard problem, and therefore begin with a horizontal tiling model, categorical data types. We then show how its formal underpinnings give rise to a software development methodology.

Chapter 5 ——————————————————

The Categorical Data Type of Lists

So far we have discussed the properties that a model of parallel computation ought to have and have claimed that models built from categorical data types have these properties. In this chapter we show how to build a simple but useful categorical data type, the type of join or concatenation lists, and illustrate its use as a model. We show how such a model satisfies the requirements, although some of the details are postponed to later chapters.

The language we construct for programming with lists is not different from other parallel list languages in major ways in the sense that most of the list operations are familiar maps, reductions, and prefixes. The differences are in the infrastructure that comes from the categorical data type construction: an equational transformation system, a deeper view of what operations on lists are, and a style of program development. When we develop more complex types, the construction suggests new operations that are not obvious from first principles.

For the next few chapters we concentrate on aspects of parallel computation on lists. We describe the categorical data type construction in more detail in Chapter 9 and move on to more complex types. The next few sections explain how to build lists in a categorical setting. They may be skipped by those who are not interested in the construction itself. The results of the construction and its implications are summarised in Section 5.5.

5.1   Categorical Preliminaries

We begin with some elementary category theory definitions:

Definition 5.1 *(Category)* A category is a structure with objects $A, B, \ldots$, arrows $f, g, \ldots$, and an associative binary operation $\cdot$ *(compose)* on arrows such that

$$\frac{f : A \to B \quad g : B \to C}{(g \cdot f) : A \to C} \tag{5.1}$$

that is, whenever there are arrows $f : A \to B$ and $g : B \to C$ then there is an arrow, called $(g \cdot f)$ from A to C, and

$$\overline{id_A : A \to A} \tag{5.2}$$

such that for every arrow $f : A \to B$,

$$f \cdot id_A = f$$
$$id_B \cdot f = f$$

In other words, a category can be thought of as an edge-labelled directed graph whose edge structure is "sufficiently rich" that it includes transitive closures and single vertex cycles.

We will assume that we are working within the category *Type* or *Set* whose objects are sets and whose arrows are total functions. The properties we need of this category are:

- It has an initial object **0**. There is a unique arrow from this object to every other object in the category.

- It has a final object **1**. There is a unique arrow from every object in the category to this object.

- It has products, that is for all pairs of objects A and B, there is an object $A \times B$, and projections from it to A and B.

- It has coproducts, that is for all pairs of objects A and B, there is an object $A + B$, and injections to it from A and B.

- For every pair of arrows $f : A \rightarrow C$ and $g : B \rightarrow C$ there is an arrow, called the junction, $f \triangledown g : A + B \rightarrow C$.

Background reading in category theory can be found in [127, 158].

In *Type*, products are ordered pairs of types. So the product $\mathbb{N} \times Bool$ is the type whose elements are pairs of natural number with True or False. There are two arrows, the right and left projections, from the product to each of its component types. For example, the right projection from $\mathbb{N} \times Bool$ to $Bool$ maps each ordered pair to its second component.

Coproducts are unions of types. The coproduct $\mathbb{N} + Bool$ is the type whose elements are either natural numbers or True or False, labelled to say which type each element is. There are two injections from the underlying types to the coproduct type. The left injection from $\mathbb{N}$ to $\mathbb{N} + Bool$ maps a natural number to itself, labelled with the information that it is a natural number.

A functor is a category homomorphism.

Definition 5.2 *(Functor)* A functor $\mathsf{F} : \mathcal{C} \rightarrow \mathcal{D}$ maps objects of a category $\mathcal{C}$ to objects of a category $\mathcal{D}$ and maps arrows in $\mathcal{C}$ to arrows in $\mathcal{D}$ in such a way as to preserve compositions and identities, that is

$$\begin{aligned}
\mathsf{F}(f : A \rightarrow B) &= \mathsf{F}f : \mathsf{F}A \rightarrow \mathsf{F}B \\
\mathsf{F}(g \cdot f) &= \mathsf{F}g \cdot \mathsf{F}f \\
\mathsf{F}id_A &= id_{\mathsf{F}A}
\end{aligned}$$

5.2 Data Type Construction

The first step of the categorical data type construction is to choose an endofunctor, that is a functor from the base category onto itself, of a particular kind. In order to know what the functor should be, we first consider the constructors we wish the constructed type to possess.

The lists we will build are homogeneous and so have elements of some underlying type, which we write A. We write the (so far hypothetical) type of join or concatenation lists as $A*$. The three required constructors for this type are then:

$$[] \ : \ 1 \to A*$$
$$[\cdot] \ : \ A \to A*$$
$$\mathbin{+\!\!+} \ : \ A* \times A* \to A*$$

The first constructor, *emptylist* or $[]$, defines the distinguished element of the type that represents the empty sequence. The second constructor, *makesingleton* or $[\cdot]$, takes a value of the underlying type and makes it into a singleton list. The third constructor, *concatenate* or $\mathbin{+\!\!+}$, takes two lists and makes them into a single list by concatenating them. To get the type of lists rather than simply binary trees we also need a pair of equations, one of which states that $\mathbin{+\!\!+}$ is associative, and the other that the codomain of $[]$ is the identity for $\mathbin{+\!\!+}$. Using these three constructors we can build any list of As, including the empty list. A list is an object such as

$$[a_1] \mathbin{+\!\!+} [a_2] \mathbin{+\!\!+} [a_3]$$

which can be conveniently abbreviated to

$$[a_1, a_2, a_3]$$

These three constructors correspond to a single arrow in the base category, namely $[] \triangledown [\cdot] \triangledown \mathbin{+\!\!+} \ : \ 1 + A + A* \times A* \to A*$. We have not yet shown that the object $A*$ exists, but the endofunctor we want is the one whose action is to unpack the hypothetical constructed type into its components. If this functor exists and has certain properties, we define $A*$ to be the object part of its fixed point.

We define a functor T whose effect is

$$T : A* \mapsto 1 + A + A* \times A*$$

For lists, functor T is clearly
$$T = K_1 + K_A + I \times I$$

where K_X is the constant X functor that maps every object to X, and every arrow to id_X. Functor T takes $A*$ to $1 + A + A* \times A*$ as required. The functor T depends on the type over which we are building lists, A, so we write it T_A to remember this dependence. Later on we show how to make the construction polymorphic.

Notice that the form of the functor T_A is a combination of constant functors, and products and coproducts of functors. Such a functor is called *polynomial*.

In the base category, polynomial functors have fixed points. We define $A*$ to be the object part of the fixed point of the functor T_A [186].

The arrow part of the fixed point is an isomorphism between $A*$ and $T_A A*$. $A*$ is isomorphic to $T_A A* = 1 + A + A* \times A*$, that is it is isomorphic to the components from which it was built, in their proper arrangement. Intuitively, this seems obvious; there is nothing about an object of a constructed type that does not depend on the pieces from

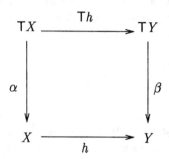

Figure 5.1: Homomorphism between T_A-Algebras

which it was built, and their mutual relationships.

One instance of this isomorphism is the constructor arrow

$$\tau = [] \triangledown [\cdot] \triangledown \mathbin{+\!\!+} : 1 + A + A* \times A* \to A*$$

and the inverse pattern-matching arrow τ^{-1}

$$\tau^{-1} : A* \to 1 + A + A* \times A*$$

This arrow maps an object of type $A*$ to an empty list, a single value, or a pair of sublists depending on its argument. This mutually inverse pair of arrows plays an important role in the use of categorical data types.

5.3 T-Algebras

Given a functor, T, a T-algebra is a pair (TX, X) and an arrow between them $TX \to X$. By the definition of T_A, there is a T_A-algebra,

$$[] \triangledown [\cdot] \triangledown \mathbin{+\!\!+} : T_A A* \to A*$$

Now consider the category whose objects are such T_A-algebras, and whose arrows are T_A-algebra homomorphisms. T_A-algebra homomorphisms are maps that preserve T_A-algebra structure, that is they are pairs of arrows in the original category. For example, if h is a T_A-algebra homomorphism from $T_A X \to X$ to $T_A Y \to Y$, it must consist of two component arrows, one from $T_A X$ to $T_A Y$ and another from X to Y such that the diagram in Figure 5.1 commutes. The fact that the diagram commutes can be expressed equationally as

$$h \cdot \alpha \;=\; \beta \cdot Th$$

This category is called the category of T_A-algebras. We know that there is at least one object in this category, the T_A-algebra corresponding to the type of lists of As. This T_A-

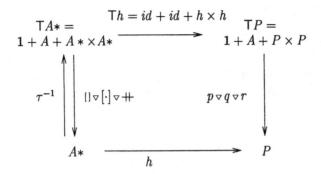

Figure 5.2: Homomorphism from an Initial T_A-Algebra

algebra is actually rather special in this category; it is the category's *initial object*, that is there is a unique T_A-algebra homomorphism from it to any other T_A-algebra [186]. These unique T_A-algebra homomorphisms are called *catamorphisms* and they turn out to be the homomorphic operations on objects of the categorical data type.

We have already seen that the initial algebra is more than just a T_A-algebra – it is also an isomorphism, with the arrows

$$\tau = []\triangledown[\cdot]\triangledown\!\!+\!\!+ : 1 + A + A* \times A* \rightarrow A*$$

and

$$\tau^{-1} : A* \rightarrow 1 + A + A* \times A*$$

An arbitrary T_A-algebra consists of three pieces: a type P, a type $T_A P$, that is $1 + A + P \times P$, and an arrow $p\triangledown q\triangledown r : 1 + A + P \times P \rightarrow P$. The algebra inherits the equational properties that r is associative and the codomain of p is its identity. Thus an arbitrary T_A-algebra is a *monoid* whose underlying type, P, is computable from A (via q), with an associative binary operation, r, whose identity is $p(1)$.

In summary, the category of T_A-algebras is the category of monoids whose underlying types are computable from the type A, and whose initial object is the *free list monoid* $(A*, [], +\!\!+)$.

Consider the special case of the diagram in Figure 5.1 where the left hand algebra is chosen to be the initial algebra. This is shown in Figure 5.2. The diagram shows that there is an indirect way to compute the function h, by following the left, top, and right sides of the diagram and using the fact that it commutes. The first step is the inverse to the constructors, τ^{-1}, which selects which of the three possible constructors was used to build the argument to which h is being applied. The second step is to use the appropriate part of $T_A h$ – if the argument was an empty list use id_1, if it was a singleton use id_A, and if it was a larger list, use h applied to the sublists that were used to build it. The third step is to put back together the results of these subcomputations by applying p, q, and r as appropriate. It is the middle step that makes the alternative form of the computation interesting. When

```
eval_catamorphism(p, q, r, l)
case l of
      [] : return p ([])
      [a] : return q (a)
      l1 ++ l2 : return r ( eval_catamorphism(p, q, r, l1),
                            eval_catamorphism(p, q, r, l2))
end
```

Figure 5.3: Evaluating a Catamorphism

the argument is a list of length greater than two, the middle step consists of two independent recursive calls to h. These calls can be executed concurrently, opening up the possibility of parallelism of the order of the number of elements of the list.

Another way to understand the diagram in Figure 5.2 is to look at the equations that are implied by the commuting square:

$$
\begin{aligned}
h \cdot [] &= p \cdot id_{[]} \\
h \cdot [\cdot] &= q \cdot id_A \\
h \cdot \mathbin{+\!\!+} &= r \cdot (h \times h)
\end{aligned}
$$

The left hand sides of these equations describe the application of h to objects of the constructed type, already assembled from component pieces. The right hand sides show that the same results can be computed by applying functions to the pieces, and then putting them together in a different but consistent way.

The diagram encapsulates a recursive schema that shows how to compute any catamorphism in terms of operations on subobjects of the argument, reassembled using the algebra structure of the codomain. The diagram gives a purely syntactic way to write recursive computations on a structured data type – a form of packaged recursion. For types whose objects are expressed as combinations of two or more subobjects of the same type, this recursive structure is the basis for the parallel computation of catamorphisms.

The computation strategy in the diagram is expressed as a program in Figure 5.3. The evaluation of a list catamorphism is a recursive function in which decisions are based on the form of the argument. Because the list concatenation operation is associative, we are free to divide the argument list in two in any way. It is clearly going to be best to divide it as nearly in half as possible.

There is a one-to-one connection between catamorphisms and the algebraic objects that are their codomains because of the uniqueness of catamorphisms as arrows whose domains are the initial object. Therefore we express the catamorphism arrow in terms of its codomain, the target monoid. We write

$$(\, p, q, r \,)$$

for the catamorphism from $(A*, [], \mathbin{+\!\!+})$ to (P, p, r) which maps As to Ps using q.

This one-to-one connection is important because it implies a decomposition strategy for

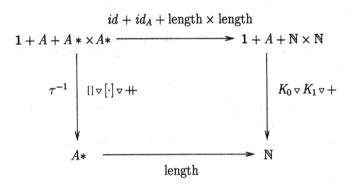

Figure 5.4: Length expressed as a Catamorphism

homomorphic programs on lists. All such homomorphisms are catamorphisms, and therefore have corresponding target monoids. These target monoids in turn correspond to a type and a triple of functions with type signatures involving this type. The construction of a list homomorphism can be reduced to the simpler problem of finding such a triple of functions.

Catamorphisms depend heavily on initiality, an idea which is not particularly new in the area of data type construction. Much work was done in the Seventies and Eighties on abstract data types using initiality [72, 87]. This work concentrated on a syntactic notion of data type, whose semantics was given by many-sorted algebras. Reasoning about data types occurred in the syntactic domain, using first-order logic and the powerful tools associated with it. OBJ represents an implementation of these ideas. The categorical data type approach emphasises mathematical reasoning, rather than logic, and is purely semantic.

Catamorphisms include most of the interesting functions on lists. Let us consider some simple examples.

Example 5.3 The function *length* computes the length of a list. It is a catamorphism from $(A*, [], +\!\!\!+)$ to the monoid $(\mathbb{N}, 0, +)$ where the function q maps elements of type A to the constant 1, that is $q : A \to \mathbb{N}$. This catamorphism is written as $(\!| K_0, K_1, + |\!)$ (where K_x is the constant x function). The diagram corresponding to this catamorphism is shown in Figure 5.4. Notice that knowing that the codomain is a monoid forces us to define the length of an empty list, something that is often omitted in *ad hoc* definitions of this function. From the diagram, we get the following equations that show how to compute *length* on different arguments:

$$\begin{aligned} length \cdot [] &= K_0 \cdot id_{[]} \\ length \cdot [\cdot] &= K_1 \cdot id_A \\ length \cdot +\!\!\!+ &= + \cdot (length \times length) \end{aligned}$$

The length of an empty list can be computed by applying the constant 0 function, so the length of any empty list is 0. The length of a singleton list can be computed by applying the constant 1 function. The length of any longer list can be computed by dividing the list into two pieces (in any way, because of associativity), computing the length of each, and summing the result.

Example 5.4 Another example of a useful catamorphism is the function *sum* which sums the elements of a list (we assume that A is the type of natural numbers for this example). It is the catamorphism

$$\text{sum} = (\!| \, K_0, id, + \, |\!)$$

that is, the sum of an empty list is 0, the sum of a singleton list is the value of the element it contains, and to compute the sum of any other list, apply *sum* to each of the sublists recursively and apply + to the values returned by these recursive calls.

As a general rule, the effect of a catamorphism can be seen by taking a constructed object of the free type and replacing each constructor by the corresponding part of the catamorphism. For example, for *sum*

$$
\begin{array}{ccccccc}
[a_1] & +\!\!+ & [a_2] & +\!\!+ & [a_3] & & [] \\
\downarrow & \downarrow & \downarrow & \downarrow & \downarrow & & \downarrow \\
a_1 & + & a_2 & + & a_3 & & 0 = K_0[]
\end{array}
$$

where the [] constructor has been replaced by K_0, the [·] constructor has been replaced by the identity on As, and the +\!\!+ constructor has been replaced by +.

Although all catamorphisms can be computed using a single recursive schema, it is worth considering some special cases – special because they occur often in computations, and also because they can be computed without all the operations required by the full recursive schema and so offer opportunities for optimisation. The two special kinds of catamorphisms are *list reductions* and *list maps*.

The *sum* catamorphism is an example of a list reduction. For list reductions the component function corresponding to the constructor that introduces singleton elements of the underlying type is the identity. Reductions do not affect the elements of the list, but only the list structure itself.

The second kind of special catamorphism is the list map. Suppose that there exists a computable function $f : A \rightarrow B$. Then we define a map to be a catamorphism of the form

$$\text{map } f = (\!| \, [], [\cdot] \cdot f, +\!\!+ \, |\!)$$

and write it $f*$. Its effect on a list of As is

$$
\begin{array}{ccccccc}
[a_1] & +\!\!+ & [a_2] & +\!\!+ & [a_3] & & [] \\
\downarrow & \downarrow & \downarrow & \downarrow & \downarrow & & \downarrow \\
[fa_1] & +\!\!+ & [fa_2] & +\!\!+ & [fa_3] & & []
\end{array}
$$

that is, it applies the function f to each of the singleton values in the structure, without altering the structure. The effect of this catamorphism is to "lift" f so that it applies to lists pointwise, that is it maps lists of As into lists of Bs. Thus whenever there is an arrow in the base category, there is a corresponding map arrow in the category of T-algebras. Of course, computing a list map can be done by simple applications of f at each singleton node, without the need for pattern matching at all.

The category of T_A-algebras has other arrows besides the catamorphisms. These other arrows are monoid homomorphisms. However, the initiality of the free list algebra has one other useful implication. Suppose that we wish to compute a function that is a composition of a catamorphism followed by some sequence of monoid homomorphisms. The codomain of this program is a monoid. Therefore there is a unique arrow from the free list monoid directly to it. In other words, all such functions can be transformed to a canonical form consisting of a single catamorphism. Furthermore, the transformations involved are just equational substitutions corresponding to commuting diagrams in the category.

This result is important for two reasons. First, it tells us that programs can be built by applying a simple catamorphism to lists and then applying further operations to the resulting monoid (as long as they are monoid homomorphisms). Building in this way loses no generality, because the resulting program can always be transformed into a single catamorphism. Second, it shows that there is a canonical representation for every homomorphic program on lists, and that the equations of the T-algebra category form a canonical rewrite rule set. This gives us a completeness property for the program transformation system built from these equations – any initial representation of a given function can be transformed into any other representation, including the efficient ones. Furthermore, transformations cannot lead to 'dead ends' because they are all reversible, being equational.

Categorical data types in which the components of $T_A A*$ can be divided into two coproduct terms, one of which is a coproduct of products involving only the underlying type A, and the other of which does not contain a reference to A, are called *separable*. Such types have the important and useful property that any catamorphism factors into the composition of a map and a reduction (the proof can be found in Chapter 9). Thus only implementations of two special cases of the general recursive schema need to be built to compute any homomorphism on the constructed type.

Lists are a separable type, since the type functor T_A can be written as $K_A + (K_1 + id \times id)$. Any homomorphism on lists can therefore be factored into the composition of a list map and a list reduction. For example, the catamorphism *length* factors as

$$
\begin{aligned}
length \; &= \; (\!| \; K_0, K_1, + \; |\!) \\
&= \; (\!| \; K_0, id, + \; |\!) \cdot (\!| \; [], [\cdot] \cdot K_1, +\!+ \; |\!) \\
&= \; +/ \cdot K_1 *
\end{aligned}
$$

5.4 Polymorphism

There was nothing special about the type A with which we began the construction. We could have equally well begun with another type, B, and all of the details would have worked out the same. Doing so, we end up with a category of T_B-algebras with an initial object of lists of Bs and catamorphisms from it to monoids whose underlying types are computable from B.

All of the T-algebras are related to each other via the map catamorphisms. If there is a function $f : A \to B$ then there is a catamorphism from the free list monoid on A to the free list monoid on B. The catamorphisms from the list monoid on B are certainly monoid homomorphisms, so there must exist catamorphisms from the list monoid on A corresponding to the composition of the map and B catamorphisms.

Now, recall that our underlying category has an initial object, **0**. The T_0-algebra category includes all of the other T_X-algebra categories, because there is a suitable computable function from **0** to any other type that can be lifted to a map. We can think of T as a bifunctor, one of whose arguments records the underlying type. This is made more formal in Chapter 9.

Now for any object in the underlying category, there is an object (the free list monoid on that object) in the category of T_0-algebras, and every arrow in the underlying category lifts to a map in the category of T_0-algebras. Thus we can define a functor *map* (written ∗), from the underlying category to the category of T_0-algebras.

5.5   Summary of Data Type Construction

The construction of lists as a categorical data type has the following properties:

1. Every homomorphism on lists should properly be regarded as a function from the free list monoid (whose objects are lists of As, with binary concatenation ($+\!\!+$) and identity the empty list) to another monoid (whose objects are of a type P computable from A, with a binary associative operation and identity). Such homomorphisms are called catamorphisms.

   Target monoids are determined by three operations

   $$
   \begin{aligned}
   p &: \; \mathbf{1} \to P \\
   q &: \; A \to P \\
   r &: \; P \times P \to P
   \end{aligned}
   $$

   where r is associative with identity $p(\mathbf{1})$.

   Every catamorphism is in one-to-one correspondence with a target monoid. We can therefore write each catamorphism in the form $(\!|\, p, q, r \,|\!)$.

2. A useful strategy for finding catamorphisms is to look instead for a suitable target monoid. This allows decomposition of concerns, since it separates the structural part, which is the same for every list catamorphism, from the specific part of each individual catamorphism.

3. Every catamorphism on lists can be computed by a single recursive schema (which contains opportunities for parallelism and for which computation and communication patterns can be inferred). The schema is shown in Figure 5.3.

4. Maps and reductions are special cases of catamorphisms. They are important special cases because every list catamorphism can be expressed as a map followed by a reduction.

5. Any syntactic form of a list homomorphism can be reached from any other form by equational transformation using a set of equations that come automatically from the construction of the type of lists.

5.6 Practical Implications

All of this may seem remote from a programming language. However, the recursive schema for evaluating catamorphisms has an obvious operational interpretation. We can view it in several related ways.

Taking an object-oriented view, we could regard the recursive schema as an object containing a single method, *evaluate_catamorphism*. It is given two objects as arguments: the first is a free list monoid object, the second a monoid object. A free list monoid object consists of a type and six methods, three constructor methods and three pattern-matching methods. A list monoid consists of a type and three methods, the component functions. A C++ library showing this is included in Appendix A.

In this view, categorical data types have obvious connections to object-oriented models in which parallelism is hidden inside objects (such as Mentat [91, 92] and C** [128]). There is a clear separation between the semantics of *evaluate_catamorphism* and potential implementations, either sequential or parallel. None of the objects possess state, since we are working in a functional setting, but there is an obvious extension in which the base category has arrows that are something other than *functions*.

A more standard functional view is to regard the evaluation of a catamorphism as a second-order function. Strictly speaking, *evaluate_catamorphism* takes

$$p \triangledown q \triangledown r \cdot \mathsf{Th} \cdot \tau^{-1}$$

as its argument. However, since $p \triangledown q \triangledown r$ and h are in one-to-one correspondence, and the remaining machinery comes from the data type being used, it is hardly an abuse of notation to regard the catamorphism evaluation function as taking p, q, and r as its arguments. This is the view that has been taken in work on software development within the CDT framework (usually called the Bird–Meertens Formalism (BMF) [32, 144]).

It might seem as if any CDT program on lists consists of a single catamorphism evaluation. This is not true for two reasons. First, programs are calculated, so that their intermediate forms are usually a catamorphism followed by a sequence of homomorphisms. Second, since lists can be nested, programs can involve mapping of catamorphisms over the nested structure of lists.

We illustrate some of the catamorphisms that are so useful that it is convenient to think of them as built-in operations on lists. We will then show how the CDT model satisfies the requirements that were listed in Chapter 2.

Because of the factorisation property of lists, only two basic building blocks are needed. These are a way of evaluating list maps, a *map* skeleton, and a way of evaluating list reductions, a *reduction* skeleton. Each of these satisfies equations, derived from the recursive schema, which are the familiar equations satisfied by the second-order map and reductions of ordinary functional programming.

Given a function $f : A \to B$ in the underlying category, a *map* is defined by the following three equations:

$$f*[a_1, a_2, \ldots a_n] = [fa_1, fa_2, \ldots fa_n]$$
$$f*[a_1] = [fa_1]$$

$$f * [] \ = \ []$$

When f is a function of two variables (usually a binary operation) it is convenient to define a form of map called *zip*. It is defined by the equations:

$$[a_1, a_2, \ldots a_n] \curlyvee_\oplus [b_1, b_2, \ldots b_n] \ = \ [a_1 \oplus b_1, a_2 \oplus b_2, \ldots a_n \oplus b_n]$$
$$[a_1] \curlyvee_\oplus [b_1] \ = \ [a_1 \oplus b_1]$$
$$[] \curlyvee_\oplus [] \ = \ []$$

for $\oplus$ a function of two variables.

A reduction is the catamorphism from $(A*, [], +\!\!\!+)$ to a monoid $(P, e, \oplus)$ given by

$$\oplus/ \ \triangleq \ (\!|\, K_e, id, \oplus \,|\!)$$

or

$$\oplus/\,[a_1, a_2, \ldots a_n] \ = \ a_1 \oplus a_2 \oplus \ldots \oplus a_n$$
$$\oplus/\,[a_1] \ = \ a_1$$
$$\oplus/\,[] \ = \ e$$

Another convenient catamorphism is *filter*, which selects those elements of a list that satisfy a given predicate and returns them as a new list. If p is a predicate (that is a computable function $p : A \rightarrow Bool$), then

$$p \triangleleft \ \triangleq \ +\!\!\!+ \,/ \cdot (\text{if } p \text{ then } [\cdot] \text{ else } [])*$$

Any injective function f on lists is a homomorphism. The proof is as follows [84]: since f is injective it has an inverse g such that $g \cdot f = id$. Define an operation @ by

$$u @ v = f \sim (g \sim u +\!\!\!+ g \sim v)$$

where $\sim$ indicates that application associates to the right. Then

$$f \sim (x +\!\!\!+ y) \ = \ f \sim (g \sim f \sim x +\!\!\!+ g \sim f \sim y)$$
$$= \ f \sim x @ f \sim y$$

It is is easy to check that @ is associative. Thus f is a homomorphism on the list type and hence a catamorphism. This result generalises to any categorical data type.

This result assures us that many interesting functions are catamorphisms. One such function computes the list of initial segments of its argument list, that is

$$\text{inits}[a_1, a_2, \ldots, a_n] = [[a_1], [a_1, a_2], \ldots [a_1, a_2, \ldots, a_n]]$$

Clearly *last* $\cdot$ *inits* $= id$, so *inits* is a catamorphism. In fact, it is the catamorphism

$$\text{inits} \ = \ (\!|\, A**, [], [[\cdot]], +\!\!\!+ \,|\!)$$

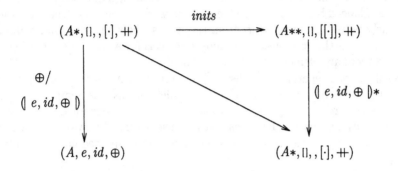

Figure 5.5: Defining Prefix

If $\oplus/$ is any reduction, then we can define a *prefix* operation based on it by

$$\oplus/\!\!/ \cong (\oplus/)* \cdot \text{ inits}$$

This exactly corresponds to the operation defined by Ladner and Fisher [126] sometimes called *scan*. Figure 5.5 shows the diagram from which this definition arises.

We can generalise the *prefix* operation in the following way: an operation is a *generalised prefix* if it is of the form

$$\text{generalised prefix} \cong (\!\!|\ f\ |\!\!)* \cdot \text{ inits}$$

for an arbitrary catamorphism $(\!\!|\ f\ |\!\!)$. Generalised prefixes are the most general operations that have the computation and communication structure of the prefix operation.

Programs can be written using these operations, which are not very different from those developed for other data-parallel programming languages on lists. The benefit of having built them as CDTs is in the extra power for software development by transformation, and the knowledge that all of these apparently diverse operations have an underlying regularity which may be exploited when evaluating them. We illustrate their use in software development in Chapter 6.

5.7   CDTs and Model Properties

We now turn our attention to the properties of catamorphisms as a model of parallel computation, in the sense of the last few chapters.

We begin by considering the communication requirements of the two operations, list map and list reduction. If we use the full recursive schema, then all catamorphisms require exactly the same communication pattern. However, as we have already noted, we can often optimise. List map requires no communication at all between the subcomputations representing the application of the argument function at each element of the list. Reduction can also be optimised. Strictly speaking, evaluating a reduction involves pattern matching and dividing a list into sublists to which recursive reductions are applied. However, the binary operation involved is associative, so that we are free to divide list in any way that suits us. The obvious best way is to divide each list in half, or as close as can be managed. The end result is that the recursion is a balanced binary tree, in which all the work is done after the recursive calls return. It is clearly better to simply start from the leaves, the singletons, and combine the results of subtrees. Thus the communication requirement is for a complete binary tree with as many leaves as there are elements of the argument list.

Using the result on the separability of lists, all catamorphisms on lists can be computed if we provide a balanced binary tree topology for which the list elements are the leaves. This is called the *standard topology* for the list type. It can be determined, even before the type is constructed, by inspecting the types of the constructors. We will use the standard topology to show that these operations can be efficiently implemented across a wide range of architectures.

We now consider the six properties that a model of parallel computation should possess and measure the categorical data type of lists against them.

Architecture Independence. It is immediate that the categorical data type of lists is architecture-independent.

Intellectual Abstractness. The CDT of lists satisfies the requirement for intellectual abstraction because it decouples the semantics of catamorphisms from their implementation (although the recursive schema provides one possible implementation). Programs are single-threaded compositions of second-order operations, inside which all of the parallelism, communication, and decomposition are hidden. Only compiler writers and implementers really need to know what goes on inside these operations. As far as programmers are concerned, the operations are monolithic operations on objects of the data type. Furthermore, compositions of operations can themselves be treated as new operations and their implementations hidden, providing a way to abstract even further. Almost any level of detail other than the kind of data type being used can be hidden in this way.

Software Development Methodology. A software development methodology is provided by the categorical framework in which CDTs are built. This has a number of components:

- The one-to-one correspondence between catamorphisms (programs) and monoids provides an unusual method for searching for programs. We have already commented on the abstraction provided by being able to specify what is to be computed rather than how it is to be computed. A further abstraction is provided by being able to think only about the type of the result (that is, which codomain the result of the program lies in) rather than what is to be computed.

  Furthermore, finding a catamorphism reduces to the problem of finding an algebra, which reduces to finding a particular set of functions. This is a powerful way to limit concerns during software design.

- The recursive schema for catamorphisms provides a set of equations that shows how to evaluate catamorphisms in terms of constructors. These equations are used for program transformation.

- There is a canonical form for any homomorphic program on the data type. Furthermore, all syntactic forms of a particular homomorphic function are mutually inter-transformable within the equational system provided by the category of T-algebras. Thus it does not matter which form of a program is used as the starting point in a development – it is still possible to reach all other forms, including the best.

We discuss software engineering aspects of CDTs further in Chapter 6.

Cost Measures. The implementation of CDT operations using a standard topology allows a reasonable cost calculus to be developed. In general, the number of degrees of freedom in decomposing and mapping a parallel program make it impractical to compute realistic costs. The standard topology simplifies the problem of mapping computations to processors in a way that makes costs of operations reasonable to calculate. However, costs of compositions of operations cannot be computed accurately in any cost system, so a limited cost calculus is the best that can be hoped for. This is discussed in more detail in Chapter 8.

No Preferred Granularity. The absence of a preferred scale of granularity occurs because the construction is polymorphic. It is possible to build not only lists of integers or lists of reals, but also lists of lists of integers, and so on. Thus the data objects to which programs are applied are in general deeply nested and there is flexibility about the level at which parallelism is exploited. In many ways it is like writing ordinary imperative programs using only nested loops – such programs can exploit both fine and coarse grained parallelism, as well as parallelism at multiple levels.

Efficiently Implementable. To implement maps and reductions efficiently on different architectures, it suffices to embed the standard topology in the interconnection network of the architecture without edge dilation (ensuring that communication time is constant). In the discussion that follows, we assume that the first-order functions (the component functions) take constant time and constant space. This is not always true, and we will return to this point in Chapter 8.

We have already seen that any computation can be implemented efficiently on shared-memory architectures and distributed-memory architectures with rich interconnect, that is whose interconnect capacity grows as $p \log p$. Doing so for shared-memory architectures requires using parallel slackness, but direct emulation can be done for some distributed-memory architectures with rich interconnect structure. Suppose that a distributed-memory machine possesses a hypercube interconnect. If the machine has 2^d processors, then a standard way to implement the interconnect is to allocate a d-bit address to each processor and join those processors whose addresses differ in any single bit. A simple routing algorithm results – on each step, route a message so that the Hamming distance between the current node and destination is reduced.

Maps can be implemented efficiently on shared-memory and distributed-memory MIMD architectures because they require no communication between threads. Direct emulations, without the use of parallel slackness, suffice.

Reductions can be implemented efficiently on shared-memory MIMD architectures using the emulation described in Chapter 3. The use of parallel slackness is required.

Reductions can be implemented on distributed-memory MIMD architectures with rich interconnect structure because they can be arranged so as to require only nearest-neighbour communication. The technique is called *dimension collapsing*. Suppose that an element of the list is placed at each processor. On the first step of the reduction, each of the processors in the upper hyperplane of dimension d sends its value to the corresponding processor in the lower hyperplane, which then applies the binary operation to produce a partial reduction. The processors in the upper plane then sleep, while the step is repeated in the hyperplanes of dimension $d - 1$. This continues until the result is computed at a hyperplane of dimension 0, that is, at a single processor. Each step takes constant time, and there are d steps, where d is the logarithm of the number of elements in the list.

The same dimension-collapsing implementation of reductions can be made to work for certain distributed-memory interconnection topologies with linear capacity. Recall that the cube-connected-cycles topology can be thought of as a hypercube of dimension d, in which each corner has been replaced by a cycle of d processors, each connected to a hypercube edge. If each processor of such a machine contains a single element of a list, a reduction is implemented as follows:

- Carry out a reduction in each cycle simultaneously, circulating the accumulating result around the cycle.

- Use the hypercube reduction algorithm to collapse the dimensions of the hypercube substructure, rotating the newly-computed value at each corner one position around the cycle between each step so that it is in position for the next reduction step.

The resulting implementation is still of logarithmic order, and therefore efficient.

The operations of map and reduction can also be implemented efficiently on SIMD architectures because they have the property that, at each step, each processor is either executing a common operation, or is idle. This choice of two possible operations is easy to implement on most SIMD machines. Maps require a single operation to be computed at each processor. Reductions require an operation to be computed at half the processors on the first step, at one quarter of the processors on the next step, and so on, with the other processors idle.

Catamorphisms on the categorical data type of lists can therefore be efficiently implemented across all four architecture classes. The model satisfies all six properties of a model of parallel computation.

5.8   Other List Languages

Functional languages have tended to use cons lists and not to restrict themselves to second-order functions. The natural set of languages with which to compare the categorical data type of lists are data-parallel list languages. Many data-parallel languages on lists have been defined and implemented. Many of these have sets of operations that are similar to some of the useful catamorphisms we have been examining. We briefly examine how the categorical data type approach differs from these other list-based models.

The chief advantages of the CDT approach to data-parallel lists compared to other list-based languages are:

- The data-parallel operations (skeletons) are not chosen as part of the construction of the data type, but arise naturally from the construction. The only choice in building lists was that of the constructors. If we had not included the [] constructor we would have built the type of non-empty join lists; the algebras would have been different; and therefore so would the catamorphisms. This avoids the two opposite questions that an *ad hoc* construction faces: have any data-parallel operations been missed, and are any of the data-parallel operations redundant?

- The categorical construction provides a software development methodology, and hence a way to build in correctness, that does not arise as naturally in *ad hoc* constructions, and may not be possible for them.

- All catamorphisms share a common communication pattern implied by the recursive schema that underlies them all. This common pattern allows us to define a standard topology for each type, which makes a restricted solution to the mapping problem possible. This in turn makes useful cost measures possible. As we have seen, separability makes things easier by allowing simpler implementations without losing expressive power. This commonality cannot be guaranteed for *ad hoc* constructions, and may be obscured in them if present.

- The constructed type is polymorphic. This is usually possible for an *ad hoc* data-parallel language, but often seems to be forgotten. Most data-parallel list languages do not allow nested lists.

The differences between the categorical data type construction and other constructions become more obvious and important as they are used to build more complex types. The benefit of the CDT construction is in the depth of understanding and regularity that it gives to the use of data-parallel operations.

5.9 Connections to Crystal

Crystal [51] is the approach that is closest to categorical data types. The Crystal view of a data type is a lower-level one than we have taken, because each data type has a concrete implied geometric topology, much more so than the standard topology of a CDT. Crystal work has concentrated on refinement of data types in the sense of replacing one geometric arrangement by one which is easier to implement. The Crystal approach is accordingly more flexible because it can handle any interconnection topology.

Crystal uses index domains as the descriptors of each type. An index domain represents that structure of a type, without implying anything about its content. Thus an index domain corresponds to a T_0-algebra or a T_1-algebra. Crystal data types are defined as arrows from an index domain to a content type, so the correspondence with a T_1-algebra is more useful. Thus in Crystal an indexed interval of natural numbers is represented by the arrow

$$[m, n] \to \mathbb{N}$$

As a CDT the equivalent construction would be an algebra of pairs

$$[(m, a_1), (m + 1, a_2), \ldots, (n, a_{n-m+1})]$$

where the a_i are elements of some type A. Thus an indexed interval of natural numbers is an arrow from the terminal algebra (with A instantiated as $\mathbf{1}$) to the algebra with A instantiated as $\mathbb{N}$.

Crystal's refinements are morphisms between index domains. From the CDT point of view, these correspond to functors between T-algebras and, say, S-algebras induced by mappings of the terminal objects. These have not been explicitly investigated within the CDT framework, but it has been observed that connections between CDTs lead to powerful new algorithms (e.g. [24]).

In summary, the approaches taken in Crystal and CDTs are complementary to one another. Progress can be expected from exploring this synthesis.

Chapter 6

Software Development Using Lists

In this chapter, we explore, in more detail, the software development methodology that is used with CDTs. It is a methodology based on transformation. Many of the transformations that are useful for list programming were already known informally in the Lisp community, and more formally in the APL and functional programming community. The chief contributions of the categorical data type perspective are:

- a guarantee that the set of transformation rules is complete (which becomes important for more complex types); and

- a style of developing programs that is terse but expressive.

This style has been extensively developed by Bird and Meertens, and by groups at Oxford, Amsterdam, and Eindhoven. A discussion of many of the stylistic and notational issues, and a comparison of the Bird–Meertens approach with Eindhoven quantifier notation, can be found in [17]. Developments in the Bird–Meertens style are an important interest of IFIP Working Group 2.1.

6.1 An Integrated Software Development Methodology

A software development methodology must handle specifications that are abstract, large, and complex. The categorical data type approach we have been advocating plays only a limited role in such a methodology because it is restricted (at the moment) to a single data type at a time. Although it is useful for handling the interface to parallel architectures, it is too limited, by itself, to provide the power and flexibility needed for large application development. In this section, we sketch how the CDT approach fits into the larger scene, some parts of which are already well understood, while others are active research areas.

One plausible view of an integrated parallel software development approach is shown in Figure 6.1. The process of refining a specification to a parallel program can be conveniently divided into three stages, although the boundaries are not nearly as well-defined as the diagram suggests. In all three stages, progress is made by refinement or by transformation, the final program resulting from a complete sequence of manipulations from specification to implementation.

In the first stage, the primary goal is to remove non-determinism from the specification. This stage is well-understood, and systems such as Z [120, 188] and VDM [36], together with the schema calculus, can be used. (Of course, these systems can do more than this and

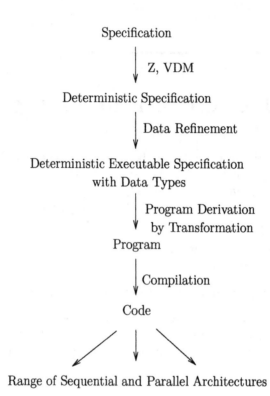

Figure 6.1: An Integrated Scheme for Parallel Software Development

can play a role in the later stages of development. However, we would argue that CDTs do better, once a data-type-dependent specification has been reached.)

The second stage involves decisions about the data types to be used in the computation. This is called *data refinement* or *data reification*, but is really the stage at which the algorithm, or kind of algorithm, is being chosen. Data refinement is an area of active research. Work by Gardiner, for example, [80, 81] is relevant. Note that the choice is of data type, not of representation, and the choice of algorithm is of the kind of algorithm (e.g. sorting lists) rather than the specific algorithm (e.g. quicksort).

The third stage is the development of code for a computation on a particular data type, and it is here that the equational development style associated with categorical data types comes into play. The form of the specification at the end of the second stage is often a comprehension involving the selected data types. Many solutions to programming problems can be expressed in the form: generate all possible solution structures, then pick the one(s) that are solutions. For example, it is easy to characterise those lists that are sorted, and thus to express sorting on lists as a comprehension. However, this does not trivially lead to good sorting algorithms. The third stage usually begins from a form of the specification in which the algorithms are expressed in a brute force way. The goal at the end of this stage is to transform them into efficient algorithms. At the beginning of the third stage specifications are usually still clear enough that their correctness is obvious; by the end this is not usually the case.

Starting from an executable specification over a particular data type, the category of algebras associated with that data type provides equations that are used to transform the specification into a more efficient form. This is not a directly automatic procedure and insights are usually required to direct the transformation process. Nevertheless, the transformational derivation style has a number of advantages:

1. The insights required to make a single transformation are small ones, involving an equational substitution at some point in the current version of the specification. This modularity of concerns brings many of the benefits of stepwise refinement in traditional software development – only one problem needs to be considered at a time.

2. There are typically only a few transformations that are applicable at each point in the derivation. This makes it possible, for example, to use a transformation assistant to display all transformation rules that apply.

3. The choice of one transformation over another is preserved in the derivation to record that there was a choice point and, if necessary, the justification for the choice can be recorded with it. The derivation becomes a kind of documentation for the eventual program, and one that encodes not just how it was built, but why it was built that way.

4. The transformations are equational and hence necessarily correctness-preserving. The only obligations on the developer are to show that the rules used are applicable. Furthermore, rules are used in software development without concern for their correctness and how they were arrived at – developing rules and ensuring their correctness can be left to specialists.

5. Complete derivations or parts of derivations can be kept and reused, and can even be parameterised and used as derivation templates. Parameterised derivations are much more powerful than reusable software, because each single derivation produces a wide range of programs, whose similarities may be subtle and hard to see from the programs themselves.

Some automation is possible. At the simplest level, transformational systems are tedious because they require much copying of text unchanged from one step to the next. We have built several simple assistants that handle text from one step to the next, and which also allow equations that apply to the current specification to be selected and applied. All of the decisions about what transformations to use are still made by the developer, but much of the housekeeping can be handled automatically.

With the development of a cost calculus (discussed in Chapter 8), a further level of automation becomes possible. For example, equations can be oriented in the direction that reduces the execution cost. However, this is not directly useful, because most derivations are not monotonically cost-reducing. Indeed, many derivations seem to involve three phases: the first in which expansions occur and costs are increased, the second in which rearrangements

$$(f \cdot g)* \ = \ f* \cdot g* \tag{6.1}$$

$$f* \cdot + \!\!\!\!+/ \ = \ + \!\!\!\!+/ \cdot f** \tag{6.2}$$

$$p\triangleleft \cdot + \!\!\!\!+/ \ = \ + \!\!\!\!+/ \cdot p\triangleleft* \tag{6.3}$$

$$+/ *. + \!\!\!\!+ / \ = \ + \!\!\!\!+/.+/** \tag{6.4}$$

$$\oplus/ \cdot + \!\!\!\!+/ \ = \ \oplus/ \cdot (\oplus/)* \tag{6.5}$$

$$\oplus /\!\!/ \ = \ \oplus/ * \cdot \text{inits} \tag{6.6}$$

$$\text{inits} \ = \ + \!\!\!\!+/\!\!/ \cdot ([\cdot]) * \tag{6.7}$$

$$\oplus /\!\!/ \cdot f* \ = \ \oplus/ * \cdot f** \cdot \text{inits} \tag{6.8}$$

$$\oplus/ \cdot f* \cdot + \!\!\!\!+/ \cdot g* \ = \ \oplus/ \cdot (\oplus/ \cdot f* \cdot g)* \tag{6.9}$$

Figure 6.2: Basic Identities for Lists

occur and the cost does not change much, and the third in which contractions take place and costs are reduced. There does not seem to be much hope of automating this process, although it would obviously be useful to be able to instruct the transformation system to automatically minimise cost at any moment in the derivation.

One difference between the calculus of CDTs and other transformational approaches is that the conditions determining whether or not a rule applies in the context of a particular specification are algebraic rather than logical – a certain transformation applies because an operation $\oplus$ is the operation of a monoid, rather than because of some logical condition on it. We have already mentioned that developers must justify the applicability of a rule. In the CDT setting this justification is an appeal to the algebraic status of some operations. This creates a new style of proof which is significantly different from standard program-proving approaches.

6.2   Examples of Development by Transformation

Deriving programs on lists in the CDT style began before a categorical view of lists was built. Examples can be found in [31–35, 144]. We give a few simple examples to provide the flavour of how such derivations look and how they are done.

Figure 6.2 gives some of the basic identities for lists, with f and g any functions, and $\oplus$ the operation of a monoid. These equations are all special cases of commuting diagrams in one or other of the categories we discussed in Chapter 5. For example, Equation 6.1 is just the action of the functor $*$ on arrows of the base category.

We begin with a simple example. Write a program to *find the maximum of the sums of the initial segments of a list*. From this specification it is easy to write down a computation that satisfies it, namely

$$\uparrow/ \cdot (+/) * \cdot inits$$

(where $\uparrow$ is the binary maximum function). The correctness of this computation is manifest, since it does exactly what the specification asks for, word by word. It is an example of the kind of initial specification that often arises in which the first step is the generation of many possible solutions, followed by the selection of one. Since the *inits* operation generates $n(n-1)/2$ elements when applied to a list of length n, we see informally that this computation does work at least quadratic in the length of its argument.

A transformation to a more efficient computation is straightforward:

$$\text{maxinitialseg} = \quad \{ \text{ initial version } \}$$
$$\uparrow / \cdot (+/) * \cdot inits$$

$$= \quad \{ \ 6.6 \ \}$$
$$\uparrow / \cdot +/\!\!/$$

The new version computes only a linear number of intermediate values, and so is much more efficient than the original. We will make this transformation again when we have developed a cost calculus, and it will be possible to see exactly how much of an improvement this transformation has made.

Now let us consider the problem of string matching, that is, *given a string of characters, and another string w, determine if w is present in the given string*. This problem is presented in detail in [35] and a good sequential algorithm derived. Again we write down a direct but expensive solution:

$$sr = \vee / \cdot (w =) * \cdot \text{segs}$$

where *segs* is the function that computes all of the substrings of a list and $\vee$ is binary **or**. One way to compute *segs* is

$$\text{segs} = +\!\!+/ \cdot \text{tails} * \cdot \text{inits}$$

where *tails* is like *inits*, but takes final segments instead. The derivation might then continue like this:

$$sr = \quad \{ \text{ initial solution } \}$$
$$\vee / \cdot (w =) * \cdot \text{segs}$$

$$= \quad \{ \text{ definition of segs } \}$$
$$\vee / \cdot (w =) * \cdot +\!\!+ / \cdot \text{tails} * \cdot \text{inits}$$

$$= \quad \{ \ 6.2, (w =) * \cdot +\!\!+ / = +\!\!+/ \cdot (w =)** \ \}$$
$$\vee / \cdot +\!\!+/ \cdot (w =)* * \cdot \text{tails} * \cdot \text{inits}$$

$$= \quad \{ \ 6.5, \vee / \cdot +\!\!+/ = \vee / \cdot (\vee/)* \ \}$$
$$\vee / \cdot (\vee/) * \cdot (w =)* * \cdot \text{tails} * \cdot \text{inits}$$

$$= \quad \{ \ 6.1 \ \}$$
$$\vee / \cdot (\vee/ \cdot (w =) * \cdot \text{tails}) * \cdot \text{inits}$$

We will see other, more complex derivations as we introduce new list operations in the next chapter.

Another major component to software development in this style is the separation of concerns that comes because any catamorphism is equivalent to a set of functions in the target algebra. Lists are so simple a type that it is less important here, but we will see, when we build more complex types, that it is very useful to be able to break up the construction of a catamorphism into the construction of a set of simpler functions. Furthermore, the simpler component functions are not functions on the constructed type, but functions *inside* the target algebra, which is usually a simpler environment. In a very real and practical sense, the CDT construction takes care of the structure of the constructed type and leaves only the construction of the component functions to be designed.

6.3   Almost-Homomorphisms

While homomorphisms include all of the injective functions and are enough to compute many common functions, there are some functions that are not homomorphic. Fortunately, some of these turn out to be almost-homomorphisms. An almost-homomorphism is a homomorphism whose argument is an instance of the data type where the base type is a tuple, followed by a projection. The use of tuples allows partial results to be available throughout the computation of a catamorphism. The final projection is used to select the desired element of the tuple as the result of the almost-homomorphism. An example (taken from [55]) will make the idea clearer. Consider the problem of determining whether a string contains a matched set of nested parentheses. As it stands, the function that determines this is not a homomorphism, for it returns *NO* when applied to n left parentheses or n right parentheses, but returns *YES* when applied to n left parentheses followed by n right parentheses.

This function can be made homomorphic by applying it to a list of tuples where each tuple consists of three values: a boolean value which is true when the current string is a matched set of parentheses, an integer giving the count of the excess of opening over closing parentheses for the current string, and an integer representing the lowest value that the excess counter would have reached in a sequential pass through the current string. Whether or not a string contains a matched set of parentheses can then be determined by the following three stage process:

1. Map the function f over the symbols of the string where

$$
\begin{aligned}
f\ (\ &= \ (\text{false}, 1, 0) \\
f\ ) \ &= \ (\text{false}, -1, -1) \\
f\ x \ &= \ (\text{true}, 0, 0)
\end{aligned}
$$

   for x any other character.

2. Compute a reduction with $\oplus$ where

$$
\begin{aligned}
(ok, final, low) &\oplus (ok', final', low') = \\
&((ok \wedge ok') \vee ((final + final' = 0) \wedge (low \geq 0) \wedge (final + low' \geq 0)), \\
&final + final', \\
&low \downarrow (final + low'))
\end{aligned}
$$

3. Project out the first element of the resulting tuple.

The second and third elements of the tuple carry information that is required to compute the next level of the reduction; Cole calls this baggage. The intuition for the reduction step is that a string has a matched set of parentheses if: each of its halves is matched independently, or the number of left and right parentheses agree, the excess count in the left substring was never negative and the excess count in the right substring *would never have been negative* had it been initialised to the final value of the left substring.

Almost-homomorphisms provide a simple but powerful way to increase the expressiveness of the catamorphic approach. We see them again used for computing recurrences in Chapter 7 and for computing costs at the end of Chapter 8.

Chapter 7

Other Operations on Lists

In this chapter we show some more complex operations defined for the theory of lists. We build new operations that compute recurrences in parallel and address the question of permutation operations.

7.1 Computing Recurrences

Consider the computation of a linear recurrence with coefficients $a_1, \ldots, a_n$ and $b_0, \ldots, b_n$ and given by

$$
\begin{aligned}
x_0 &= b_0 \\
x_i &= (x_{i-1} \otimes a_i) \oplus b_i, \quad 1 \leq i \leq n
\end{aligned}
$$

Such computations are very common because many real problems are of this kind. For example, the x_is can represent states at discrete time intervals and the a_is and b_is transformations of a state at time t to a new state at time $t + 1$. Usually x_n is to be computed, given the coefficients a_i and b_i; sometimes all of the x_is are needed.

The interesting thing about recurrences is that, although they seem absolutely sequential because of the dependence of each x_i on the previous one, there is a fast parallel algorithm for computing them (under certain conditions on $\otimes$ and $\oplus$). This has been known for a decade [123]. We include it here because we can *derive* the parallel algorithm from consideration of the recurrence equations, and because it illustrates how a composition of useful list operations can be packaged as a single useful list operation, thus increasing the level of abstraction of list programming.

Expanding the recurrence gives

$$
x_n = (\ldots(b_0 \otimes a_1 \oplus b_1) \otimes a_2 \oplus \ldots \oplus b_{n-1}) \otimes a_n \oplus b_n
$$

When the operators $\otimes$ and $\oplus$ are not associative or semi-associative, the computation of x_n is inherently linear. However, if $\otimes$ and $\oplus$ are associative and $\otimes$ distributes backwards through $\oplus$, a parallel version of the computation is possible.

With these algebraic properties on the operators their types must be

$$
\begin{aligned}
\otimes &: A \times A \;\rightarrow\; A \\
\oplus &: A \times A \;\rightarrow\; A
\end{aligned}
$$

We define an operation, recur-reduce, $\otimes/_e\oplus$ with type

$$\otimes/\_\oplus : A \rightarrow A* \times A* \rightarrow A$$

by

$$
\begin{aligned}
[\,] \otimes /_{b_0}\oplus\, [\,] &\;\hat{=}\; b_0 \\
[a_1, ..., a_n] \otimes /_{b_0}\oplus\, [b_1, ..., b_n] &\;\hat{=}\; b_0 \otimes a_1 \otimes ... \otimes a_n \oplus \\
&\qquad b_1 \otimes a_2 \otimes ... \otimes a_n \oplus \\
&\qquad ... \qquad\quad \oplus \\
&\qquad b_{n-1} \otimes a_n \oplus \\
&\qquad b_n
\end{aligned}
$$

In making this definition, we choose to make the length of the argument lists equal, and treat the initial seed value, b_0, as a third argument because it reduces the difficulty of conformance checking of the length of argument lists during derivations.

The following lemma shows that $x \otimes /_{b_0}\oplus y$ can be calculated by using $\otimes/$ and $\oplus/$:

Lemma 7.1

$$x \otimes /_{b_0}\oplus y = \oplus/\left(([b_0] + \!\!\!+\, y) \,\curlyvee_\otimes\, ((\otimes/* \cdot tails)\, x)\right), \quad \#x = \#y \qquad (7.1)$$

Proof

$$
\begin{aligned}
x \otimes /_{b_0}\oplus y \;=&\; \left\{\; \text{definition} \;\right\} \\
&\; b_0 \otimes a_1 \otimes ... \otimes a_n \oplus b_1 \otimes a_2 \otimes ... \otimes a_n \oplus ... \oplus b_{n-1} \otimes a_n \oplus b_n \\[4pt]
=&\; \left\{\; \text{inspection, } b \circledast x \,\hat{=}\, b \otimes (\otimes/x) \;\right\} \\
&\; \oplus/\left(([b_0] + \!\!\!+\, y) \,\curlyvee_\circledast\, (tails\, x)\right) \\[4pt]
=&\; \left\{\; \text{properties of zip} \;\right\} \\
&\; \oplus/\,\cdot\,(\otimes/)*\left(([[b_0]] + \!\!\!+\, [.]* \,y) \,\curlyvee_{+\!\!\!+}\, (tails\, x)\right) \\[4pt]
=&\; \left\{\; \text{promotion through zip} \;\right\} \\
&\; \oplus/\left(((\otimes/)* ([[b_0]] + \!\!\!+\, [.]* \,y)) \,\curlyvee_\otimes\, ((\otimes/)* (tails\, x))\right) \\[4pt]
=&\; \left\{\; \text{reduction on singleton, function composition} \;\right\} \\
&\; \oplus/\left(([b_0] + \!\!\!+\, y) \,\curlyvee_\otimes\, ((\otimes/* \cdot tails)\, x)\right)
\end{aligned}
$$

In this lemma, the calculation of $x\otimes/_{b_0}\oplus y$ is dominated by the operation of *tails*. Therefore, it takes $O(n)$ parallel time for lists of length n. The problem with the computation above is that it recomputes many of the $\otimes$ products – which suggests that if we wish to find a fast parallel computation, we should memoise and save the values of these intermediate computations so that they are only computed once. This suggests that we look for an operator whose type is

$$\oslash : (A, A) \times (A, A) \to (A, A)$$

where the first of the tuple arguments can be used for partial $\otimes$ products. The following lemma shows that $x \otimes /_{b_0} \oplus y$ can be computed in parallel in $O(\log n)$ time using such an associative operator. Notice that this is another example of an almost-homomorphism.

Lemma 7.2 Recur-reduce *is expressed as a reduction as follows:*

$$x \otimes /_{b_0} \oplus y = \begin{cases} b_0, & \text{if } \#x(=\#y) = 0 \\ b_0 \otimes \pi_1 A \oplus \pi_2 A, & \text{if } \#x(=\#y) \neq 0 \end{cases} \tag{7.2}$$

where

$$\begin{aligned}
A &= \oslash/(x \curlyvee_\otimes y), \\
a \otimes b &= (a, b), \\
(a, b) \oslash (c, d) &= (a \otimes c, b \otimes c \oplus d), \\
\pi_1(a, b) = a, \quad &\text{and} \quad \pi_2(a, b) = b
\end{aligned}$$

The identity element of operator $\oslash$, $id_\oslash = (id_\otimes, id_\oplus)$, exists only when $id_\otimes$ is the *left-zero* element of $\otimes$, that is, $id_\oplus \otimes a = id_\oplus, \forall a \in A$. In this case, the lemma simplifies to:

$$x \otimes /_{b_0} \oplus y = b_0 \otimes \pi_1 A \oplus \pi_2 A$$

Since $\otimes$ and $\oplus$ are both associative, and $\otimes$ distributes backwards through $\oplus$, a little algebra and an example (see Figure 7.1) make the associativity of $\oslash$ obvious. It is also clear that both $\otimes$ and $\oslash$ are constant time operators. Therefore, the above lemma expresses a logarithmic parallel time algorithm.

We compute all of the values x_i of a recurrence using a similar operator. *Recur-prefix*, written as $\otimes /\!\!/_{b_0} \oplus$, takes two lists of values (e.g., $[a_1, ..., a_n]$ and $[b_1, ..., b_n]$) and returns the list of x_i values. We informally define it as follows:

$$\begin{aligned}
[\,] \otimes /\!\!/_{b_0} \oplus [\,] &\triangleq [b_0] \\
[a_1, ..., a_n] \otimes &/\!\!/_{b_0} \oplus [b_0, \ldots, b_n] \\
&\triangleq [b_0, b_0 \otimes a_1 \oplus b_1, \\
&\quad b_0 \otimes a_1 \otimes a_2 \oplus b_1 \otimes a_2 \oplus b_2, ..., \\
&\quad b_0 \otimes a_1 \otimes ... \otimes a_n \oplus ... \oplus b_{n-1} \otimes a_n \oplus b_n]
\end{aligned}$$

where the types are

$$\begin{aligned}
\otimes &: A \times A \to A \\
\oplus &: A \times A \to A \\
\otimes /\!\!/\_\oplus &: A \to A* \times A* \to A*
\end{aligned}$$

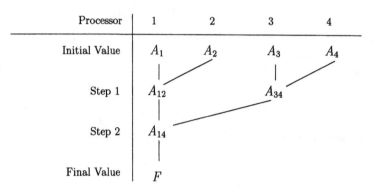

Processor	1	2	3	4
Initial Value	A_1	A_2	A_3	A_4
Step 1	A_{12}		A_{34}	
Step 2	A_{14}			
Final Value	F			

$$A_1 = (a_1, b_1), \ A_2 = (a_2, b_2), \ A_3 = (a_3, b_3), \ A_4 = (a_4, b_4)$$
$$A_{12} = (a_1 \otimes a_2, b_1 \otimes a_2 \oplus b_2), \ A_{34} = (a_3 \otimes a_4, b_3 \otimes a_4 \oplus b_4)$$
$$A_{14} = (a_1 \otimes \ldots \otimes a_4, b_1 \otimes a_2 \oplus b_2 \otimes a_3 \otimes a_4 \oplus b_3 \otimes a_4 \oplus b_4)$$
$$F = b_0 \otimes a_1 \otimes \ldots \otimes a_4 \oplus b_1 \otimes a_2 \otimes a_3 \otimes a_4 \oplus \ldots \oplus b_3 \otimes a_4 \oplus b_4$$

Figure 7.1: Parallel Algorithm for Computing x_4

Lemma 7.3 *Recur-prefix can be expressed by a prefix as follows:*

$$x \otimes /\!\!/_{b_0}\oplus y = \begin{cases} [b_0], & \text{if } \#x(= \#y) = 0 \\ [b_0] + (b_0 \circledast) * (\oslash/\!\!/(x \curlyvee_\otimes y)), & \text{if } \#x(= \#y) \neq 0 \end{cases} \tag{7.3}$$

where

$$\begin{aligned} a \otimes b &= (a, b), \\ (a, b) \oslash (c, d) &= (a \otimes c, b \otimes c \oplus d), \\ b_0 \circledast (a, b) &= b_0 \otimes a \oplus b \end{aligned}$$

Again some simple algebra shows that $\oslash$ is associative. Since $\oslash$ and $\otimes$ are constant time operations, $\oslash/\!\!/$ can be evaluated in $O(\log n)$ parallel time. Since $\circledast$ is also a constant time operation, $(b_0 \circledast)*$ can be evaluated in constant time. Therefore, overall the lemma gives a logarithmic parallel time algorithm for computing the *recur-prefix* function. Note that the definition of operator $\oslash$ is the same as in Lemma 7.2. The parallel algorithm expressed by the lemma is shown in Figure 7.2.

In the same way as *reduction* and *prefix* are related, the following lemma relates *recur-reduce* and *recur-prefix*:

Lemma 7.4

$$x \otimes /\!\!/_{b_0}\oplus y = (\otimes/_{b_0}\oplus)* (inits \ x \curlyvee_\otimes inits \ y) \tag{7.4}$$

where

$$\#x = \#y, \quad and \quad s \otimes t = (s, t)$$

The lemma states that *recur-prefix* can also be computed by applying *recur-reduce* to all

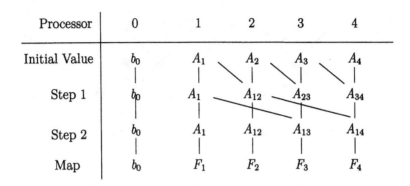

Processor	0	1	2	3	4
Initial Value	b_0	A_1	A_2	A_3	A_4
Step 1	b_0	A_1	A_{12}	A_{23}	A_{34}
Step 2	b_0	A_1	A_{12}	A_{13}	A_{14}
Map	b_0	F_1	F_2	F_3	F_4

$$A_1 = (a_1, b_1), \ A_2 = (a_2, b_2), \ A_3 = (a_3, b_3), \ A_4 = (a_4, b_4)$$
$$A_{12} = (a_1 \otimes a_2, b_1 \otimes a_2 \oplus b_2), \ A_{23} = (a_2 \otimes a_3, b_2 \otimes a_3 \oplus b_3),$$
$$A_{34} = (a_3 \otimes a_4, b_3 \otimes a_4 \oplus b_4)$$
$$A_{13} = (a_1 \otimes a_2 \otimes a_3, b_1 \otimes a_2 \otimes a_3 \oplus b_2 \otimes a_3 \oplus b_3),$$
$$A_{14} = (a_1 \otimes \dots \otimes a_4, b_1 \otimes a_2 \otimes a_3 \otimes a_4 \oplus \dots \oplus b_3 \otimes a_4 \oplus b_4)$$
$$F_1 = b_0 \otimes a_1 \oplus b_1, \ F_2 = b_0 \otimes a_1 \otimes a_2 \oplus b_1 \otimes a_2 \oplus b_2$$
$$F_3 = b_0 \otimes a_1 \otimes a_2 \otimes a_3 \oplus b_1 \otimes a_2 \otimes a_3 \oplus b_2 \otimes a_3 \oplus b_3$$
$$F_4 = b_0 \otimes a_1 \otimes \dots \otimes a_4 \oplus b_1 \otimes a_2 \otimes a_3 \otimes a_4 \oplus \dots \oplus b_3 \otimes a_4 \oplus b_4$$

Figure 7.2: Parallel Algorithm for Computing $[x_0, x_1, x_2, x_3, x_4]$

pairs of initial segments of x and y. Clearly, the right hand side of the equation takes $O(n)$ parallel time.

7.2 Permutations

Many list-based data-parallel languages include the ability to permute lists arbitrarily as a basic data-parallel operation (e.g. [39]). Such operations do not arise naturally in the construction of the theory of lists, since they are not catamorphisms. Also, they cannot be efficiently implemented in the sense that we have been working with. An arbitrary permutation takes at least logarithmic time on real machines, but its PRAM complexity is constant time. (This highlights one of the problems with measuring efficiency relative to the PRAM because it is arguable that the mismatch here is a problem with the PRAM rather than with defining permutation operations.)

We can, however, introduce a limited form of permutation operation whose communication is implemented in constant time. It has interesting applications both in common algorithms where data movement is important, and in geometric layout.

We define *Compound List Operations* (CLOs) that operate on pairs of list elements. The set of applications that can be expressed with compound list operations is large and interesting and includes sorting and FFT.

In what follows, we assume that all lists are of length $n = 2^k$.

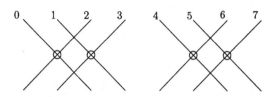

Figure 7.3: CLO with $n = 8$, $w = 1$ and $h = 0$

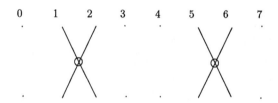

Figure 7.4: CLO with $n = 8$, $w = 0$ and $h = 1$

Definition 7.5 *Let $\oplus$ be an operation defined on pairs by $\oplus(a, b) = (f(a, b), g(a, b))$. The compound list operation (CLO) $\overline{\oplus}_w^h$ applied to the list $[a_0, a_1, \ldots, a_{n-1}]$ of n elements is the concurrent application of the pair-to-pair operations $\oplus(a_j, a_{j+2^w})$ where*

$$(j + (2^h + 1).2^w) \bmod 2^w = (j + (2^h + 1).2^w) \bmod 2^{(w+h+1)}$$

and $0 \leqslant j \leqslant n - 1$.

Such an operation is characterised by the pattern of pairing, given by the two arguments w and h, and by the underlying pair-to-pair operation. The *width* parameter w varies between 0 and $(\log n - h - 1)$ and gives the distance between members of each pair based on their position in the list. The *hops* parameter h varies between 0 and $(\log n - 1)$ and gives the distance between members of a pair based on their placement in a hypercube. Pairing patterns, for different values of w and h, are illustrated in Figures 7.3, 7.4 and 7.5.

The intuition for the CLO parameters is given by the mapping of lists onto the hypercube, placing the kth list element on the processor identified by the binary representation of k. Paired elements are 2^w apart in the list and $h+1$ communication links apart in the hypercube topology. If the operation $\oplus$ takes constant time then the CLO $\overline{\oplus}_w^h$ can be implemented on the hypercube in time proportional to h (and $h \leq \log n - 1$). Also the hypercube edges used by pair-to-pair communication are disjoint.

Another way to understand CLOs is to treat each as the composition of three functions: *pair*, *map*, and *unpair*. The function *pair(w, h)* takes a list and computes a list of pairs arranged as described above. The *map* function then applies the base operation, $\oplus$, to all of the pairs simultaneously, and then the *unpair(w, h)* function takes the list of pairs and

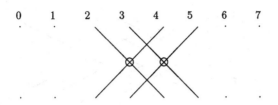

Figure 7.5: CLO with $n = 8$, $w = 1$ and $h = 1$

flattens it using the inverse of the arrangement used by *pair*. Thus CLOs can be considered as adding new functions *pair* and *unpair* to the theory of lists. They are also related to the functions in Backus's FP and FL [18].

CLOs also have an obvious geometric interpretation if they are not considered as embedded in a hypercube. Each CLO represents a particular interconnection pattern between a list of inputs and a list of outputs. If the base operation is *compare-and-exchange* then such an interconnection looks like a single stage of a comparison sorter, for example. If the base operation is a router, then the interconnection looks like a stage of a dynamic interconnection network. This connects CLOs to other geometric and functional languages such as μFP and Ruby [171, 172].

7.3 Examples of CLO Programs

Programs are functional compositions of CLOs. We use the short form $\overline{\oplus}_{b,a}^d$ to denote the composition of CLOs $\overline{\oplus}_b^d.\overline{\oplus}_{b-1}^d.\cdots.\overline{\oplus}_a^d$.

7.3.1 List Reversal and FFT

Consider the simplest composition of CLOs, namely $\overline{\oplus}_{0,\log n-1}^0$. This composition applies the base operation to groups of size $n/2$, groups of size $n/4$, down to groups of size 4, and groups of size 2 (nearest neighbours). The pairing pattern is illustrated in Figure 7.6 for $n = 8$.

If the base operation is $\oplus(a, b) = (b, a)$, pairwise interchange, then this composition represents reversal of the list as a whole. If the base operation is $\oplus(a_j, a_{j+p}) = (a_j + a_{j+p}.z^q, a_j - a_{j+p}.z^q)$ where $p = 2^w$, $z = c^p$, $q = r(j) mod(n/p)$, $r(j)$ is the reverse of the binary representation of j, and $c^0, c^1, \ldots, c^{n-1}$ are the n complex nth roots of unity, then the composition computes FFT.

On n processors, each step of the composition executes in unit time (if communication is achieved with constant locality). The time complexity of the composition is therefore $\log n$ which is the best known for either problem.

We use CLOs to define dynamic interconnection networks by using the pair-to-pair operation

$$\oplus([as], [bs]) = ([as] + [bs], [as] + [bs])$$

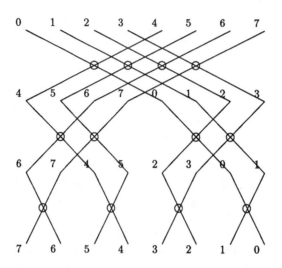

Figure 7.6: Pairing Pattern Sequence for Reversal

where as and bs are lists and $+\!\!+$ is list concatenation. Any composition of CLOs that maps the list

$$[a_1, a_2, \ldots, a_n] \longmapsto [[a_1, a_2, \ldots, a_n], [a_1, a_2, \ldots, a_n], \ldots [a_1, a_2, \ldots, a_n]]$$

is capable of routing any incoming value to any out port. Therefore if the $\oplus$ operations are replaced by suitable routers, this pattern can implement an n-to-n switch. It is easy to see that the composition of CLOs in Figure 7.6 achieves this, and thus defines the structure of a dynamic interconnection network.

7.3.2   Shuffle and Reverse Shuffle

The shuffle function takes a list $[a_0, a_1, \ldots, a_{n-1}]$ and yields the list

$$[a_0, a_{n/2}, a_1, a_{n/2+1}, \ldots, a_{n/2-1}, a_{n-1}]$$

The CLO sequence to do this is $\overline{\otimes}^1_{0,\log n-2}$ with interchange as the underlying primitive operation.

The reverse shuffle function takes the original list and yields the list

$$[a_{n/2}, a_0, a_{n/2+1}, a_1, \ldots, a_{n-1}, a_{n/2-1}]$$

The CLO sequence for this corresponds to composing the shuffle function above with the CLO $\overline{\otimes}^0_{\log n-1}$.

Figure 7.7 illustrates the pattern for these two functions for $n = 8$. The time complexity for these functions is $\log n - 1$ and $\log n$ respectively.

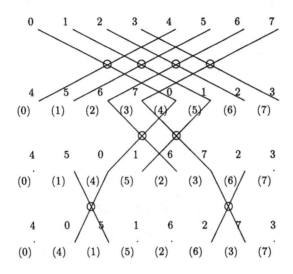

Figure 7.7: Sequence for Shuffle and Reverse Shuffle

7.3.3 Even-Odd and Odd-Even Split

The functions for even-odd and odd-even split transform the original list into the lists $[a_0, a_2, \ldots, a_{n-2}, a_1, a_3, \ldots, a_{n-1}]$ and $[a_1, a_3, \ldots, a_{n-1}, a_0, a_2, \ldots, a_{n-2}]$ respectively. The CLO sequences to do this are $\overline{\otimes}^1_{\log n-2,0}$ and the composition of $\overline{\otimes}^0_{\log n-1}$ with $\overline{\otimes}^1_{\log n-2,0}$, where $\otimes$ is interchange.

Figure 7.8 illustrates the pattern for these cases for $n = 8$. The time complexities are again $\log n - 1$ and $\log n$ respectively.

7.4 CLO Properties

We now consider the relationships between CLOs with the goal of building an algebra.

Lemma 7.6 *For all values of w and h, $\overline{\odot}^h_w$ is an identity transformation on the list whenever $\odot$ is the identity pair-to-pair operation $\odot(a, b) = (a, b)$. Such a CLO can therefore be removed from any sequence.*

Lemma 7.7 *The inverse of a CLO $\overline{\oplus}^h_w$, where it exists, is the CLO $\overline{\ominus}^h_w$ where, for all $\oplus(a, b) = (c, d)$, $\ominus(c, d) = (a, b)$.*

Lemma 7.8 *The inverse of any CLO based on the interchange primitive is the CLO itself (idempotence). The inverse of any composition of CLOs based on interchange is the CLO composition sequence in reverse.*

Some immediate consequences of this are the following:

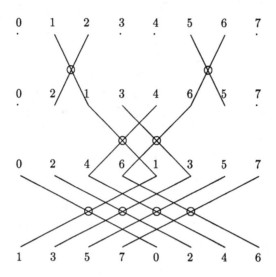

Figure 7.8: Sequence for Even-Odd and Odd-Even Split

- the inverse of reverse is reverse,

- the inverse of shuffle is even-odd split, and

- the inverse of reverse shuffle is odd-even split.

The inverse of a CLO based on the FFT primitive is the CLO whose underlying operation is defined as in the FFT primitive, but using the set $\{c^0, c^{-1}, \ldots, c^{-n+1}\}$ of inverses of nth roots of unity instead. This follows from the fundamental inversion property of the Fourier transform.

The CLOs $\overline{\oplus}_w^h$ and $\overline{\circledast}_{w'}^{h'}$ commute iff the sequences $\overline{\oplus}_w^h.\overline{\circledast}_{w'}^{h'}$ and $\overline{\circledast}_{w'}^{h'}.\overline{\oplus}_w^h$ are semantically equivalent.

Lemma 7.9 Let $\oplus$ and $\circledast$ be defined by

$$\oplus(a, b) = (f(a, b), g(a, b))$$
$$\circledast(a, b) = (f'(a, b), g'(a, b))$$

If for all a, b, c and d we have

$$f'(f(a, b), f(c, d)) = f(f'(a, c), f'(b, d))$$
$$f'(g(a, b), g(c, d)) = g(f'(a, c), f'(b, d))$$
$$g'(f(a, b), f(c, d)) = f(g'(a, c), g'(b, d))$$
$$g'(g(a, b), g(c, d)) = g(g'(a, c), g'(b, d))$$

then $\overline{\oplus}_w^0$ commutes with $\overline{\circledast}_{w'}^0$ for all w and w'.

Proof: This follows from the pairing patterns for the case $h = 0$.

Some examples of such CLOs are those based on the interchange primitive. Other examples come from choosing the functions f, f', g and g' to be basic commutative operations like arithmetic addition.

Lemma 7.10 *A sequence of two CLOs* $\overline{\oplus}_w^h \cdot \overline{\otimes}_w^h$ *for any possible primitive operations* $\oplus(a, b) = (f(a, b), g(a, b))$ *and* $\otimes(a, b) = (f'(a, b), g'(a, b))$ *is equivalent to the single CLO* $\overline{\circledast}_w^h$ *defined by* $\circledast(a, b) = (f'(f(a, b), g(a, b)), g'(f(a, b), g(a, b)))$.

The effect of a collapse of two adjacent CLOs is to eliminate the redundant *unpair* operation of the first, and the *pair* operation of the second. This reduces the data traffic and also typically increases the grain size of the computation in the resulting CLO, both benefits in most architectures.

7.5 Sorting

Sorting is an important and widely researched area and a detailed exposition of early sorting algorithms and their evolution can be found in [122]. More recent suggestions include asymptotic algorithms such as [7] that give networks of depth $\log n$. We show how a simple merge sort can be improved by transformation to achieve the time complexity of the bitonic sorting network [26].

We first derive the CLO function for a merge sort and show how it may be improved by making use of the commutativity and collapsability properties of some CLO subsequences. The time complexity of both versions of the function is $O(\log^2 n)$ which is the complexity of the standard practical sorting methods on n processors.

7.5.1 The Strategy and Initial CLO Program

The algorithm proceeds by merging in parallel pairs of sorted lists of length one into sorted lists of length two; merging in parallel pairs of these sorted lists of length two in turn into sorted lists of length four, and so on. Lists of length one are trivially sorted. Clearly, we have $\log n$ merging steps in an algorithm to sort n elements.

Our strategy for merging two sorted lists of length m involves the following sequence of steps:

- Reverse the second list.

- Perform *compare-exchange* operations in parallel on the pairs of ith elements from each list, for i varying from 1 to m.

- Perform a similar sequence of parallel *compare-exchange* operations on pairs made up of elements that are spaced $m/2, m/4, \ldots, 1$ apart, in that order, in the resulting list of length $2m$.

The resulting merged list is sorted. As we perform the merge of lists of length one, two, four and so on using this strategy, we are required to perform the reversal of segments of

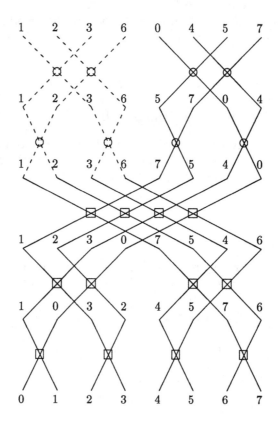

Figure 7.9: Sequence for Merging using Alternated Reversal

the original list of length one, two, four and so on respectively. This is done using a set of *partially masked* interchange CLOs that reverse only the relevant portions of the original list and leave the rest unchanged. For the case when $m = 4$, for example, the sequence of interchange CLOs reverses every alternate set of 4 list elements starting from the left. The reversal followed by the *compare-exchange* CLO sequence for this case is illustrated in Figure 7.9. Reversal takes place in the first two steps. Since the leftmost 4 elements are not involved in the reversal, this is illustrated through the use of dashed lines; $\otimes$ represents an interchange primitive indicated by a circle in the figure. The next three steps in the figure correspond to the *compare-exchange* CLO sequence with $\circledast$, a *compare-exchange* primitive, indicated by a square in the figure. Note how *compare-exchange* is performed for $m = 4$, $m = 2$ and then $m = 1$ in that order.

It is simple to see that the merge of lists of length $m = 2^k$ involves k CLO steps for the reversal described by the function $\overline{\otimes}^0_{0,k-1}$. $\otimes$ is the parameterised interchange primitive defined as $\otimes(a_j, a_{j+2^w}) = (a_j, a_{j+2^w})$ whenever $j \bmod 2^k = j \bmod 2^{k+1}$ and $\otimes(a_j, a_{j+2^w}) = (a_{j+2^w}, a_j)$ otherwise. The merger also involves $k + 1$ CLO steps for the *compare-exchange*

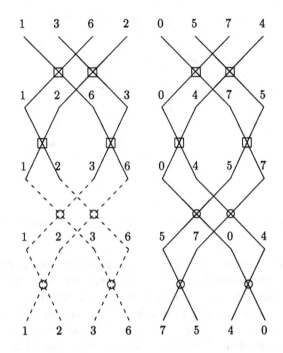

Figure 7.10: Order-Reverse Alternate Group Sequence

described by the function $\overline{\circledast}^0_{0,k}$. $\circledast$ is the *compare-exchange* primitive defined as $\circledast(a,b) = (\min(a,b), \max(a,b))$.

We use the notation $\uparrow^{\log n}_{k=1}$ to indicate a repeated composition parameterised by k increasing, and $\downarrow^{\log n}_{k=0}$ to indicate repeated composition with k decreasing. The overall function for sorting is therefore $\uparrow^{\log n-1}_{k=1}(\overline{\circledast}^0_{0,k}).\overline{\circledast}^0_{0,k-1}$. Its time complexity is $\sum^{\log n-1}_{k=0} 2.k + 1 = \log^2 n$.

7.5.2 The Improved Version

Let us consider a sequence in the function made up of the k compare-exchange CLO steps producing sorted lists of length 2^k followed by k reverse CLO steps reversing alternate groups of 2^k elements. Figure 7.10 illustrates this sequence for the case $2^k = 4$. The first two steps represent the performance of *compare-exchange* over lists of 4 elements, as the final part of the CLO sequence for merge sort of 4 element lists. The next two steps are the initial two steps of the CLO sequence for merge sort of 8 element lists, starting from two sorted 4 element lists. As in Figure 7.9, dashed lines indicate identity operations, and circles and squares represent the primitives for interchange and *compare-exchange* respectively.

The commutativity of the reverse CLOs makes it possible to reverse their order. As a result, the *compare-exchange* and reverse CLOs for the case $w = 0$ can be made adjacent. They can then be collapsed to a single CLO step and one that is a *compare-exchange*,

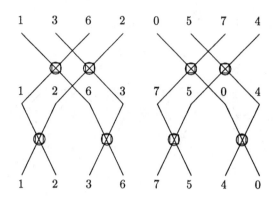

Figure 7.11: Sequence After Collapsing Ordering and Reversal

but in ascending order. Further, reverse CLOs not only commute among themselves, but also commute with the *compare-exchange* CLOs. This enables us to place every reverse CLO adjacent to a *compare-exchange* CLO with the same w value and thus to collapse them into a single CLO step. The situation resulting from this transformation on the sequence in Figure 7.10 is illustrated in Figure 7.11. The circle-square symbol represents the parameterised *compare-exchange* primitive defined below. Notice how steps 1 and 3 in Figure 7.10 collapse into step 1 in Figure 7.11 and steps 2 and 4 in Figure 7.10 into step 2 in Figure 7.11.

Using this optimisation, we now describe our optimised function as $\uparrow_{k=0}^{\log n-1}(\circledast_{0,k}^0)$, where the parameterised *compare-exchange* primitive is $\circledast(a_j, a_{j+2^w}) = $ order-ascending(a_j, a_{j+2^w}) whenever $j \bmod 2^k = j \bmod 2^{k+1}$ and $\circledast(a_j, a_{j+2^w}) = $ order-descending(a_j, a_{j+2^w}) otherwise. The time complexity of the function is clearly $\sum_{k=0}^{\log n-1} k + 1 = \log^2 n/2 + \log n/2$, which is nearly a factor of two improvement.

Chapter 8

A Cost Calculus for Lists

We have already discussed why a set of cost measures is important for a model of parallel computation. In this chapter we develop something stronger, a cost calculus. A cost calculus integrates cost information with equational rules, so that it becomes possible to decide the direction in which an equational substitution is cost-reducing. Unfortunately, a perfect cost calculus is not possible for any parallel programming system, so some compromises are necessary. It turns out that the simplicity of the mapping problem for lists, thanks to the standard topology, is just enough to permit a workable solution.

8.1 Cost Systems and Their Properties

Ways of measuring the cost of a partially developed program are critical to making informed decisions during the development. An ideal cost system has the following two properties:

1. It is compositional, so that the cost of a program depends in some straightforward way on the cost of its pieces. This is a difficult requirement in a parallel setting since it amounts to saying that the cost of a program piece depends only on its internal structure and behaviour and not on its context. However, parallel operations have to be concerned about the external properties of how their arguments and results are mapped to processors since there are costs associated with rearranging them. So, for parallel computing, contexts are critically important.

2. It is related to the calculational transformation system, so that the cost of a transformation can be associated with its rule.

A cost system with these two properties is called a *cost calculus*.

Cost systems for sequential computing exist. For example, the standard sequential complexity theory is built on the RAM (Random Access Memory) model. In this system, ordinary instructions take unit time, memory references take zero time, and space used is the largest number of variables in use at any point of the computation. Since costs are only distinguished by orders, only loops and recursions need to be examined in computing execution time. This cost system is compositional, since the cost of a program is simply the sum of the costs of its pieces.

This approach does not quite work for functional programming because there is no well-defined flow of control. A functional program may not even execute all of the program text if non-strictness is allowed. However, it is usually possible to deduce the total amount of work that must be done, and therefore how long it will take regardless of the execution order. The usual approach is to count function calls as taking unit time. Because of the clean semantics of functional languages, it is possible to automate the computation of the cost of a program [129, 168, 169].

Cost systems for parallel computing hardly exist. There is of course the PRAM which has provided a useful complexity theory for parallel algorithms. However, as we have seen (Section 3.2), it is inaccurate for costing computations on real machines because it ignores communication. Furthermore, its underestimate of execution time is not systematic, so there is no obvious way to improve it.

A better cost system is that associated with the Bulk Synchronous Parallelism of Valiant [199, 200], and variants of it [68, 180]. These all depend on the implementing architectures using techniques such as memory hashing to give bounded delivery time of permutations of messages. In the BSP approach, the cost of an arbitrary computation is computed based on four parameters: n the virtual parallelism (that is the number of threads in the computation), p the number of processors used, l the communication latency, and g the ratio of computation speed to communication speed. This cost system can be used to determine a program's cost once it has been completely constructed, with all of the computation assigned to threads and the necessary communication worked out. However, it cannot help with the construction of the program. It also depends on knowing some parameters of the proposed target architecture, so that knowing costs requires violating architecture independence. If a program's costs are unsatisfactory, perhaps because it communicates too frequently, then it may need to be completely redesigned.

Neither of these two approaches to parallel cost systems is particularly satisfactory, and the reason is that cost systems are fundamentally more difficult in a parallel setting than in a sequential setting. There are many more implementation decisions to be made for a parallel computation, particularly one that abstracts from parallel hardware in the way that we have been advocating. Decisions made by the compiler and run-time system must be reflected by the cost system even though they are hidden from the programmer. The cost system makes the model abstraction partly transparent, so that programmers can see enough to make the crucial choices between this algorithm or that, while being unable to see details of the architecture.

Some of the decisions that can be made by compiler and run-time system that affect costs include:

1. The decomposition into threads to execute on different processors, which determines virtual parallelism;

2. The communication actions between threads and how they are synchronised, which determines latency;

3. How the threads (the virtual parallelism) are mapped to processors (the physical parallelism), which determines contention for processor cycles;

4. How communication actions are overlapped in the interconnection network, which determines contention for network bandwidth.

The cost of a program depends on the precise choices that are made for all of these possible decisions, and also depends on properties of the target architecture. It is no wonder that building cost systems is difficult.

One way to build a cost system is to make the programming model low-level enough that all of the decisions are made by the programmer. Computing costs then becomes an exercise in analysing program structure. However, there are a number of reasons why this is not satisfactory:

1. We want models that are as abstract as possible, given the model requirements discussed in Chapter 2.

2. In any case, the level of detail required is probably too great to be feasible. Imagine arranging all of the scheduling and communication for a 1000 processing element architecture without hiding any detail that could affect costs.

3. It wouldn't help with the problem of finding the best version of a program, since there is no practical way to search the space of possible arrangements. For example, finding an optimal mapping of a task graph onto a particular arrangement of processors has exponential complexity.

However, making models more abstract does make the development of a cost system more difficult. The challenge is to find the best trade-off between abstraction and usefulness.

There is a further, and more fundamental, difficulty that arises in trying to get the compositional property. We want the cost of $g \cdot f$ to be computable from the cost of g and the cost of f in some easy way that does not depend on knowing architectural properties in detail. For example, in sequential imperative programming, the cost of such a composition is just the sum of the costs of the two pieces. Without this kind of compositionality we cannot do program derivations in a modular way because, to decide between choices in some particular place we have to consider the costs of everything else in the program.

Expecting the cost of a composition to be the sum of the costs of its pieces fails, in a parallel setting, in two possible ways:

1. The computation of the second piece may begin before the computation of the first piece has completed, because the operations involved occur in different processors. The critical paths of g and f do not meet and so may overlap in time. The sum of the costs of g and f overestimates the cost of $g \cdot f$. A possible scenario is shown in Figure 8.1, where the critical path of the first operation does not connect with the critical path of the second operation.

2. The function $g \cdot f$ may have some implementation that is not built from the implementations of g and f at all and the other implementation is cheaper.

The costs of individual operations are not enough to give an accurate cost system because of these difficulties with compositionality – which are fundamental, and cause difficulties in any system of parallel costs.

8.2   A Strategy for a Parallel Cost Calculus

A workable cost calculus must solve the two problems of manageable abstractions from the details of execution on parallel architectures, and of compositionality. The first problem is

Processors

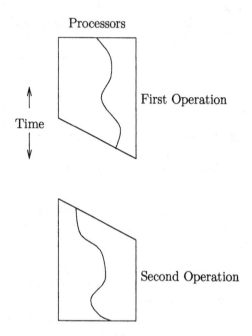

Time

First Operation

Second Operation

Figure 8.1: Critical Paths that may Overlap in Time

solved in the categorical data type setting because of the restricted programming domain
– we have given up the ability to write arbitrary programs (for other reasons), and the
structured programs we do write can be neatly mapped to architectures via the standard
topology. The second problem is fundamental, but we suggest a pragmatic solution that
seems useful.

The first step is to design implementations for the basic catamorphic operations. Building
one single implementation for the recursive schema is possible, but is not good enough to
achieve the performance on certain operations that optimised versions can.

It is not clear exactly what should be the standard for efficient implementation but, as in
Chapter 5, we assume that achieving the same complexity as the PRAM will do. Since the
costs we compute account for communication, and the PRAM does not, achieving the same
complexity as PRAM algorithms is a strong requirement. Any implementation for basic
catamorphic operations is acceptable, provided the work it does is equivalent to the work
of the corresponding PRAM implementation. Catamorphisms are naturally "polymorphic"
over the size of the arguments to which they are applied. Implementations therefore are
already parameterised by argument sizes, which translate into virtual parallelism. Implementations also need to be parameterised by the number of physical processors used, since
this is in general different from the number of virtual processors. In the next section we give
such parameterised implementations for the basic operations on lists that were introduced
in Chapter 5.

For the more intractable problem of composition, we suggest the following general approach. Whenever a composition of two operations has an implementation that is cheaper than the sum of the costs of its pieces because of the overlapping of their critical paths, define a new operation to represent the combined cheaper operation, thus:

$$\text{newop} \;\triangleq\; g \cdot f$$

Now we take two views of programs. In the functional view, this equation is a tautology, since both sides denote the same function. However, in the operational view, the left hand side denotes a single operation, while the right hand side denotes an operation f, followed by a barrier synchronisation, followed by an operation g. The operational view amounts to giving an operational semantics to composition in which all processors must have completed f before any processors may begin computing g.

Costs can only be associated with programs by taking the operational view. However, cost differences can be expressed by directing equations, while maintaining the functional view. Having defined *newop*, we can now assign it the cheaper cost of the composition, while the cost of the right hand side is the sum of the costs of g and f. The equation can be recognised as cost-reducing when it is applied right to left.

The second possibility is that the composition $g \cdot f$ has a cheaper implementation that is independent of the implementations of g and f. This case is much easier, for this different implementation is some composition of other operations, say $j \cdot h$ and an equation

$$g \cdot f = j \cdot h$$

already exists or else they do not compute the same function. The operational view allows the costs of both sides to be computed and the equation to be labelled with its cost-reducing direction.

There are two difficulties with this in practice. The first is that the number of different functions is infinite and we have to label a correspondingly infinite set of equations. Fortunately, most of the cases where compositionality fails in these ways are because of *structural* differences in the costs of the equations' sides. Thus it suffices to label equation schemas.

The second difficulty is that it is always possible that some long, newly-considered composition of operations has a cheap implementation, using some clever technique, and hence that a new definitional equation needs to be added. So the process of adding new definitional equations is not necessarily a terminating one. The absence of some equations means that the cost calculus overestimates some costs. Adding new equations removes particular cases of overestimation, but it can never get rid of them all. In practice, this is not perhaps too important, because once all short compositions of operations have been considered it is unlikely that long compositions will hold surprises.

The different representations of each function as compositions of subfunctions are partially ordered by their costs, and equations involving them used as cost-reducing rewrite rules. So at least partial automation is possible.

This pragmatic solution to the problem of compositionality induces two different views of operations and equations on them. On the one hand, programmers really do have a cost calculus, because costs are determined in a context-independent way, and the cost of a function is computed (additively) from the cost of its component pieces. Programmers do not need to be aware of the operational view of programs. They get enough operational information indirectly in the labelling of equations with their cost-reducing directions.

On the other hand, implementers have a stock of parameterised implementations for the named operations. When a CDT implementation is built, all compositions of operations up to some pragmatically determined length are examined for ways to build overlapped implementations; new operations are defined, and equations and equation schemas labelled with their cost-reducing directions. Composition is seen as an opportunity to find new ways of overlapping the execution of components.

Thus cost measures breach the abstraction provided by the computation model but in two covert ways: the labelling of equations with a cost-reducing direction, and the definition of new operations, that appear monolithic to the programmer. This seems to be the best kind of solution we can hope for, given the fundamental nature of the problem.

In the next sections we work out a cost system of this kind for the theory of lists. However, the approach works for any programming language for which deterministic, parameterised costs can be obtained for the basic operations. This certainly includes other data-parallel languages on lists, bags, and sets, and probably certain hardware design languages as well.

8.3   Implementations for Basic Operations

Because join lists are a separable type, all catamorphisms factor into the composition of a list map and a list reduction. Thus maps and reductions are the basic operations on which implementations are built. To implement both we need to embed the standard topology in the interconnection network of target architectures in such a way that near-neighbour communication in the standard topology uses near-neighbour communication in the interconnect. This is not possible for every target architecture, but we have seen that it can be done for at least one architecture in each class. Once such an embedding has been done, communication of single values takes unit time and we treat it as free in subsequent considerations of cost.

We have already seen how to build such implementations for basic operations on lists when the length of the list argument matches the number of processors used to compute the operations (Chapter 5). These implementations must be extended to take into account the use of fewer processors.

List map requires no communication since the computation of its component function takes place independently on each element of the list. As we have seen, list reduction is best implemented using a binary tree, up which the results of subreductions flow. Elements of lists have an implicit order and it is convenient to reflect this ordering in the communication topology. Thus we wish to embed a binary tree with n leaves, and a cycle through the leaves, into the interconnection topology of each target architecture.

Let t_p to denote the parallel time required for a computation on p processors, and n denote the length of a list argument. The cost of a structured operation depends on what it does itself, but also on the cost of its component functions. As long as the component functions are constant space, that is the size of their results are the same as the size of their arguments, they affect the cost of a structured operation multiplicatively. Let $t_p(f)$ denote the time required to compute f on p processors. Then, the costs of list map and list reduction when $p = n$ are

$$t_n(f*) = 1 \cdot t_1(f) \tag{8.1}$$

$$t_n(\oplus/) = \log n \cdot t_1(\oplus) \tag{8.2}$$

provided that f and $\oplus$ are constant space.

Notice that the equations hold even if the argument list is deeply nested, and f or $\oplus$ are themselves complex functions that involve other catamorphisms. This means that costs can be computed from the top level of a program down, computing the cost of the operations applying to the outer level of list first, then (independently) computing the cost of operations applied to the next level and so on. But only if the operations are constant space. If they are not, cost computation becomes much more difficult. To avoid this, we compute costs of reductions with non-constant space operations as their components individually. At the end of the chapter we show how to do cost computations in full generality, but also why doing so isn't practical.

Since costs are expressed in terms of the size of arguments, we need notation to describe the size of an arbitrarily nested list. A *shape vector* is a list of natural numbers; a shape vector $[n, m, p]$ denotes a list of n elements (at the top level), each of which is a list of no more than m elements, each of which is an object of size no larger than p. Two properties are important: except for the top level, the shape vector entry gives the *maximum* length of list at each level; and the last entry in a shape vector gives the *total* size of any substructure. Thus the shape vectors $[n, m, p]$ and $[n, mp]$ describe the same list. In the first case we are interested in three levels of nesting structure, in the second only two.

Since the shape vector of the result of an operation is not usually the same as the shape vector of its argument, it is convenient to be able to annotate programs with the shape vectors of their (unnamed) intermediate results. We do this by writing the shape vector as a superscript before, after, or between operations. So if f takes an argument of size m and produces a result of size p then an annotation of $f*$ is

$$^{[n,p]}f*^{[n,m]}$$

(Note that the shape vector can be regarded as part of the type of arguments and results.)

As an example of what happens when a reduction applies a non-constant space but constant time component function, let us extend the cost equation for reduction above (Equation 8.2). An obvious example of a reduction of this kind is $+\!\!+/$, where the size of the lists computed at each step of the reduction increases. Because these lists are moved between processors in an implementation of reduction, larger lists require longer times.

On the first step of the reduction, a list element of size 1 is moved between processors, and a constant time operation applied in each destination processor to compute a list of length 2. Now on the second step a list of length 2 must be moved between processors. On the third step, a list of length 4 is moved, and so on. The total time for $+\!\!+/$ is therefore dominated by the communication time which is

$$t_n(+\!\!+/) = 2^0 + 2^1 + \ldots + 2^{\log n - 1} = n - 1 \tag{8.3}$$

Thus an operation with a logarithmic number of steps actually takes linear time.

We now turn to considering how to implement the basic operations on fewer processors than the number of elements of the list. Such implementations require some mapping of the virtual parallelism to physical processors, and there are several separate choices. They are

1. Allocate elements to processors in a round-robin fashion or

2. Allocate elements to processors by segments, so that the first n/p of them are placed in the first processor, the next n/p in the second processor and so on;

and

   a. Allocate top-level elements, that is if the list has shape vector $[n, m, q]$, allocate n objects each of size up to mq; or

   b. Allocate bottom-level elements, that is allocate nmq distinct objects.

Alternative (2) is better than (1) because it reduces traffic in the interconnection network for operations in which adjacency in the list is important (reductions, for example). Alternative (a) is better than (b) because list operations are hierarchically structured, with maps on the outer levels. Thus the work gets more evenly distributed across processors if the allocation respects the list nesting structure. We therefore assume that the standard topology is embedded in smaller machines so that computations in subtrees that include leaves take place within a single processor, and so that adjacent subtrees are mapped to adjacent processors.

It would be conceivable to use different embedding strategies for different operations, one kind for maps and another for reductions, say. However, this introduces difficulties whenever one kind of operation is followed by another, because some implicit rearrangement operation must be inserted between them. We prefer to avoid this extra complexity.

We now give implementations of list maps and list reductions using this embedding. Each physical processor is responsible for applying a component function to more than one element of its argument list, so we need a new notation to distinguish parallel application from sequential application. We first add a subscript to each operation to denote how many times it is being applied; and we use an overbar to denote that an operation is being applied sequentially. Thus we write

$$^{[n]}(f*)_n^{[n]}$$

and

$$^{[1]}(\oplus/)_n^{[n]}$$

to denote the functions we described earlier (Equations 8.1 and 8.2), and we omit the shape vector annotations when they are unnecessary. On the other hand

$$\overline{f*}_n$$

denotes $f*$ applied sequentially to a list of length n, that is this denotes a sequential loop in a single processor.

We assume in what follows that $p \leq n$. This is too strong an assumption in practice. For example if we apply $f*$ to a list with shape vector $[2, 100, 50]$ then we are only able to exploit 2-way parallelism, whereas we would like to be able to exploit all of the 10000-way parallelism possible. Extending the cost calculus to allow this is straightforward [125] but it complicates the exposition. To avoid using ceiling functions repeatedly, we also assume that p divides n.

A list of length n is stored on a p-processor system with about n/p (top level) elements in each processor. Computing $f*$ applied to such a list means, in parallel, applying f sequentially to the n/p elements in each processor. The *implementation equation* for *list map* is

$$f*_n = (\overline{f*}_{n/p}) *_p \qquad (8.4)$$

which is read as "a parallel map applied to a list of size n is implemented by p parallel applications of the function that sequentially applies f to n/p elements of a list." This is a functional equation, but the right hand side contains operational information that the left hand side does not.

List reduction is implemented in a similar way – reductions are first done sequentially on the list segments stored in each processor, and the results are then reduced in parallel between processors. The implementation equation for *list reduction* is therefore

$$\oplus/_n = \oplus/_p \cdot (\overline{\oplus/}_{n/p}) *_p \qquad (8.5)$$

which is read as "a parallel reduction applied to a list of length n is implemented by p parallel applications of a sequential reduction applied to n/p elements of a list, followed by a parallel reduction on the results." From these two implementation equations we see that the implementation of a program requires transforming it until it consists of a composition of functions all of which are p-way parallel maps or reductions at the outer level.

A complete program begins with a distribution of the argument list to processors, and ends with a collection of results in a single place. The distribution function is of type

$$\text{distribute} : A* \to A**$$

which fixes the type error that is implicit in the equations above. A more formal approach to implementation equations is provided by Roe [163], who observes that

$$+\!\!+/ \cdot \text{parts}_p = id$$

Adding this to the end of a program and then transforming it so that the $+\!\!+/$ moves leftwards naturally produces implementation equations.

It is clear that

$$f = \overline{f}$$

from which it follows that

$$\overline{g}_m \cdot \overline{f}_m = \overline{(g \cdot f)}_m$$

This equation just states that two sequential loops computing different functions can be joined into a single loop in which the body computes the composition of the functions. It is a common optimisation in sequential compilers. Another useful equation is

$$\left(\overline{f}_m\right)_n = \overline{f}_{mn}$$

This equation states that nested sequential loops can be collapsed to a single loop with the same body and an appropriate change to its bounds.

We now use the implementation equations for the basic operations to compute their execution times. For an implementation equation, the total execution time is just the sum of the execution times of the components. For list map we have, from Equation 8.4,

$$t_p(f*_n) = \frac{n}{p}$$

and for list reduction we have, from Equation 8.5,

$$t_p(\oplus/_n) = \log p + \frac{n}{p}$$

Again each of these can be multiplied by $t_1(f)$ and $t_1(\oplus)$ respectively if these are not constant time.

We also compute the cost of a reduction using a function with non-constant space such as $+\!\!+/$. The cost on p processors comes first from the cost of the sequential reductions on the segments of the list of length n/p stored in each processor. This takes time $n/p - 1$ and produces partial results of size n/p. The second step is the parallel reduction on arguments of size n/p which takes time $(p-1)n/p$, using Equation 8.3 with p processors and operands of size n/p. The total execution time is the sum of these two times, that is

$$
\begin{aligned}
t_p(+\!\!+/_n) &= (p-1)\frac{n}{p} + (\frac{n}{p} - 1) \\
&= n - 1
\end{aligned}
$$

This is perhaps surprising – the cost depends only on the length of the argument list, and not on the number of processors used.

We have been using explicit constants when we determine costs. These constants are not of any practical interest because implementations conceal constants that are much larger. However, making constants explicit helps to show how cost expressions are arrived at.

8.4   More Complex Operations

We have defined several other useful operations on lists and now we compute their costs. Again we are satisfied with any implementation whose total work (product of time and processors) is that of the equivalent PRAM computation. If there are several different implementations, we can choose any of them.

Inits.   Recall that *inits* computes the initial segments of a list, that is

$$\text{inits } [a_1, a_2, \ldots, a_n] = [[a_1], [a_1, a_2], [a_1, a_2, a_3], \ldots, [a_1, a_2, \ldots, a_n]]$$

One way to implement this operation is to circulate values around the Hamiltonian cycle, with each processor accumulating the values it needs to form its segments. On the initial step each processor computes the local initial segments of the part of the list it contains. The concatenation of its local part is then passed to the processor immediately to its right, where it is prepended to each of the partial initial segments held by that processor. When the values from the first processor have reached the last processor (after p steps) the computation is complete. The process is illustrated below.

P0	P1	P2	P3
a_1	a_3	a_5	a_7
a_2	a_4	a_6	a_8

After the first step, each processor has computed the following partial initial segments:

P0	P1	P2	P3
a_1	a_3	a_5	a_7
$a_1 a_2$	$a_3 a_4$	$a_5 a_6$	$a_7 a_8$

Each processor then passes its sublist to its right neighbour, where it is prepended to give:

P0	P1	P2	P3
a_1	$a_1 a_2 a_3$	$a_3 a_4 a_5$	$a_5 a_6 a_7$
$a_1 a_2$	$a_1 a_2 a_3 a_4$	$a_3 a_4 a_5 a_6$	$a_5 a_6 a_7 a_8$

The same values are then passed on a further step to a neighbour two steps from their original processor and the prepending repeated, for a total of p steps. We write this as

$$\text{inits}_n = \left(\overline{\left(\overline{\text{prepend}}_{n/p} \cdot \text{passright} \right)}_p \right) *_p \cdot (\overline{\text{inits}}_{n/p}) *_p$$

where *passright* and *prepend* are local processor actions, not part of the language. The operation *passright* receives a string from the processor to its left and passes it to the processor to its right, and *prepend* adds it to the front of the n/p segments held in each processor. A sequential implementation of *inits* computes $n(n+1)/2$ values. So the number of steps in this computation is: $n(n/p-1)/2p$ for the local *inits*, then p sequential repetitions of a *passright* followed by n/p prepends. Each of these steps uses an argument whose size is n/p, so that the total cost is

$$t_p = p \left(\frac{n}{p} + 1 \right) \frac{n}{p} + \frac{n}{2p} (\frac{n}{p} - 1)$$

or

$$t_p = \frac{n^2}{p} + n + \frac{n^2}{2p^2} - \frac{n}{2p}$$

Since *inits* requires the computation of about n^2 values, it is clear that its execution time is bounded below by n^2/p. Thus the implementation above is of the right order. *Inits* has an analogue, *tails*, which computes the suffix segments of its argument list, and has the same cost.

Both of these operations illustrate composition problems of the first kind – operations that have an implementation more efficient than the direct one as a composition of map and reduction. This justifies giving them names and adding definitional equations to the theory.

Prefix.   Another useful operation is *prefix*. The operation $\oplus\!/\!\!/$ applied to a list is defined by

$$\oplus\!/\!\!/[a_1, a_2, \ldots, a_n] = [a_1, a_1 \oplus a_2, a_1 \oplus a_2 \oplus a_3, \ldots a_1 \oplus a_2 \oplus \ldots \oplus a_n]$$

Prefix is computed using a two-phase algorithm. The upsweep phase of the algorithm computes a reduction over the argument list. The downsweep phase passes global information back to be merged with values computed on the upsweep. Consider a list of integers of length n. The data flow of the algorithm is shown in Figure 8.2(a), where the columns represent the operations needed to compute each position in the result list, and the arrows between columns show the communication that takes place.

On the first step, the values of all even-numbered elements of the list are passed to adjacent odd-numbered elements. During the upsweep phase, the operation carried out at the nodes is shown in Figure 8.2(b). The value received from the left is kept, and the $\oplus$ operator applied to it and the most recent retained value. The result of this reduction operation is then passed right.

The time taken for the upsweep is

$$t_n(\oplus\!/\!\!/_{up}) = \log n$$

as we have already seen, since it is a slight variant on the reduction computation.

For the downsweep, the operations performed at each node are illustrated in Figure 8.2(c). Values passed from the right are copied to the left, and the $\oplus$ operation is applied to that value and the value at the beginning of the list at that node. One value is transmitted on the first step, three values on the second, and so on, with all but one processor active on the last step. Thus the time for this step is also

$$t_n(\oplus\!/\!\!/_{down}) = \log n$$

and the total execution time for prefix is

$$t_n(\oplus\!/\!\!/) = 2\log n$$

The algorithm is easy to adapt to p processors, by making each processor responsible for computing n/p elements of the result list. The overall prefix is computed by:

- computing a sequential prefix in each processor on the segment of length n/p it contains;

- computing the parallel prefix of the last value in each processor in a parallel way, using the tree algorithm, and then shifting the resulting values to the right (inserting zero at the left and discarding the rightmost value).

- adding the shifted value at each processor to each of the values in that processor sequentially.

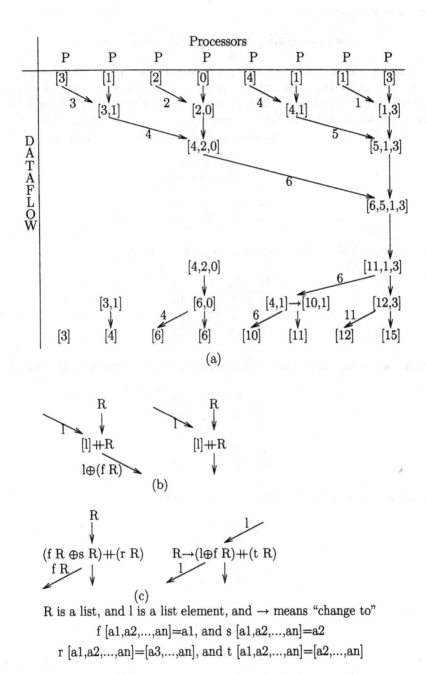

R is a list, and l is a list element, and → means "change to"

f [a1,a2,...,an]=a1, and s [a1,a2,...,an]=a2

r [a1,a2,...,an]=[a3,...,an], and t [a1,a2,...,an]=[a2,...,an]

Figure 8.2: Data Flow for Prefix (using a list of length 8, node labels are the values held at each node, edge labels are the values flowing on arcs)

Its implementation equation is

$$\oplus/\!\!/_n = (\overline{(x\oplus)*}_{n/p}) *_p \cdot \text{shift} \cdot \oplus/\!\!/_p \cdot (\overline{\oplus/\!\!/}_{n/p})*_p$$

where $x\oplus$ adds the element of the parallel prefix local to each processor to each element of the local segment of the list. The *shift* operation, a local processor action, is necessary to realign the results of the parallel prefix since each processor requires the result of the prefix held in the processor to its left to finish computing its own prefix values. This is illustrated on the following list, stored in four processors. The initial value of the list is

P0	P1	P2	P3
1	4	7	10
2	5	8	11
3	6	9	12

After the first sequential prefix in each processor, the values are

P0	P1	P2	P3
1	4	7	10
3	9	15	21
6	15	24	33

A parallel prefix is computed for the values $[6, 15, 24, 33]$ which are then shifted right to get

P0	P1	P2	P3
0	6	21	45
1	4	7	10
3	9	15	21
6	15	24	33

and these values are added to the values below them to give

P0	P1	P2	P3
1	10	28	55
3	15	36	66
6	21	45	78

The resulting cost is

$$t_p(\oplus/\!\!/_n) = \frac{n}{p} + 1 + 2\log p + \frac{n}{p}$$

Since a prefix computation generates n values, its execution time is bounded below by n/p; since one of these values depends on all the other values in the list, and hence requires communication from all the other processors, its execution time is also bounded below by $\log p$. Hence the time derived for the implementation above is (up to constants) as good as we can hope to do.

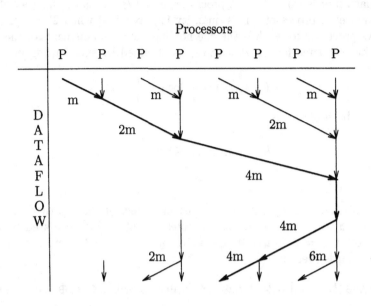

Figure 8.3: Data Flow for Concatenation Prefix (using a list of length 8 where initial elements are of size m, edge labels are the sizes of data flowing on arcs). Critical path shown bold.

Prefix with non-constant space component functions. Prefix is an operation, like *reduce*, whose complexity changes when applied to a first-order function whose result is larger than its arguments. Consider the implementation of $+\!\!\!/\!\!/$ shown in Figure 8.3. The analysis of the upsweep is exactly the same as for $+\!\!\!/$ so the time for the upsweep is

$$t_p(+\!\!\!/\!\!/_{up}) = n - 1$$

Consider the data flow on the downsweep. The amount of information required by the rightmost n/p elements held in the last processor is large, all of the list elements held in the other processors. On the other hand, this information has accumulated in the last processor during the upsweep, so need only be replicated within this processor. The second-to-last processor needs less information, but it takes longer to get it since it must be transmitted by the last processor.

Divide the processors into groups, depending on their distance in the tree from the last processor – thus the last processor is in group 0, the second last processor in group 1, the next two processors preceding it in group 2, and so on. The time taken to correctly deliver the required data to a processor in group i is

$$t_p = \frac{n}{p}(p - 2^i)(i + \frac{n}{p} - 1)$$

where the term $n(p - 2^i)/p$ is the volume of data sent to a processor in group i, i is the distance the data travels from the last processor, and $n/p - 1$ is the number of times it is replicated within each processor. This quantity is maximised when $2^i = p/2$, that is the most expensive processor to reach is the one holding the initial elements of the second half of the list. Thus the time for the downsweep is obtained by substituting in the equation above to give

$$t_p(\#\!/\!/\,_{down}) = \frac{n}{2}(\log p + \frac{n}{p} - 2)$$

and the time for both phases is

$$t_p(\#\!/\!/\,_n) = \frac{n}{2}(\log p + \frac{n}{p}) - 1$$

Recur-reduce. The next operation we consider is *recur-reduce* (written $\otimes/\!_{b_0}\!\oplus$), which given coefficients $a_1, ..., a_n$ and $b_1, ..., b_n$ computes the nth value generated by a linear recurrence function $x_{i+1} = x_i \otimes a_{i+1} \oplus b_{i+1}$ where $x_0 = b_0$, $\otimes$ and $\oplus$ are associative, and $\otimes$ distributes backwards over $\oplus$:

$$[a_1, ..., a_n] \otimes/\!_{b_0}\!\oplus [b_1, ..., b_n] = b_0 \otimes a_1 \otimes ... \otimes a_n \oplus b_1 \otimes a_2 \otimes ... \otimes a_n \oplus ... \oplus b_{n-1} \otimes a_n \oplus b_n$$

Recur-reduce is expressed as a reduction as follows:

$$x \otimes/\!_{b_0}\!\oplus y = \begin{cases} b_0, & \text{if } \#x(=\#y) = 0 \\ b_0 \otimes \pi_1 A \oplus \pi_2 A, & \text{if } \#x(=\#y) \neq 0 \end{cases}$$

where

$$\begin{aligned} A &= \oslash/(x \,\mathsf{Y}_{\!\oslash}\, y), \\ a \oslash b &= (a, b), \\ (a, b) \oslash (c, d) &= (a \otimes c, b \otimes c \oplus d), \\ \pi_1(a, b) = a, \quad \text{and} \quad \pi_2(a, b) &= b \end{aligned}$$

The operation *zip* has implementation equation

$$(\text{-}\,\mathsf{Y}_{\!\oplus}\,\text{-})_n = (\overline{(\text{-}\,\mathsf{Y}_{\!\oplus}\,\text{-})}_{n/p})*_p$$

so its cost, like *map*, is

$$t_p = n/p \cdot t_1(\oplus)$$

The implementation equation for *recur-reduce* is therefore

$$A = \oslash/\,_p \cdot \overline{(\oslash/\,_{n/p})} *_p \cdot \overline{((\text{-}\,\mathsf{Y}_{\!\oslash}\,\text{-})_{n/p})}*_p$$

so the cost of computing it is

$$\begin{aligned} t_p &= 4 + 3\log p + 3n/p + n/p \\ &= 4 + 3\log p + 4n/p \end{aligned}$$

since computing $\oslash$ takes 3 operations and the final projection step takes 4 operations.

Recur-prefix. Recall *recur-prefix* (written $\otimes /\!\!/_{b_0}\oplus$), which computes all values generated by the same linear recurrence:

$$[a_1, ..., a_n] \otimes /\!\!/_{b_0}\oplus [b_1..., b_n] = [b_0, b_0 \otimes a_1 \oplus b_1, ..., b_0 \otimes a_1 \otimes ... \otimes a_n \oplus ... \oplus b_{n-1} \otimes a_n \oplus b_n]$$

Recur-prefix is expressed as a prefix as follows:

$$x \otimes /\!\!/_{b_0}\oplus y = \begin{cases} [b_0], & \text{if } \#x(= \#y) = 0 \\ [b_0] + (b_0 \circledast)*(\oslash /\!\!/ (x \curlyvee_\otimes y)), & \text{if } \#x(= \#y) \neq 0 \end{cases}$$

where

$$\begin{aligned} a \otimes b &= (a, b), \\ (a, b) \oslash (c, d) &= (a \otimes c, b \otimes c \oplus d), \\ b_0 \circledast (a, b) &= b_0 \otimes a \oplus b \end{aligned}$$

Its implementation equation is

$$\text{shiftright}_{b_0} \cdot (\overline{(b_0\circledast)}*_{n/p}) *_p \cdot (\overline{((x,y)\oslash)}*_{n/p}) *_p \cdot \text{shift} \cdot \oslash /\!\!/_p \cdot (\overline{\oslash /\!\!/}_{n/p}) *_p \cdot (\overline{(-\curlyvee_\otimes -)}_{n/p})*_p$$

where *shiftright* rotates the entire list right one place, moving a single element from each processor to the next and inserting b_0 at the left hand end. Its execution cost is

$$\begin{aligned} t_p &= (n/p + 1) + 2n/p + 3n/p + 2 + 3\log p + 3n/p + n/p \\ &= 3 + 3\log p + 10n/p \end{aligned}$$

For simplicity, when $[b_1, ..., b_n] = [id_\otimes, ..., id_\otimes]$ and $b_0 = id_\otimes$, we write

$$[a_1, ..., a_n] \otimes /_{b_0}\oplus [b_1, ..., b_n] \quad as \quad \otimes /_{id_\otimes}\oplus [a_1, ..., a_n]$$
$$[a_1, ..., a_n] \otimes /\!\!/_{b_0}\oplus [b_1, ..., b_n] \quad as \quad \otimes /\!\!/_{id_\otimes}\oplus [a_1, ..., a_n]$$

The complexity of these operations is the same as the general forms except for the first step of each, and the map and concatenation steps at the end of the prefix computation.

Figure 8.4 summarises the costs of the operations covered in this section.

8.5 Using Costs with Equations

We have seen how to annotate operations with the shape vectors of their arguments and results. When operations are composed, these annotations appear between each pair of operations, representing the size of the first's result and the second's argument. They must be computed from right to left in programs because in general operations produce results of different sizes from their arguments.

Operation	t_p
$f*$	n/p
$\oplus/$	$\log p + n/p$
$+\!\!+/$	$n - 1$
inits	$n^2/p + n + n^2/2p^2 - n/2p$
$\oplus/\!\!/$	$2\log p + 2n/p + 1$
$+\!\!+/\!\!/$	$n/2(\log p + n/p) - 1$
$\otimes/_{bo}\oplus$	$4n/p + 3\log p + 4$
$\otimes/\!\!/_{bo}\oplus$	$10n/p + 3\log p + 3$

Figure 8.4: Summary of Operation Costs

Here is an example:
$$\oplus/\cdot\otimes/\cdot f* \tag{8.6}$$
As long as f is constant space, this can be annotated as
$$^{[q]}\oplus/\cdot^{[m,q]}\otimes/\cdot^{[n,m,q]}f*^{[n,m,q]} \tag{8.7}$$
so that applied to a list with $q = 1$ it computes a list of length 1. Note that we treat a list of length 1 and a scalar as the same.

We now show how the cost information is used to direct equations of the theory and to add new equations which can then be directed.

Example 8.1
$$(f \cdot g)* = f* \cdot g* \tag{8.8}$$
The cost of the left hand side is given by
$$LHS\ t_p = \frac{2n}{p}$$
and the cost of the right hand side by
$$RHS\ t_p = \frac{n}{p} + \frac{n}{p}$$
This equation is cost-neutral, with both sides requiring the same number of operations.

(Note, though, that the left hand side is to be preferred on many architectures since it requires fewer synchronisations.)

Example 8.2

$$f * \cdot +\!\!+/ = +\!\!+/ \cdot f **$$ (8.9)

The equation annotated with shape vectors is

$$^{[nm]}f * \cdot^{[nm]} +\!\!+/^{[n,m]} = {}^{[nm]} +\!\!+/ \cdot^{[n,m]} f **^{[n,m]}$$

The cost of the left hand side is

$$LHS \ t_p = \frac{nm}{p} + (n-1)m$$

However, the cost of the right hand side is much smaller. After the step $f**$, each processor holds n/p items of the original list, each of which is a sublist of length m. The effect of the $+\!\!+/$ is to merge these sublists into a single list so that each processor finishes holding about nm/p list elements. This merging is really just a housekeeping operation within each processor and can reasonably be accounted as taking constant time (or perhaps time proportional to m). Thus the cost of the right hand side formulation is

$$RHS \ t_p = 1 + \frac{n}{p}m$$

This equation is an example of both composition problems discussed earlier. The right hand side is a cheaper implementation than the left hand side, *and* the right hand side has a cheaper implementation than the sum of its component operations. In this situation, we define a new operation, say *concatmap*, by

$$\begin{aligned} \text{concatmap} &\triangleq f * \cdot +\!\!+/ \\ \text{concatmap} &\triangleq +\!\!+/ \cdot f ** \end{aligned}$$

direct the first equation from right to left, and label the second equation as cost-neutral.

Example 8.3

$$+/ * \cdot +\!\!+/ = +\!\!+/ \cdot +/ **$$ (8.10)

This equation is a special case of the equation above; it is interesting because it illustrates how the use of a suboperation that reduces argument sizes affects the cost of two different computation forms. The annotated form of the equation is

$$^{[nm]}+/ * \cdot^{[nm,q]} +\!\!+/^{[n,m,q]} = {}^{[nm]} +\!\!+/ \cdot^{[n,m]} +/ **^{[n,m,q]}$$

The cost of the left hand side is

$$LHS \ t_p = \frac{nm}{q} + (n-1)mq$$

while the cost of the right hand side is

$$RHS \ t_p = 1 + \frac{n}{p}(mq)$$

Here the left hand side is clearly much more costly. The reason is that the right hand side has reduced the volume of data that must be moved in the prefix step by applying the reduction with + early in the computation. The formulation on the left hand side moves much larger volumes of data around, condensing it only at the last operation. We direct the equation from left to right.

Example 8.4

$$\oplus / \cdot + / = \oplus / \cdot (\oplus/)* \tag{8.11}$$

The annotated version is

$$^{[1]} \oplus / \cdot^{[nm]} + /^{[n,m]} = ^{[1]} \oplus / \cdot^{[n]} (\oplus/)*^{[n,m]}$$

The cost of the left hand side is

$$LHS \ t_p = \frac{nm}{p} + \log p + (n-1)m$$

while the cost of the right hand side is

$$RHS \ t_p = \frac{n}{p} + \log p + \frac{n}{p}m$$

The right hand side formulation is less costly, again because it applies the reduction with $\oplus$ early and therefore reduces the volume of data to which the second reduction is applied. The left hand side "wastes" data movement. We direct the equation from left to right.

Example 8.5

$$\oplus /\!/ = (\oplus/) * \cdot inits \tag{8.12}$$

If we annotate this with size information we get

$$^{[n]} \oplus /\!/^{[n]} = ^{[n]}(\oplus/) * \cdot^{[n,n]} inits^{[n]}$$

The cost of the left hand side is

$$LHS \ t_p = 2\log p + \frac{2n}{p}$$

and the cost of the right hand side is

$$
\begin{aligned}
RHS \ t_p &= (\frac{n}{p}n) + (\frac{n^2}{p} + n + \frac{n^2}{2p^2} - \frac{n}{2p}) \\
&= \frac{2n^2}{p} + n + \frac{n^2}{2p^2} - \frac{n}{2p}
\end{aligned}
$$

so the left hand side formulation is much less costly. We direct the equation from right to left.

Example 8.6

$$inits = +\!\!/\!\!/ \cdot ([\cdot]) * \qquad (8.13)$$

or annotated with size information

$$inits = {}^{[n,n]} +\!\!/\!\!/ \, .^{[n,1]} ([\cdot]) *^{[n]}$$

The cost of the left hand side is

$$LHS \ t_p = \frac{n^2}{p} + n + \frac{n^2}{2p^2} - \frac{n}{2p}$$

while the cost of the right hand side is

$$RHS \ t_p = \frac{n}{2}(\log p + \frac{n}{p}) - 1 + \frac{n}{p}$$

The left hand side formulation is less costly. We direct the equation from right to left.

Example 8.7

$$\otimes /_{id_\otimes}\oplus = \oplus / \cdot \otimes / * \cdot tails \qquad (8.14)$$

The annotated version is

$${}^{[1]} \otimes /_{id_\otimes}\oplus^{[n]} = {}^{[1]} \oplus / \, .^{[n]} \otimes / * \, .^{[n,n]} tails^{[n]}$$

The cost of the left hand side is

$$LHS \ t_p = \frac{4n}{p} + 3\log p + 4$$

while the cost of the right hand side is

$$\begin{aligned} RHS \ t_p &= (\frac{n}{p} + \log p) + (\frac{n}{p}n) + \frac{n^2}{p} + n + \frac{n^2}{2p^2} - \frac{n}{2p} \\ &= \frac{2n^2}{p} + n + \frac{n}{2p} + \frac{n^2}{2p^2} + \log p \end{aligned}$$

The left hand side is clearly less costly since it represents a much more direct way of computing the desired result. In fact, this equation is the general form of Horner's Rule for evaluating polynomials. We direct the equation from right to left.

Example 8.8

$$\otimes /\!\!/_{id_\otimes}\oplus = (\otimes /_{id_\otimes}\oplus) * \cdot inits \qquad (8.15)$$

The annotated version of the equation is

$${}^{[n]} \otimes /\!\!/_{id_\otimes}\oplus^{[n]} = {}^{[n]} (\otimes /_{id_\otimes}\oplus) * \, .^{[n,n]} inits^{[n]}$$

$$(f \cdot g)* \rightleftharpoons f* \cdot g* \qquad \text{Equation 8.8}$$

$$f* \cdot +\!\!/ \rightharpoonup +\!\!/ \cdot f** \qquad \text{Equation 8.9}$$

$$\oplus/ \cdot +\!\!/ \rightharpoonup \oplus/ \cdot (\oplus/)* \qquad \text{Equation 8.11}$$

$$\oplus/\!\!/ \leftharpoonup (\oplus/) * \cdot inits \qquad \text{Equation 8.12}$$

$$inits \leftharpoonup +\!\!/\!\!/ \cdot ([\cdot])* \qquad \text{Equation 8.13}$$

$$\otimes/_{id_\otimes}\oplus \leftharpoonup \oplus/ \cdot \otimes/ * \cdot tails \qquad \text{Equation 8.14}$$

$$\otimes/\!\!/_{id_\otimes}\oplus \leftharpoonup (\otimes/_{id_\otimes}\oplus)* \cdot inits \qquad \text{Equation 8.15}$$

Figure 8.5: Summary of Cost-Reducing Directions

The cost of the left hand side is

$$LHS \; t_p = \frac{10n}{p} + 3\log p + 3$$

while the cost of the right hand side is

$$RHS \; t_p = \frac{n}{p}(4n+4) + (\frac{n^2}{p} + n + \frac{n^2}{2p^2} - \frac{n}{2p})$$

Again the direct formulation on the left hand side is much less costly. We direct the equation from right to left. Note the parallel with the equation defining *prefix* in Example 8.5.

Figure 8.5 summarises the cost-reducing directions of the equations considered in this section.

With this information about equations and their effects on costs we illustrate a derivation driven by cost minimisation. Of course, minimising costs does not automatically lead to optimal programs, so at best transformation assistants still need human input. However, it suggests the usefulness of a "minimise cost" button that could be provided in such systems to reduce the drudgery of some of the steps.

The example we use here, the derivation of a new parallel solution to the maximum segment sum problem, is almost entirely driven by cost minimisation. The maximum segment sum problem is: given a list of integers, find the greatest sum of values from a contiguous sublist. It is of interest because there are efficient but non-obvious algorithms to compute it, both sequentially and in parallel. The derivation of a sequential algorithm is given in [33]. The algorithm derived here uses the recur-reduce and recur-prefix operations. It begins from an obviously correct solution: compute all of the subsegments, sum the elements of each, and select the largest of the sums.

$$mss \;=\; \{ \text{ definition } \}$$
$$\uparrow/ \cdot +/ * \cdot segs$$

$$=\; \{ \text{ by definition, } segs = +\!\!\!+/ \cdot tails * \cdot inits \}$$
$$\uparrow/ \cdot +/ * \cdot +\!\!\!+/ \cdot tails* \cdot inits$$

$$=\; \{ \text{ equation 8.10, cost-reducing } \}$$
$$\uparrow/ \cdot +\!\!\!+/ \cdot +/ ** \cdot tails* \cdot inits$$

$$=\; \{ \text{ equation 8.11, cost-reducing } \}$$
$$\uparrow/ \cdot \uparrow/ * \cdot +/ ** \cdot tails* \cdot inits$$

$$=\; \{ \text{ map promotion, equation 8.8 , cost-neutral } \}$$
$$\uparrow/ \cdot (\uparrow/ \cdot +/ * \cdot tails)* \cdot inits$$

$$=\; \{ \text{ equation 8.14, cost-reducing } \}$$
$$\uparrow/ \cdot (+\!\!/_0\!\uparrow)* \cdot inits$$

$$=\; \{ \text{ equation 8.15, cost-reducing } \}$$
$$\uparrow/ \cdot +\!\!/\!\!/_0\!\uparrow$$

We can compute the difference in cost between the initial version and the final version. We begin with the expanded initial version, applied to a list of length n and annotated with the shape vectors of the intermediate results.

$$^{[1]}\uparrow / \cdot^{[n^2]} +/ * \cdot^{[n^2,n]} +\!\!\!+/ \cdot^{[n,n,n]} tails* \cdot^{[n,n]} inits^{[n]}$$

If we sum the costs for each step of this composition beginning from the right, we get

	t_p
$inits$	$\frac{n^2}{p} + n + \frac{n^2}{2p^2} - \frac{n}{2p}$
$tails*$	$\frac{n(n-1)n}{2p}$
$+\!\!\!+/$	$(n-1)n^2$
$+/*$	$\frac{n^2}{p}n$
$\uparrow/$	$\frac{n^2}{p} + \log p$

The overall cost is $t_p = O(n^3)$, regardless of p, that is the naive solution takes cubic time regardless of parallelism. The final version is

$$[1] \uparrow / \ .^{[n]} + /\!\!/_0 \uparrow^{[n]}$$

with costs

$$
\begin{aligned}
t_p &= \frac{n}{p} + \log p + 3\log p + \frac{10n}{p} + 3 \\
&= \frac{11n}{p} + 4\log p + 3
\end{aligned}
$$

which is much smaller and can make use of linear parallelism. The efficient algorithm can be computed in logarithmic parallel time on n processors, a big improvement over cubic parallel time.

There are a number of weaknesses in the cost calculus presented here. Costs do not take into account load-balancing between processors. Although lists appear to be distributed equally at the beginning, processors may not do equal work because the shape vectors give maximal sizes at different nesting depths. So although processors have equal segments of top-level elements, they do not have equal amounts of data. Furthermore, as computations proceed these imbalances become larger. The approach proposed here is a first attempt to limit the complexity of a general cost calculus so that it is of practical usefulness. The problem of compositionality means that an exact cost calculus cannot be made context-free, so some trade-off is necessary.

8.6   Handling Sizes Explicitly

In this section we show what happens when sizes and costs are manipulated explicitly. The resulting cost system is accurate but it is not of great practical interest in its most general form.

Since cost measures depend on arrangements of elements of data types, as well as their values and the sizes of these values, accurate costs are only obtainable by manipulating all of these values. Fortunately, this can also be done catamorphically.

Embed each list

$$[a_1, a_2, \ldots, a_n]$$

in an extended list

$$[(1, c_1, s_1, a_1), (2, c_2, s_2, a_2), \ldots, (i, c_i, s_i, a_i), \ldots, (n, c_n, s_n, a_n)]$$

where the is represent the position in the list (necessary so that we can deduce communication cost from placement), the c_is represent the cost of computing the ith element (so far), the s_is represent the size of the ith argument, and the a_is are from the original list are also present. Note that such an embedding is already a kind of implementation decision.

The data type of extended lists is not a particular case of the type of join lists. "Concatenation" is no longer associative, because position in the list is meaningful, so that concatenation involves moving the second argument list to new positions. Also "concatenation" no longer has an identity.

If h is a list catamorphism $(e, f, \oplus)$, then there is a cost catamorphism which exactly describes the effect of h in this extended domain. The "cost of h" catamorphism is (g_1, g_2, g_3) with

$$
\begin{aligned}
g_1 [] &= (0, 1, 1, e) \\
g_2(i, c_i, s_i, a_i) &= (i, c_i + cost(f\ a_i), size(f\ a_i), f\ a_i) \\
g_3(i, c_i, s_i, a_i)(j, c_j, s_j, a_j) &= (j, \\
& \quad \uparrow(c_i, c_j) + comm(s_i, i, j) + cost(a_i \oplus a_j), \\
& \quad size(a_i \oplus a_j), \\
& \quad a_i \oplus a_j)
\end{aligned}
$$

where the implementation is parallel and uses the usual algorithm with a right skew (that is the reductive step on two values at locations i and j takes place at location j) and $comm(s_i, i, j)$ describes the communication cost in moving an object of size s_i from location i to location j. Notice that this is another almost-homomorphism.

The reason that this approach to costs is impractical is that it is at least as much work to compute the cost of a catamorphism as it is to compute the catamorphism itself. The cost catamorphism above cannot be sectioned in any useful way – computing the cost requires knowing the size of the arguments as well as their values, and computing their sizes requires knowing their values. Thus there is no obvious way to compute only part of the information by a kind of abstract interpretation.

It only seems possible to use this approach if special cases in which closed forms for some of the terms in the cost catamorphism can be found, that is in which some of the recursion can be precomputed. This is essentially what we have done in treating reductions differently depending on how they alter the sizes of their intermediate results.

Chapter 9 ————————————————————

Building Categorical Data Types

We have shown how to build categorical data types for the simple type of concatenation lists. In this chapter we show the data type construction in its most general setting. While there is some overhead to understanding the construction in this more general setting, the generality is needed to build much more complex types. We illustrate this in subsequent chapters by building types such as trees, arrays, and graphs.

More category theory background is assumed in this chapter. Suitable references are [127, 158].

9.1 Categorical Data Type Construction

The construction of a categorical data type is divided into four stages:

1. The choice of an underlying category of basic types and computations on them. This is usually the category *Type*, but other possibilities will certainly be of interest.

2. The choice of an endofunctor, T, on this underlying category. The functor is chosen so that its effect on the still-hypothetical constructed type is to unpack it into its components. Components are chosen by considering the type signatures of constructors that seem suitable for the desired type. When this endofunctor is polynomial it has a fixed point; and this fixed point is defined to be the constructed type.

3. The construction of a category of T-algebras, T-Alg, whose objects are algebras of the new type and their algebraic relatives, and whose arrows are homomorphisms on the new type. The constructed type algebra (the free type algebra) is the initial object in this category. The unique arrows from it to other algebras are catamorphisms.

4. The construction of a type functor between the underlying category and T-Alg, showing that the new type is polymorphic over the objects of the underlying category.

The category T-Alg can be regarded as a different view of the underlying category in which pairs of arrows are associated as a single algebra arrow. Thus T-Alg is a way of viewing the structure of the underlying category so that its interesting structure is revealed; in particular parallel computations using recursive schemas. The commuting diagrams in T-Alg are the basis for the equations used in program transformation.

The construction we describe works for any category $\mathcal{C}$ which has binary products and coproducts, and an initial and a terminal object. We will assume, however, that the underlying category is *Type* for the remainder of the book. The following definition outlines the properties required.

Definition 9.1 *(Underlying Category $\mathcal{C}$)* $\mathcal{C}$ is a category with objects $A, B, \ldots$, arrows $f, g, h, \ldots$ and the following objects, arrows, rules of inference, and equations:

Objects.

For every pair of $\mathcal{C}$-objects A and B, there are $\mathcal{C}$-objects $A \times B$ and $A + B$ (the product and coproduct of A and B respectively).

$\mathcal{C}$ has an initial object **0**.

$\mathcal{C}$ has a terminal object **1**.

Arrows.

The following arrows exist:

$$id_A : A \rightarrow A \tag{9.1}$$
$$\overleftarrow{\pi}_{A,B} : A \times B \rightarrow A \tag{9.2}$$
$$\overrightarrow{\pi}_{A,B} : A \times B \rightarrow B \tag{9.3}$$
$$\overleftarrow{\iota}_{A,B} : A \rightarrow A + B \tag{9.4}$$
$$\overrightarrow{\iota}_{A,B} : B \rightarrow A + B \tag{9.5}$$
$$! : 0 \rightarrow A \tag{9.6}$$
$$\mathbf{i} : A \rightarrow 1 \tag{9.7}$$

Rules of Inference

A binary operation $\cdot$ *(compose)* such that

$$\frac{f : A \rightarrow B \quad g : B \rightarrow C}{(g \cdot f) : A \rightarrow C} \tag{9.8}$$

A binary operation $\vartriangle$ *(split)* such that

$$\frac{f : A \rightarrow B \quad g : A \rightarrow C}{f \vartriangle g : A \rightarrow (B \times C)} \tag{9.9}$$

A binary operation $\triangledown$ *(junc)* such that

$$\frac{f : B \rightarrow A \quad g : C \rightarrow A}{f \triangledown g : (B + C) \rightarrow A} \tag{9.10}$$

Equations.

For every arrow $f : A \rightarrow B$,

$$f \cdot id_A = f \tag{9.11}$$
$$id_B \cdot f = f \tag{9.12}$$

For any three arrows $f : A \rightarrow B$, $g : B \rightarrow C$, and $h : C \rightarrow D$

$$h \cdot (g \cdot f) \;=\; (h \cdot g) \cdot f \tag{9.13}$$
$$h = f \vartriangle g \;\equiv\; \hat{\pi}_{B,C} \cdot h = f \;\land\; \hat{\pi}_{B,C} \cdot h = g \tag{9.14}$$
$$h = f \triangledown g \;\equiv\; h \cdot \hat{\iota}_{B,C} = f \;\land\; h \cdot \hat{\iota}_{B,C} = g \tag{9.15}$$

The existence of binary product and coproduct arrows follow from this definition. They are:

Definition 9.2 *(Product)* If $f : A \rightarrow C$ and $g : B \rightarrow D$ are arrows, the arrow $f \times g : A \times B \rightarrow C \times D$ is defined by:

$$f \times g \triangleq (f \cdot \hat{\pi}) \vartriangle (g \cdot \hat{\pi}) \tag{9.16}$$

Definition 9.3 *(Coproduct)* If $f : C \rightarrow A$ and $g : D \rightarrow B$ are arrows, the arrow $f + g : C + D \rightarrow A + B$ is defined by:

$$f + g \triangleq (\hat{\iota} \cdot f) \triangledown (\hat{\iota} \cdot g) \tag{9.17}$$

9.2   Type Functors

Definition 9.4 *(Functor)* A functor $\mathsf{F} : \mathcal{C} \rightarrow \mathcal{D}$ is a mapping of objects in category $\mathcal{C}$ to objects in category $\mathcal{D}$ and of arrows in $\mathcal{C}$ to arrows in $\mathcal{D}$ that preserves category structure, that is it is a category homomorphism. Therefore it preserves identity arrows and composition.

$$\mathsf{F}(f : A \rightarrow B) \;=\; \mathsf{F}f : \mathsf{F}A \rightarrow \mathsf{F}B \tag{9.18}$$
$$\mathsf{F}(g \cdot f) \;=\; \mathsf{F}g \cdot \mathsf{F}f \tag{9.19}$$
$$\mathsf{F}id_A \;=\; id_{\mathsf{F}A} \tag{9.20}$$

A functor $\mathsf{F} : \mathcal{C} \rightarrow \mathcal{C}$ is called an endofunctor.

Definition 9.5 *(Polynomial Functor)* The identity functor I is a polynomial type functor defined by:
$$\mathsf{I}(f : A \rightarrow B) \triangleq f : A \rightarrow B \tag{9.21}$$
For any $\mathcal{C}$-object X, the constant functor K_X is a polynomial type functor, defined by:

$$\mathsf{K}_X(f : A \rightarrow B) \triangleq id_X : X \rightarrow X \tag{9.22}$$

If F and G are polynomial type functors then $\mathsf{F} \times \mathsf{G}$, $\mathsf{F} + \mathsf{G}$ and $\mathsf{G} \cdot \mathsf{F}$ are polynomial type functors defined by:

$$\mathsf{F} \times \mathsf{G}(f : A \rightarrow B) \;\triangleq\; (\mathsf{F}f \times \mathsf{G}f) : (\mathsf{F}A \times \mathsf{G}A) \rightarrow (\mathsf{F}B \times \mathsf{G}B) \tag{9.23}$$
$$\mathsf{F} + \mathsf{G}(f : A \rightarrow B) \;\triangleq\; (\mathsf{F}f + \mathsf{G}f) : (\mathsf{F}A + \mathsf{G}A) \rightarrow (\mathsf{F}B + \mathsf{G}B) \tag{9.24}$$
$$\mathsf{G} \cdot \mathsf{F}(f : A \rightarrow B) \;\triangleq\; \mathsf{G}(\mathsf{F}(f : A \rightarrow B)) \tag{9.25}$$

If A is an object of C then $(A\times)$, $(\times A)$, $(A+)$ and $(+A)$ are polynomial type functors (known as left and right sections of $\times$ and left and right sections of $+$ respectively) defined by:

$$(A\times)(f : B \to C) \;\;\triangleq\;\; (id_A \times f) : (A \times B) \to (A \times C) \tag{9.26}$$

$$(\times A)(f : B \to C) \;\;\triangleq\;\; (f \times id_A) : (B \times A) \to (C \times A) \tag{9.27}$$

$$(A+)(f : B \to C) \;\;\triangleq\;\; (id_A + f) : (A + B) \to (A + C) \tag{9.28}$$

$$(+A)(f : B \to C) \;\;\triangleq\;\; (f + id_A) : (B + A) \to (C + A) \tag{9.29}$$

Definition 9.6 *(Bifunctor)* A bifunctor $\dagger : C \times C \to C$ is a functor which maps pairs of arrows into arrows, and pairs of objects into objects as follows:

$$\dagger(f \times g : A \times B \to C \times D) = f\dagger g : A\dagger B \to C\dagger D \tag{9.30}$$

Definition 9.7 *(Sectioned Bifunctor)* Sectioned bifunctors are defined according to the rules:

$$(A\dagger)(f : B \to C) \;\;=\;\; id_A \dagger f : A\dagger B \to A\dagger C \tag{9.31}$$

$$(\dagger A)(f : B \to C) \;\;=\;\; f \dagger id_A : B\dagger A \to C\dagger A \tag{9.32}$$

9.3   T-Algebras and Constructors

Constructors make objects of a constructed type by putting together their component parts in particular ways. We build a category in which the objects are pairs consisting of components and constructed objects. Homomorphisms have the property that their behaviour on a composite object can be expressed as a function of their behaviour on the components from which it is built. Thus homomorphisms correspond to "parallel" arrows from pairs to pairs, mapping each element of the pair in a consistent way.

The new category consists of other pairs with cognate structure; these turn out to be algebraic objects whose internal workings are "like" the constructed type in a sense we make precise. Homomorphisms on the constructed type are arrows from the constructed pairs to these other algebraic objects that resemble them.

We begin by defining a T-algebra.

Definition 9.8 *(T-Algebra)* Let C be a category, and T an endofunctor on C. A T-algebra is an arrow $f : \mathsf{T}A \to A$, where A is an object called the carrier of f.

T-algebra homomorphisms are functions that respect T-algebra structure.

Definition 9.9 *(T-Homomorphism)* Given an endofunctor $\mathsf{T} : C \to C$, and T-algebras $f : \mathsf{T}A \to A$ and $g : \mathsf{T}B \to B$, a T-homomorphism $h : A \to B$ is an arrow such that

$$h \cdot f = g \cdot \mathsf{T}h$$

Example 9.10 For any T-algebra $\psi : TA \to A$, the arrow id_A is a T-homomorphism:

$$
\begin{aligned}
id_A \cdot \psi \;=\;& \{\text{ identity of composition }\} \\
& \psi \\[2mm]
=\;& \{\text{ identity of composition }\} \\
& \psi \cdot id_{TA} \\[2mm]
=\;& \{\text{ functors preserve identities }\} \\
& \psi \cdot T id_A
\end{aligned}
$$

Example 9.11 Given T-algebras $\phi : TA \to A$, $\psi : TB \to B$, and $\xi : TC \to C$, and T-homomorphisms $f : \psi \to \phi$ and $g : \phi \to \xi$, the arrow $g \cdot f$ is a T-homomorphism.

$$
\begin{aligned}
g \cdot f \cdot \psi \;=\;& \{\text{ Definition 9.9 }\} \\
& g \cdot \phi \cdot Tf \\[2mm]
=\;& \{\text{ Definition 9.9 }\} \\
& \xi \cdot Tg \cdot Tf \\[2mm]
=\;& \{\text{ functors respect composition }\} \\
& \xi \cdot T(g \cdot f)
\end{aligned}
$$

Thus we can define categories whose objects are T-algebras and whose arrows are T-algebra homomorphisms. This category is called T-Alg. If C is a category such as *Type*, then the category T-Alg is just another, more structured, way of looking at the same category. This is shown in Figure 9.1.

Now consider the constructors for some hypothetical data type $A\varpi$ which we wish to construct. The constructors are arrows of the form:

$$
\begin{aligned}
\tau_1 : X \to A\varpi & \qquad\qquad (9.33) \\
\tau_2 : Y \to A\varpi & \qquad\qquad (9.34) \\
\tau_3 : Z \to A\varpi & \qquad\qquad (9.35)
\end{aligned}
$$

A non-trivial type makes some reference to the type of underlying objects from which it is built. For a polymorphic construction this is essential, but it is hard to think of interesting types that do not do so. We have indicated this by using a "base type" A in the naming of the constructed type $A\varpi$. Thus some of X, Y and Z usually contain some reference to A.

Non-trivial types also usually have some recursive structure, that is instances of the type are built up from smaller instances. Thus some of X, Y and Z contain some reference to $A\varpi$.

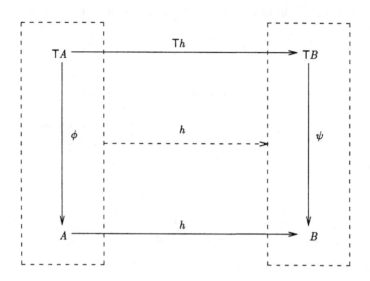

Figure 9.1: T-Algebras and a T-Algebra Homomorphism

Now consider the question of the existence of a functor that maps the constructed type (as an object) to its components X, Y and Z. Call this functor T, the endofunctor used to build algebras. Its effect must be

$$\mathsf{T} : A\varpi \mapsto X + Y + Z \tag{9.36}$$

Example 9.12 The type of cons lists has two constructors:

$$\mathbf{nil} : 1 \to A\star$$
$$\mathbf{cons} : A \times A\star \to A\star$$

where **nil** builds an empty list and **cons** appends a single element to the beginning of an existing list. The functor T is

$$\mathsf{T} : A\star \mapsto 1 + A \times A\star$$

and can be written

$$\mathsf{T} = \mathsf{K_1} + \mathsf{K}_A \times \mathsf{I}$$

Recall that K_X is the constant X functor.

Under certain conditions on the base category and the functor T, T has a fixed point in $\mathcal{C}$. The weakest possible conditions are still a subject for research (see for example [53, 187]) but it is enough for us that any polynomial functor in a category $\mathcal{C}$ with the properties defined above has such a fixed point. The object that is this fixed point is called the constructed categorical data type (CDT) and is written $\mu\mathsf{T}$ or, more conveniently, $A\varpi$.

Since $A\varpi$ is the fixed point of the functor T, there is an isomorphism between $A\varpi$ and the components from which it is built, $\mathsf{T}A\varpi$. This is illustrated in Figure 9.2. One half

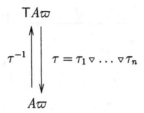

Figure 9.2: Relationship of a Data Type to its Components

of the isomorphism is the junction arrow based on the constructors; the other is a pattern matching arrow.

Recall that a T-algebra is a pair $TP \to P$. The pair $TA\varpi \to A\varpi$ is certainly one of these T-algebras. It is initial in the category of T-algebras.

Example 9.13 Consider the cons list data type introduced in Example 9.12. A T-algebra is a pair

$$f_1 \triangledown f_2 : 1 + A \times P \to P \tag{9.37}$$

with

$$f_1 \ : \ 1 \to P \tag{9.38}$$
$$f_2 \ : \ A \times P \to P \tag{9.39}$$

That is, T-algebras are sets with a distinguished element and a binary operation of type $A \times P \to P$.

Because the pair $TA \to A$ is initial in T-Alg, there is a unique arrow from it to any other T-algebra and these are the *catamorphisms*.

Definition 9.14 *(Catamorphism)* Let $\tau : TA\varpi \to A\varpi$ be the initial object in T-Alg, and $\psi : TP \to P$ be any other T-algebra. The unique T-Alg-arrow (T-homomorphism) from $\tau : TA\varpi \to A\varpi$ to $\psi : TP \to P$ is called a *catamorphism*.

Since the catamorphism depends only on the arrow ψ of the codomain algebra, it is written (ψ). The one-to-one correspondence between T-algebras and catamorphisms is of great practical usefulness.

Catamorphisms are characterised by the following property.

Property 9.15 The catamorphism $(\psi) : \tau \to \psi$ is the unique $h : A \to B$ in $\mathcal{C}$ satisfying

$$h : A \to B = (\psi) \quad \equiv \quad h \cdot \tau = \psi \cdot Th \tag{9.40}$$

Catamorphisms are homomorphisms between the constructed type and other T-algebras which are algebraic objects whose structure is "like" that of the constructed type.

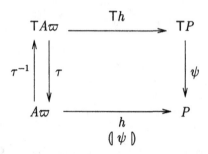

Figure 9.3: General Computation of a Catamorphism

Figure 9.3 illustrates the general strategy for computing a catamorphism. If h is the catamorphism (ψ) then it is computed by

$$\psi \cdot \mathsf{T}h \cdot \tau^{-1} \tag{9.41}$$

The operation τ^{-1} is the inverse of the junction arrow of the constructors of the new type. It is a kind of pattern matching. The arrow $\mathsf{T}h$ is a call to recursive subcomputation(s). The arrow ψ puts together the results of the recursive calls consistently (that is, in the same way as $A\varpi$ is built) to give a result. For some types, such as cons lists, this process does not have opportunities for parallelism, but for others, such as join lists, it does. Notice that the potential for parallelism can be detected purely from the form of the type's constructors.

Consider the composition of a catamorphism with a T-algebra homomorphism. The codomain of this composition is itself a T-algebra, so there is a catamorphism corresponding to the composition. This property is called *promotion* and is really a generalised form of loop fusion.

Theorem 9.16 (*Promotion*) The composition of the catamorphism $(\psi) : \tau \rightarrow \psi$ and a homomorphism $f : \psi \rightarrow \phi$ is the catamorphism $(\phi) : \tau \rightarrow \phi$.

Proof

$f \cdot (\psi) : \tau \rightarrow \phi$ is a T-homomorphism (Example 9.11) and, since its domain is τ and its codomain is ϕ, it must be the catamorphism (ϕ) (Definition 9.14).

$\square$

The diagram illustrating this proof is shown in Figure 9.4.

9.4   Polymorphism

The definition of the functor T depends on the particular type A with which we began. We wish to capture the essential similarities of all of the constructions beginning with different types in one polymorphic construction.

The construction above used a functor T that should really have been written T_A to

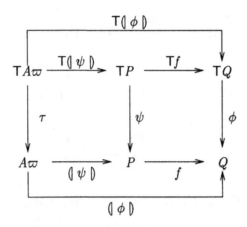

Figure 9.4: Promotion

indicate its dependence on A. We capture this by making the functor in question a bifunctor, one of whose arguments is the base type.

The constructors of a polymorphic type ought to be written

$$\tau_{i_A} : X \to A\varpi \qquad (9.42)$$

to establish that they depend on the base type A. Similarly, the functor T should be written as $A \dagger A\varpi$ with

$$A \dagger A\varpi : A\varpi \to X + Y + Z \qquad (9.43)$$

The fixed point of the bifunctor $\dagger$ is now considered to be a polymorphic data type which can be instantiated at a particular type A using the sectioned functor $A\dagger$. We are now able to talk about the relationship of CDTs built on different base types, that is the relationship between the types built by $A\dagger$ and $B\dagger$.

One of the most important operations on a CDT is the generalised map catamorphism. This catamorphism behaves as its name suggests – it applies some function pointwise to the components from which an object of the data type was built, without otherwise altering its structure.

Definition 9.17 *(Generalised Map)* Given a function $f : A \to B$, and CDTs $A\varpi$ and $B\varpi$, we define the pointwise map function $f\varpi : A\varpi \to B\varpi$ by:

$$f\varpi \triangleq (\!| \ \tau_B \cdot f \dagger id_{B\varpi} \ |\!)$$

That this is a valid definition is seen from the diagram in Figure 9.5. We also see from this diagram how to evaluate a generalised map: pattern match on the structure of the argument

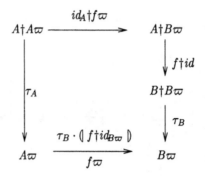

Figure 9.5: Building a Generalised Map

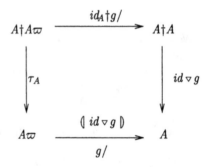

Figure 9.6: Building a Generalised Reduction

(τ_A^{-1}); recursively apply generalised map to the substructures, if any; use the function f on any components that are single elements of A, mapping them to single elements of B; and reassemble into the same structure as we began with.

A second important class of operations on a CDT are the generalised reduction catamorphisms. These catamorphisms are complementary to generalised maps in the sense that reductions affect structure.

Definition 9.18 *(Generalised Reduction)* Given a function $id \triangledown g : A\dagger A \rightarrow A$, define the generalised reduction $g/ : A\varpi \rightarrow A$ to be $(\!| \; id \triangledown g \; |\!)$.

The validity of this definition is seen from the diagram in Figure 9.6.

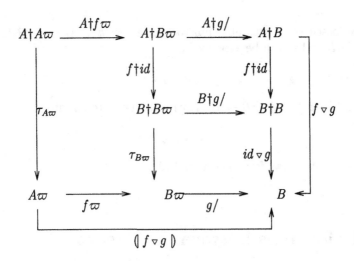

Figure 9.7: Factoring Catamorphisms

9.5 Factorisation

Under certain circumstances, catamorphisms factor into a composition of a generalised map and a generalised reduction.

Theorem 9.19 *(Factorisation)* If $h : A\dagger B \to B$ can be expressed in the form

$$h = (id \triangledown g) \cdot (f \dagger id) \tag{9.44}$$

for $f : A \to B$ and $id \triangledown g : B \dagger B \to B$ then

$$(h) = g/ \cdot f\varpi \tag{9.45}$$

Proof

If h can be factored as above then we build the diagram in Figure 9.7, from which the result can be read.

□

For certain common functors, it turns out that all catamorphisms factor in this way.

Definition 9.20 *(Separable Functor)* If a type functor $A\dagger$ can be written in the form $\mathsf{G} + \mathsf{F}$ where G is a product term involving K_A and F contains no occurrence of the type functor K_A, then the functor $A\dagger$ is called *separable*.

Corollary 9.21 For a type based on a separable functor, all catamorphisms can be factored into the composition of a generalised map and a generalised reduction.

Proof

For a type based on a separable functor, an arrow $h : A\dagger B \to B$ is actually $h : GA + FB \to B$ and so can be expressed as

$$h = f \triangledown g \tag{9.46}$$

where $f : GA \to B$ and $g : FB \to B$. Thus h can be factored into

$$id \triangledown g \cdot f + id \tag{9.47}$$

whence the result follows from Theorem 9.19.

$\square$

9.6   Relationships between T-Algebras

We have seen that each T_X-algebra is the initial object of a category T-Alg$_A$. The other algebras in this category are those whose underlying types are computable from A in $\mathcal{C}$. In principle, T-Alg$_A$ is a different category from T-Alg$_B$. However, the generalised map shows how a T_A-algebra can be related to a T_B-algebra, and this connection can be used to "paste together" the different T_X-algebras into a single category.

Consider the category T-Alg$_0$ built by using T_0. Since 0 is initial in $\mathcal{C}$, there is a unique arrow from 0 to any other object A. This arrows lifts to a T_0-catamorphism in T-Alg$_0$. Thus T-Alg$_0$ is a single category that contains all of the T-Alg$_X$ categories as subcategories. Figure 9.8 shows this for a simple category $\mathcal{C}$.

In fact, we can regard ϖ as a functor from $\mathcal{C}$ to a subcategory of T-Alg$_0$ consisting of all of the T_X-algebras for X in $\mathcal{C}$. Clearly a well-formed definition is possible; objects are mapped to algebras, and arrows f are mapped to T-algebra homomorphisms, $f\varpi$. Such a mapping preserves identities and composition.

We conclude with a theorem that is actually a special case of promotion, but which itself provides many useful corollaries.

Theorem 9.22 The composition of an A-map with a B-catamorphism is an A-catamorphism.

Proof

The proof is read from the diagram in Figure 9.9. An A-map is the lifting of some underlying function that maps A to B. The B-catamorphism is therefore certainly an A-homomorphism, and hence, by Theorem 9.16, there is a unique catamorphism to its codomain.

$\square$

The construction we have shown in this chapter is actually quite old, although its application to computation is newer. Separable types correspond to triples or monads, and the category of T-algebras to a resolution of the monad. Non-separable types correspond

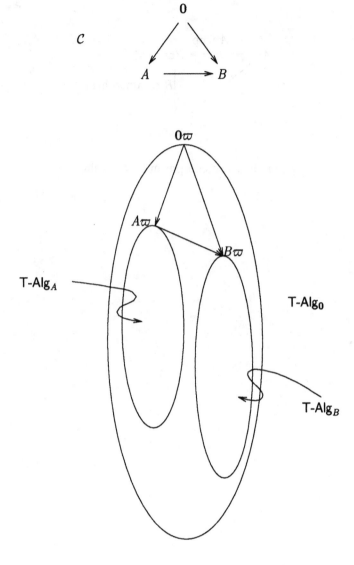

Figure 9.8: Relationships between T-Algebra Categories

to free triples, which share many of the properties of monads. The use of equations on the constructors of a data type can be seen as the use of a theory in a category such as *Set* or *Type*. Further details and a more categorical presentation can be found in the book by Barr and Wells [25].

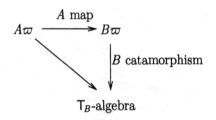

Figure 9.9: Catamorphism Relationships

Chapter 10 ─────────────

Lists, Bags, and Finite Sets

We illustrate the construction of Chapter 9 by building the three closely-related types of lists, bags and finite sets and contrasting their properties. We have already shown how to build the categorical data type of lists in Chapter 5, but we do it again here in full generality using the notation of Chapter 9.

10.1 Lists

As we have seen, the type of join or concatenation lists, which we write as $A*$ for A an arbitrary type, has three constructors:

$$[] \; : \; 1 \to A* \tag{10.1}$$
$$[\cdot] \; : \; A \to A* \tag{10.2}$$
$$+\!\!\!+ \; : \; A* \times A* \to A* \tag{10.3}$$

where 1 is the terminal object of the underlying category. The constructor $[]$ defines a constant of type $A*$ corresponding to the empty list; the constructor $[\cdot]$ takes an element of type A and makes it into a singleton list; and the constructor $+\!\!\!+$ is list concatenation. To make this correspond to lists, we add two equations, one making concatenation associative, and the other making the empty list its identity. Such side equations are handled neatly by the CDT construction [78]; they carry over to become equations on algebras.

The functor T_A whose effect is to decompose an object of this constructed type must be

$$\mathsf{T}_A \cong \mathsf{K}_1 + \mathsf{K}_A + \mathsf{I} \times \mathsf{I}$$

which maps an object $A*$ to $1 + A + A* \times A*$ as required. It is a polynomial functor and hence it has a fixed point, which we define to be $A*$.

The initial T_A-algebra is the free list monoid on A, that is the monoid whose elements are lists of elements of A, with an associative binary operation, concatenation, and identity the empty list.

A T_A-algebra is an arrow

$$p : 1 + A + P \times P \to P \tag{10.4}$$

where $p = p_1 \triangledown p_2 \triangledown p_3$ with

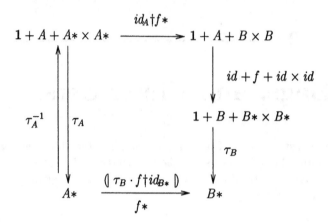

Figure 10.1: Map for Lists

$$p_1 \; : \; 1 \to P \tag{10.5}$$
$$p_2 \; : \; A \to P \tag{10.6}$$
$$p_3 \; : \; P \times P \to P \tag{10.7}$$

in which p_3 is associative with identity $p_1 1$. Thus T_A-algebras are *monoids* whose underlying type is computable from A. For any monoid with this property there is a unique arrow from the free list monoid on A, a catamorphism. Catamorphisms are computed by a recursive scheme as shown in the previous chapter (Figure 9.3).

The bifunctor $\dagger$ of the functor T_A is

$$A \dagger A* : A* \mapsto 1 + A + A* \times A* \tag{10.8}$$

Given an arrow f in $\mathcal{C}$ from A to B we construct the diagram in Figure 10.1 from which we deduce the existence of a unique map arrow from $A*$ to $B*$, given by $(\!| \; \tau_B \cdot f \dagger id \; |\!)$ which we call $f*$. The composition of the left hand, top, and right hand arrows shows that $f*$ can be evaluated by applying f independently to each of the elements of a list of As.

A reduction on the type $A*$ requires the existence of a function $id \triangledown g : A \dagger A \to A$. The diagram in Figure 10.2 shows that it is of the form

$$g = \eta \triangledown id \triangledown \oplus \tag{10.9}$$

for some $\eta : 1 \to A$ and $\oplus : A \times A \to A$. A reduction is an arrow from a free list monoid to a monoid on A (whose identity is the image of 1 under η and whose binary operation is $\oplus$).

The factorisation theorem for lists is illustrated in the diagram in Figure 10.3. Any homomorphism on a list can be expressed as the composition of a map and a reduction.

Recall that *inits*, *prefix*, and *generalised prefix* are all list catamorphisms.

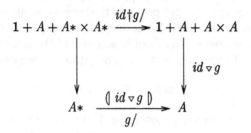

Figure 10.2: Reduction for Lists

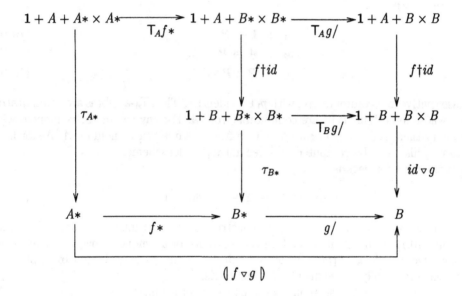

Figure 10.3: Factorisation for Lists

10.2   Bags

We now consider the type of bags, that is sets in which repetitions are significant (sometimes called *multisets*). Bags relax the ordering requirement of lists, and hence are midway between lists and sets in expressiveness. Suppose that we write this type $A_\uplus$ for A an arbitrary type. The three constructors are:

$$\mathopen{\mathrm{{\textstyle\int}\!\!\int}} \; : \; 1 \to A_\uplus \tag{10.10}$$

$$\mathopen{\tau\!\!\int} \; : \; A \to A_\uplus \tag{10.11}$$

$$\uplus \; : \; A_\uplus \times A_\uplus \to A_\uplus \tag{10.12}$$

The constructor $\{\!\!\{\,\}\!\!\}$ defines the empty bag, $\{\!\!\{\cdot\}\!\!\}$ is the singleton bag constructor, and $\uplus$ is bag union. As before we add equations to get precisely the type we want: one to make bag union associative and commutative, and the other to make the empty bag its identity. Because it is in the extra equations that bags differ from lists, much of the construction is identical.

The functor T_A whose effect is to decompose a bag into its components is

$$\mathsf{T}_A \cong \mathsf{K_1} + \mathsf{K_A} + \mathsf{I} \times \mathsf{I}$$

The initial T_A-algebra is the free bag monoid on A, that is the monoid whose elements are bags of elements of A, with an associative and commutative binary operation, bag union, and identity the empty bag.

A T_A-algebra is an arrow

$$p : 1 + A + P \times P \to P \tag{10.13}$$

with $p = p_1 \triangledown p_2 \triangledown p_3$ and

$$p_1 \ : \ 1 \to P \tag{10.14}$$
$$p_2 \ : \ A \to P \tag{10.15}$$
$$p_3 \ : \ P \times P \to P \tag{10.16}$$

and p_3 associative and commutative, with $p_1 1$ its identity. Thus T_A-algebras are *commutative monoids* whose underlying type are computable from A. For any commutative monoid with this property there is a (unique) catamorphism from the free bag monoid on A. As for lists, any catamorphism can be computed by a recursive parallel scheme.

The bifunctor $\dagger$ for bags is

$$A \dagger A\uplus : A\uplus \mapsto 1 + A + A\uplus \times A\uplus \tag{10.17}$$

Given an arrow f in $\mathcal{C}$ from A to B we construct a diagram much the same as that for lists (Figure 10.1) from which we deduce the existence of a unique arrow, bag map, from $A\uplus$ to $B\uplus$, given by $(\!\!| \ \tau_B \cdot f \dagger id \ |\!\!)$, which we call $f\uplus$. Again $f\uplus$ is evaluated by applying f independently to each of the elements of a bag of As.

A reduction on the type $A\uplus$ requires the existence of a function $id \triangledown g : A\dagger A \to A$. As before, the diagram in Figure 10.2 shows that it must be of the form

$$g = \eta \triangledown id \triangledown \oplus \tag{10.18}$$

for some $\eta : 1 \to A$ and $\oplus : A \times A \to A$. Thus a reduction is an arrow from a free bag monoid to a commutative monoid on A.

We get a factorisation theorem for bags, illustrated by the diagram in Figure 10.3. Any homomorphism on a bag can be expressed as the composition of a bag map and a reduction.

There is no analogue of *inits* for the type of bags because the equivalent function is not injective. We would require an analogue for *last*, but such a function doesn't exist because bags do not have an ordering on their elements. Because *prefix* is defined in terms of *inits*, we cannot define *prefix* or *generalised prefix* functions for bags either.

The implementation of the operations on bags is similar to the implementations on lists.

Maps of course are exactly the same. Reductions are still done most effectively using a binary tree pattern of applications of the base function, but there is some added flexibility about the order in which base functions are applied that can be exploited by some architectures. For instance, several architectures include mechanisms for computing reductions of simple operations in hardware, with evaluation order depending on detailed hardware performance. It is useful to be able to make use of this without semantic difficulties.

10.3 Finite Sets

Next we consider the type of finite sets. We write this type $A\cup$ for A an arbitrary type. The three constructors are:

$$\{\} \quad : \quad 1 \to A\cup \tag{10.19}$$
$$\{\cdot\} \quad : \quad A \to A\cup \tag{10.20}$$
$$\cup \quad : \quad A\cup \times A\cup \to A\cup \tag{10.21}$$

where $\{\}$ defines the empty set, $\{\cdot\}$ the singleton set, and $\cup$ is set union. The operation $\cup$ is associative, commutative, and idempotent and has identity $\{\}$.

The functor T_A that decomposes sets into their components is

$$T_A \triangleq K_1 + K_A + I \times I$$

A T_A-algebra is an arrow

$$p : 1 + A + P \times P \to P \tag{10.22}$$

with $p = p_1 \triangledown p_2 \triangledown p_3$ and

$$p_1 \quad : \quad 1 \to P \tag{10.23}$$
$$p_2 \quad : \quad A \to P \tag{10.24}$$
$$p_3 \quad : \quad P \times P \to P \tag{10.25}$$

with p_3 satisfying equations for associativity, commutativity, and idempotence. Thus T_A-algebras are *commutative, idempotent monoids*, or *semilattices*, whose underlying type is computable from A. For any such monoid there is a catamorphism from the free set monoid on A and a recursive scheme as before.

The bifunctor $\dagger$ for sets is

$$A \dagger A\cup : A\cup \mapsto 1 + A + A\cup \times A\cup \tag{10.26}$$

As before, given an arrow in $\mathcal{C}$ from A to B we deduce the existence of a unique arrow from $A\cup$ to $B\cup$, set map, given by $(\!| \tau_B \cdot f \dagger id |\!)$ which we call $f\cup$. Again $f\cup$ is evaluated by applying f independently to each of the elements of a set of As.

A reduction on the type $A\cup$ requires the existence of a function $id \triangledown g : A \dagger A \to A$. It is of the form

$$g = \eta \triangledown id \triangledown \oplus \tag{10.27}$$

for some $\eta : 1 \to A$ and $\oplus : A \times A \to A$. Thus a reduction is an arrow from a free set monoid to a commutative idempotent monoid on A (whose identity is the image of 1 under η and whose binary operation is $\oplus$).

As an example consider the commutative idempotent monoid on the set $\{a, b, c\}$, with identity a and operation $\oplus$ given by:

$$
\begin{array}{c|ccc}
\oplus & a & b & c \\
\hline
a & a & b & c \\
b & b & b & a \\
c & c & a & c
\end{array}
$$

Then the reduction $\oplus/$ applied to the set $\{a, b, c\}$ gives $\{a, a\}$ and finally $\{a\}$.

We get a factorisation theorem for finite sets. Thus any homomorphism on a set can be expressed as the composition of a map and a reduction.

As for bags, there is no analogue of the *inits* function for sets, and hence no analogue of *prefix*.

Implementation of these set operations is rather different from the previous two types, because of the idempotence of set union. The operations that join two subobjects together to make a larger object for lists and bags are constant-time operations, even though they conceptually manipulate large amounts of data. However, for sets idempotence must either be handled by removing duplicates during unions or by allowing them to remain but being careful to handle them properly during the computation of catamorphisms. The first strategy is to be preferred, since reductions and the like can then use the binary tree pattern, much as if they were bag reductions. However, set union then becomes an expensive operation, requiring linear time to check for duplicates in its arguments.

The language Gamma [22] takes the opposite view, regarding sets as a pool of objects into which binary operators dip, find a pair of arguments, compute a result and place it in the same or another pool. Reduction operations lose their structure in this view, since individual applications of a reductive operator act independently. As a result completion time cannot be bounded, and the reduction abstraction is lost. Nevertheless, it does avoid the difficulty of implementing an idempotent set union.

Chapter 11 ———————————

Trees

The types we have built so far have been relatively simple, and many of the results of the CDT construction had already been discovered by more *ad hoc* approaches. As we turn to more complex types, the benefits of our approach become clearer: in more sophisticated operations, in simple derivations of powerful programs, and in effective and subtle implementations. In this chapter we build the type of trees. There are several different possibilities for tree data types. We consider only full, homogeneous (all nodes have the same type), binary trees.

11.1 Building Trees

The categorical construction of trees as a data type can be found in Gibbons' thesis [83] and we use his notation here. Suppose that we write $A\underline{t}$ for the type of full, homogeneous, binary trees over an arbitrary type A. This type has two constructors written as:

$$\triangle : A \to A\underline{t}$$

$$\underline{t} : A\underline{t} \times A \times A\underline{t} \to A\underline{t}$$

The first constructor, Leaf or $\triangle$, takes a value of type A and makes it into a singleton tree, that is a single leaf holding a value. The second constructor, Moo or $\underline{t}$, takes two subtrees and joins them, placing a value of type A at the join.

The type functor needed to unpackage this hypothetical type is

$$T = K_A + I \times K_A \times I$$

and this functor is polynomial, so its fixed point exists. This fixed point becomes the new data type. Notice that, for the first time, we have a data type that is not separable. The domains of the constructors cannot be factored into two coproduct terms, one of which is product terms in A and the other does not contain A.

A T_A-algebra is an arrow

$$A + P \times A \times P \overset{f}{\longrightarrow} P$$

with $p = p_1 \triangledown p_2$ and

$$p_1 : A \to P$$
$$p_2 : P \times A \times P \to P$$

They are sets whose underlying type are computable from A and which have a ternary operation of type $P \times A \times P \to P$.

Some examples of T_A-algebras and catamorphisms are:

$$\mathrm{root} = (\!|\ id, \pi\ |\!) : (A, \triangle, \bot) \to (A, id, \pi)$$

where π is the middle projection, i.e. $\pi(b_1, a, b_2) = a$.

$$\mathrm{depth} = (\!|\ K_1, p_2\ |\!) : (A, \triangle, \bot) \to (\mathbb{N}, K_1, p_2)$$

where $p_2(u, a, v) = 1 + \uparrow(u, v)$.

$$\mathrm{leaves} = (\!|\ K_1, p_2\ |\!) : (A, \triangle, \bot) \to (\mathbb{N}, K_1, p_2)$$

where $p_2(u, a, v) = u + v$.

$$\mathrm{internal\ nodes} = (\!|\ K_1, p_2\ |\!) : (A, \triangle, \bot) \to (\mathbb{N}, K_0, p_2)$$

where $p_2(u, a, v) = u + 1 + v$.

The polymorphic form of the type functor is the bifunctor † with

$$A \dagger B = A + B \times A \times B$$

If f is an arrow from A to B, we deduce from the diagram (Figure 11.1) the existence of an arrow

$$f\bot = (\!|\ \tau_B \cdot f \dagger id\ |\!)$$

the tree map operation. Notice that its application to a tree maps f over all the nodes of the tree, not just the leaves. As usual, the computation of $f\bot$ takes place (conceptually) by decomposing the argument tree recursively into subtrees, applying f to each of the A values so created, and then rebuilding the tree.

Whenever there is an operation $\oplus : A \times A \times A \to A$, we define a function

$$g = id \triangledown \oplus : A + A \times A \times A \to A$$

from which the existence of a tree reduction $g/ = (\!|\ g\ |\!)$ follows. This is shown in Figure 11.2. Tree reductions do not explicitly affect the values in the nodes of a tree, but instead reduce the tree to a single value. They correspond to tree contractions.

The type of homogeneous binary trees is not separable, so that arbitrary catamorphisms cannot in general be factored into maps followed by reductions. Intuitively, this is because catamorphisms can act differently on the values at leaves and at internal nodes. This different action can be made context-dependent, that is dependent on the structure of the tree around an internal node. Such action cannot be factored out into a preliminary map step.

However, under certain circumstances, a limited form of factorisation exists. Theorem 9.19 gives the conditions under which factorisation occurs.

Theorem 11.1 (*Limited Factorisation*) Suppose that h is the arrow of a T_A-algebra, so

$$h : A + B \times A \times B \to B$$

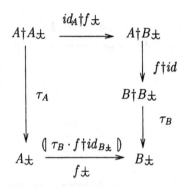

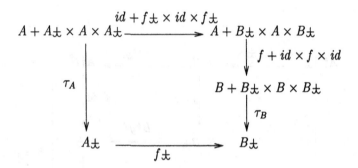

Figure 11.1: Map for Trees

Then $h = h_1 \triangledown h_2$ with $h_1 : A \to B$ and $h_2 : B \times A \times B \to B$. If $h_1 = f$ and h_2 can be factored as $g \cdot id \times f \times id$ then

$$(\!| h |\!) = g/ \cdot f\pm$$

Proof

The proof follows from the factorisation of the junction arrow $h_1 \triangledown h_2$ and is read from Figure 11.3.

□

The recursive schema for evaluating catamorphisms on trees is shown in Figure 11.4.

11.2 Accumulations

Accumulations are operations that replace each node of a structure by the results of some computation on a related substructure. We have seen such operations on lists – they are the generalised prefix operations, which replace each element of a list by a catamorphism applied to the sublist of which it is the last element.

There are two such operations on lists, **prefix** and **suffix**, but they are intimately related via *reverse*. For trees, there are two fundamentally different accumulations. The first, *upwards*

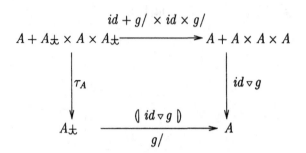

Figure 11.2: Reduction for Trees

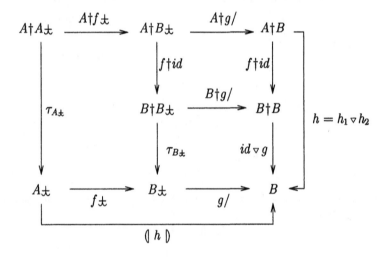

Figure 11.3: Factoring Tree Catamorphisms

```
eval_catamorphism(p1, p2, t)
case t of
     △ a : return p1( a )
     ⋔ (t1, a, t2) : return p2 ( eval_catamorphism(p1, p2, t1 ),
                               a,
                               eval_catamorphism(p1, p2, t2 ))
end
```

Figure 11.4: Evaluating a Tree Catamorphism

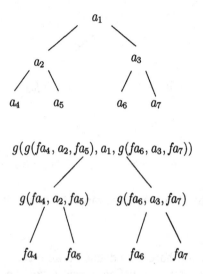

Figure 11.5: An Upwards Accumulation

accumulation, replaces each node of a tree by a catamorphism applied to the subtree of which it is the root. The second, *downwards accumulation*, replaces each node by a catamorphism applied to the path between it and the root.

We begin by considering upwards accumulations. Consider the function *subtrees* that replaces each node of a tree by the subtree rooted at that node. Since root · subtrees = *id*, *subtrees* is injective and hence a catamorphism. It is the catamorphism

$$\text{subtrees} \mathrel{\hat{=}} (\!| \ \triangle \cdot \triangle, g \ |\!)$$

where $g(u, a, v) = \pm(u, z, v)$ and $z = \pm(\text{root}\, u, a, \text{root}\, v)$. Notice that *subtrees* is the tree analogue of *inits*.

Definition 11.2 *(Upwards accumulation)* The catamorphism h is an upwards accumulation if

$$h = (\!| \ f \ |\!) \pm \cdot \text{subtrees}$$

where *subtrees* is the function defined above.

Figure 11.5 illustrates the application of the upwards accumulation based on the catamorphism $(\!| \ f, g \ |\!)$ to a tree. Notice that the computations at each node can use the results of computations from deeper nodes, if any. Thus the total amount of computation required is linear in the size of the tree, suggesting that fast parallel algorithms are possible. We return to this in the next section.

Upwards accumulations allow nodes of a tree to compute properties of their descendants. They occur naturally in a number of important problems, most notably in the computation of synthesised attributes in attribute grammar evaluation.

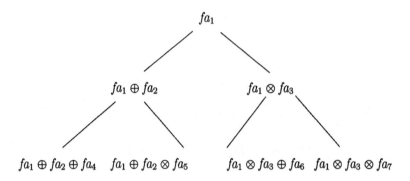

Figure 11.6: A Downwards Accumulation

Downwards accumulations are harder to define because they are less related to the construction of trees. As a first step, we define a new type, the type of non-empty *paths*. Paths are like lists except that they have two join constructors, *left turn*, $\smile$, and *right turn*, $\frown$. They model the kinds of paths that occur between the root and any other node of the tree. Such paths are a sequence of left and right turns, following right and left branches respectively. These two constructors are mutually associative, that is

$$(a?b)??c = a?(b??c)$$

where ? and ?? represent either of the constructors, $\smile$ and $\frown$. We say that they *cooperate*. Catamorphisms on these paths are unique arrows to algebraic structures $(P, f : A \rightarrow P, \oplus, \otimes : P \times P \rightarrow P)$ where $\oplus$ and $\otimes$ cooperate. Thus

$$(\!| f, \oplus, \otimes |\!) : a \smile b \frown c \mapsto fa \oplus fb \otimes fc$$

Now we can define a downwards accumulation.

Definition 11.3 *(Downwards accumulation)* The catamorphism h is a downwards accumulation if

$$h = (\!| f, \oplus, \otimes |\!) * \cdot \text{paths}$$

where *paths* is the function that replaces each node in a tree by the path between the root and that node, and the catamorphism is a path catamorphism.

A downwards accumulation is shown in Figure 11.6.

Downwards accumulations are used in algorithms that involve distributing central information to all nodes. The most obvious example is the catamorphism in which each node computes its depth in the tree.

11.3 Computing Tree Catamorphisms

In this section we consider implementations of the four special tree catamorphisms: tree maps, tree reductions, upwards accumulations, and downwards accumulations.

A *tree map*, like the maps over other types we have seen, can be optimised so that it does not decompose its argument, nor reconstruct it, but simply applies its component function in place. Its parallel time complexity is the time complexity of the component function, or $t_1(f)$ on p processors.

There is a trivial implementation of *tree reduction* with parallel time complexity of the order of the height of the tree, using the recursive schema directly. However, under conditions that are weak enough to apply often in practice, tree reductions can be evaluated in logarithmic parallel time using *tree contraction* [82]. This is possible not only on the EREW PRAM, but also on realistic models such as the hypercube [139].

The key to fast tree contraction is making it possible for some useful progress to be made towards the eventual result at many nodes of the tree, regardless of whether or not the contractions for the subtrees of which they are the root have been completed.

Suppose that we wish to evaluate $(\!|\ id, p_2\ |\!)$ on a tree argument. We first define a local contraction step that applies to any node and its two descendants, if at least one of the descendants is a leaf. Suppose that each internal node u contains a pointer u.p to its parent, a boolean flag u.*left* that is true if it is a left descendant, a boolean flag u.*internal* that is true if the node is an internal node, a variable u.g describing an auxiliary function of type $A \to A$, and, for internal nodes, two pointers, u.l and u.r pointing to their left and right descendants respectively. Initially the auxiliary function at each internal node is the identity on A but it is replaced, as the global computation proceeds, by partial compositions.

The local contraction operation replaces u, u.l, and u.r, where u.l is a leaf, by a single node u.r as shown in Figure 11.7. A symmetric operation contracts in the other direction when u.r is a leaf. The operations required are

$$
\begin{aligned}
\text{u.r.g} \quad &\leftarrow \quad \lambda x.\text{u.g}(p_2(\text{u.l.g}(\text{u.l.a}), \text{u.a}, \text{u.r.g}(x))) \\
\text{u.r.p} \quad &\leftarrow \quad \text{u.p} \\
\text{if u.left then} \quad &\text{u.p.l} \leftarrow \text{u.r else u.p.r} \leftarrow \text{u.r} \\
\text{u.r.left} \quad &\leftarrow \quad \text{u.left} \\
\text{if u} = \text{root} \quad &\text{then} \quad \text{root} \leftarrow \text{u.r}
\end{aligned}
$$

The first step is the most important one. It 'folds' in an application of p_2 so that the function computed at node u.r after this contraction operation is the one that would have been computed at u before the operation. The contraction algorithm is only efficient if this step can be done quickly and the resulting expression does not grow long. We return to this point below.

The contraction operations must be applied to about half of the leaves on each step if the entire contraction is to be completed in about a logarithmic number of steps. The algorithm for deciding where to apply the contraction operations is the following:

1. Number the leaves left to right beginning at 0 – this can be done in $O(\log n)$ time using $O(n/\log n)$ processors [56].

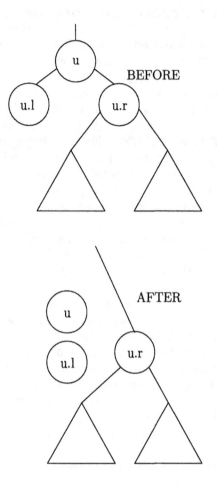

Figure 11.7: A Single Tree Contraction Step

2. For every u such that $u.l$ is an even numbered leaf, perform the contraction operation.

3. For every u that was not involved in the previous step, and for which $u.r$ is an even numbered leaf, perform the contraction operation.

4. Renumber the leaves by dividing their positions by two and taking the integer part.

For each local contraction step to remain constant time it must be possible to compute a new auxiliary function from the previous one in constant time. The sizes of the representations must not grow without bound either.

A way to handle both problems is to imagine the set of possible auxiliary functions as forming an indexed set. Partial compositions then become computations on indexes. The following conditions on indexed sets of functions are sufficient to ensure constant time local contractions [1]:

1. For all nodes u, the sectioned function $p_2(\_, u.a, \_)$ of type $A \times A \to A$ is drawn from an indexed set of functions F, and the function $u.g$ is drawn from an indexed set of functions G. Both F and G contain the identity function.

2. All functions in F and G can be applied in constant time.

3. For all p_i in F, g in G, and a in A, the functions $\lambda x.p_i(g(x), a)$ and $\lambda x.p_i(a, g(x))$ are in G and their indices can be computed from a and the indices of p_i and g in constant time.

4. For all g_i, g_j in G, the composition $g_i \cdot g_j$ is in G and its indices can be computed from i and j in constant time.

Under these conditions, tree contraction can be computed in parallel time $O(\log n)$ using $O(n/\log n)$ processors on the EREW PRAM [1, 82]. The same performance can be achieved on the hypercube [139] and the technique can presumably be extended to the cube-connected-cycles topology.

Computing an upwards accumulation using its expression as a tree catamorphism mapped over the result of applying *subtrees* is very expensive. However, the number of partial results computed in an upwards accumulation is linear in the number of tree nodes, so it is plausible that there should be a fast parallel algorithm, and indeed there is. The algorithm is an extension of tree contraction; when a node u is removed, it is stacked by its remaining child. When this child receives its final child, it unstacks u and computes its final value. Upwards accumulations can be computed in parallel time $O(\log n)$ but require $O(n)$ processors on the EREW PRAM. Details may be found in [85].

It is also expensive to compute a downwards accumulation by computing all of the paths and then mapping a path contraction over them. Again there is an adaptation of tree contraction. Downwards accumulations can again be computed in parallel time $O(\log n)$ but require $O(n)$ processors on the EREW PRAM [85].

11.4 Modelling Structured Text by Trees

One important area of application for the CDT of trees is to model structured text, which of course includes software, and document archives of structured text. Such archives are extremely large, and the uses that are made of them are sophisticated enough that parallelism can be put to good use. In this section we derive some fast algorithms based on tree catamorphisms.

We assume that documents are modelled as binary trees in which each node contains a set of functions. These functions have unit domains and have attributes as their codomains. In particular, one of the attributes is text. Binary trees can be extended to trees in which each internal node has a list of subtrees (so-called Rose trees [83]), but it complicates the exposition. The complexity of the algorithms we present only changes by a constant factor, since any Rose tree can be replaced by a binary tree without a change in the order of the number of nodes.

11.4.1   Global Properties of Documents

We now turn to applications of tree catamorphisms to problems in structured text manipulation. We begin with the use of maps and reductions to determine structural properties of documents.

We distinguish several different ways in which documents are represented in order to adequately address the complexity of these operations. For some applications, the entire document is parsed into tree form – as for example with programs. In other cases, the document is only parsed to the level of some coarse structures, such as sections or paragraphs, while the leaves contain a representation of the more deeply nested structure. In the former case, the tree data type can be used directly. In the latter, it may need to be extended to a type in which internal nodes and leaves are of distinct types.

A broad class of such applications are those that count the number of occurrences of some text or node class in a document. In such catamorphisms, the pair of functions used are of the general form

$$p_1(a) \quad = \quad \text{if object in } a \text{ then 1 else 0}$$
$$p_2(t_1, a, t_2) \quad = \quad t_1 + t_2 + (\text{if object in } a \text{ then 1 else 0})$$

We compute this catamorphism in a logarithmic number of steps, using tree contraction, but each step involves the application of the function p_1. If there is a processor associated with each node of the tree, then the total parallel time complexity is given by:

$$\text{total time} \quad = \quad \log n \ t(p_2) + t(p_1) \tag{11.1}$$

Suppose that p_2 can be evaluated in constant time. If individual nodes of the tree are of constant size, then the overall complexity is $\log n$. However, if nodes are of size m, say, then the computation of p_1 takes time proportional to m. The overall complexity is then $\log n + m$.

Catamorphisms of this form factor into the composition of a map step followed by a reduction step. The counting catamorphism above factors as

$$\text{count objects} \quad = \quad \oplus / \cdot p_1 \npreceq$$

where $\oplus$ is ternary addition.

It follows that the following document properties can be determined in the parallel time given by the expression above (Equation 11.1):

- number of occurrences of a word

- number of occurrences of a structure or node class (section, subsection, paragraph)

- number of reference points (labels)

An extension of these counting catamorphisms produces simple data types as results. For example, to produce a list of the different kinds of node classes used in a document, we need a catamorphism

$$p_1(a) = \{\text{name of node class } a\}$$
$$p_2(t_1, a, t_2) = \cup(t_1, t_2, \{\text{name of node class } a\})$$

which produces a set containing the different types of node classes present in a document. Each leaf is replaced by the name of the node class that it represents. Internal nodes merge the sets of node class names of their descendants with the name of the node class they represent. Using sets means that we record each node class type only once in the final set. To determine the number of different node classes present in a document, we need only to compute the size of the set produced by this catamorphism. As before, if the leaves of the tree represent tree structure, the function p_1 must be extended to compute the set of node classes of the tree structure at that node.

Changing the set used in this catamorphism to a list we can define a catamorphism to produce a table of contents. It is

$$p_1(a) = [\text{text of } a]$$
$$p_2(t_1, a, t_2) = \text{text of } a + t_1 + t_2$$

where $+$ is list concatenation. A similar catamorphism produces the list of all labels defined in a document. The parallel time complexity of these catamorphisms is not as straightforward to compute as the earlier example for two reasons: the operation of concatenation is not necessarily constant time, so the computation of p_2 will not be; and the size of lists grows with the distance from the leaves, creating a communication cost that must be accounted for on real machines. The function p_2 resembles $+/$ addressed in Chapter 8.

Another useful class of catamorphisms computing global properties are size catamorphisms. The most obvious example computes the length of a document in characters. It is

$$p_1(a) = \text{number of characters in } a$$
$$p_2(t_1, a, t_2) = t_1 + t_2 + \text{number of characters in } a$$

Similarly, the catamorphism that computes the deepest nesting depth of structures in a document is

$$p_1(a) = 0$$
$$p_2(t_1, a, t_2) = \uparrow(t_1, t_2) + 1$$

Program text is an example of structured text. Some catamorphisms that apply to programs are: computing the number of statements, and building a simple (that is, unscoped) symbol table.

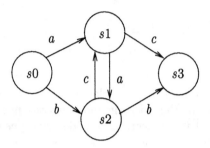

Figure 11.8: A Simple Finite State Automaton

11.4.2   Search Problems

There is a parallel list-based algorithm for recognising whether a given string is a member of
a regular language in time logarithmic in the length of the string. We explain this algorithm
briefly and then show how it can be adapted to allow fast searches in trees for strings given
by regular expressions.

Suppose that we want to determine if a given string is a member of a regular language over
some alphabet $\{a, b, c\}$. The regular language can be defined by a finite state automaton,
whose transitions are labelled by elements of the alphabet. This automaton is preprocessed
to give a set of tables, each one labelled with a symbol of the alphabet, and consisting of
pairs of states such that the labelling symbol labels a transition from the first pair in each
state to the second. For example, given the automaton in Figure 11.8, the tables are:

a	b	c
$(s0, s1)$	$(s0, s2)$	$(s2, s1)$
$(s1, s2)$	$(s2, s3)$	$(s1, s3)$

The catamorphism (on lists) consists of three functions:

$$
\begin{aligned}
p_1(a) &= \text{the empty table} \\
p_2(a) &= \text{the table labelled by } a \\
p_3(t_1, t_2) &= \text{compose all entries of the tables using } \circledast
\end{aligned}
$$

where

$$
\begin{aligned}
(s1, s2) \circledast (s2, s3) &= (s1, s3) \\
(s1, s2) \circledast (s3, s4) &= \text{null when } s2 \neq s3
\end{aligned}
$$

The function p_2 replaces each symbol in the input string with the table defining how that
symbol maps states to states. The function p_3 then performs a (list) reduction, composing tables to reflect the state-to-state mapping of longer and longer strings. Consider the

reduction step applied to the tables for a and b.

$$
\begin{array}{ccc}
a & b & ab \\
\hline
\end{array}
$$

a		b		ab
$(s0, s1)$	compose_	$(s0, s2)$	$=$	$(s1, s3)$
$(s1, s2)$	with_⊛	$(s2, s3)$		

When the reduction is complete, the table is labelled with the entire input string. If it contains a pair whose first element is the initial state and whose second element is a final state, the string is in the regular language.

The parallel time complexity of this algorithm is logarithmic in the length of the input string. All of the tables are of finite size (no larger than the number of states in the automaton) and hence each table composition takes no longer than quadratic in the number of states of the automaton. The reduction itself takes time logarithmic in the number of initial alphabet symbols on a variety of parallel architectures [178].

The regular language recognition problem is easily adapted for query processing. Suppose we wish to determine if some regular expression is present in an input string. We construct the finite state automaton for the regular language using the regular expression. New transitions labelled with all of the other symbols are added from every state to the initial state, creating an augmented regular language. The search string is present in the input string if and only if the input string is a member of the augmented language.

Notice that the list-based regular language recognition algorithm easily extends to the type of paths. We will shortly use this extension.

Queries that are boolean expressions of simpler regular language queries could be evaluated by evaluating the simple queries independently and then carrying out the required boolean operations on the results. However, the closure of the class of regular languages under union, intersection, complementation, and concatenation means that such complex queries can be evaluated in a single pass through the data by constructing the appropriate deterministic finite state automaton. For example, a query of the form "are x and y in the text" amounts to asking if the text is a string of the augmented language of the intersection of the regular languages of the strings x and y.

This algorithm is easily generalised to apply to trees. The first step applies a tree map that replaces each node of the tree by a table, mapping states to states, that is the catamorphism:

$$(\! | \ p_1(a) = \text{the table labelled by } a, p_2 = \text{±} \cdot id \times p_1 \times id \ | \!)$$

The second step is a tree contraction, in which the tables of a node and its two subtrees are composed using the same composition operator as in the string algorithm above:

$$(\! | \ id, p_2(t_1, t_2, t_3) = \text{compose\_with\_} \circledast (t_2, t_1, t_3) \ | \!)$$

Notice that the composition of tables composes the table belonging to the internal node first, followed by the tables corresponding to the subtrees in order. This represents the case where the text in the internal node represents some kind of heading. The order may or may not be significant in an application, but care needs to be taken to get it right so that strings that cross node class boundaries are properly detected.

This algorithm takes parallel time logarithmic in the number of nodes of the tree, using the tree contraction algorithm discussed in the previous section. The automaton can be extended as before to solve query problems, giving a fast parallel query evaluator for a useful class of queries.

Query evaluation problems that are of this kind include:

- word and phrase search

- boolean expressions involving phrase search

11.4.3   Accumulations and Information Transfer

Accumulations are used in both the upwards and downwards direction. Upwards accumulations allow each node of a tree to accumulate information about the nodes below it. Downwards accumulations allow each node to accumulate information about those nodes that lie between it and the root. Powerful combination operations are formed when an upwards accumulation is followed by a downwards accumulation, because this makes it possible to get arbitrary information flow between nodes of the tree.

Some examples of upwards accumulations are: compute the length in characters of each object in the document; and compute the offset from each segment to the next similar segment (for example the offset from each section heading to the next section heading).

Some examples of downwards accumulations are: structured search problems, that is searching for a part of a document based on its content and its structural properties; and finding all references to a single label.

Upwards accumulations followed by downwards accumulations are important combinations because they allow information to flow through the whole tree. Gibbons gives a number of detailed examples of the usefulness of such combinations of operations in [83]. Some examples that are important for structured text are: evaluating attributes in attribute grammars (which can represent almost any property of a document); generating a symbol table for a program written in a language with scopes; rendering trees, which is important for navigating them; determining which page each object would fall on if the document were produced on some device; and determining the font of each object (in systems where font is relative not absolute, such as LaTeX).

Operations such as resolving all cross-references and determining all of the references to a particular point can also be cast as upwards followed by downwards accumulations, but the volume of data moved on some steps makes this an expensive implementation.

11.4.4   Queries on Structured Text

Queries on structured text involve finding nodes in the tree based on information about the content of the node (its text and other attributes) and on its context in the tree. Here are some examples, based on [136]:

Example 11.4 **document where** *('database'* **in document***)*
This returns those documents that contain the word 'database'.

Example 11.5 **document where** *('Smith'* **in Author***)*
This returns those documents where the word 'Smith' occurs as part of the Author structure within each document. This query depends partly on structural information (that an
Author substructure exists) as well as text. Notice that the object returned depends on a
condition on the structure below it in the tree.

Example 11.6 *Section* **of document where** *('database'* **in document***)*
This returns all sections of documents that contain the word 'database'. The object
returned depends on a condition of the structure above it in the tree. Notice that there is
a natural way to regard this as a two-step operation: first select the documents, then select
the sections.

Example 11.7 *Section* **of document where** *('database'* **in SectionHeading***)*
This returns those sections whose headings contain the word 'database'. Notice that the
object returned depends on a condition of a structure that is neither above or below it in
the tree, but is nevertheless related to it.

One way to regard such queries is as functions from bags (that is, sets in which repetitions
count) to bags. The contents of the bags are nodes of the tree or, equivalently, paths between
the nodes and the root of the tree. Usually the query is applied to a single node, the root of
the tree, and returns a bag of nodes satisfying the query. However, it is useful to make this
slight generalisation because it allows queries to be composed to make bigger queries.

There are two kinds of bag operations in the query examples above. The first are *filters*
that take a bag of nodes and return those elements of the bag that satisfy some condition.
The second are *maps* that take a bag of nodes and return a bag in which each node has been
replaced either by a node related to it (its ancestor, its descendant, its sibling to the right)
or by one of its attributes. A simple query is usually a filter followed by the value of an
attribute at all of the nodes that have passed the filter. More complex queries such as the
last example above require more complex maps.

This insight is the critical one in the design of *path expressions* [137] which are a general
query language for structured text applications. The crucial property of path expressions
that we require is that filters and maps involve regular expressions over structure and text,
that is over paths.

The filters used in evaluating path expression queries are downwards accumulations. The
path homomorphism required is the regular expression recognition operation described in
section 11.4.2. A filter is computed by: replacing each node of the structured text tree by
the path from it to the root, and then applying the regular string recognition algorithm to
each of these paths. Those nodes for which the string recognition algorithm returns True
are the nodes selected by the filter. However, we know that there is a fast parallel algorithm
to compute downwards accumulations, provided that the base operation is constant time.
For filters used in path expression evaluation, the base operation is table composition, which
is certainly constant time. The downwards accumulation is preceded by a step in which
the table for the text in each individual node is computed. If we assume that each node is

associated with a single processor, this takes parallel time linear in the maximum size of the text in a node. Thus the time complexity of filtering path expressions is

$$O(\log n + m)$$

for trees with n nodes and maximum text per node of size m.

Chapter 12

Arrays

In this chapter we build a much more complex type, the type of arrays. The construction of arrays as a categorical data type is significantly different and more complex than the constructions seen so far, so this chapter illustrates new aspects of the construction technique.

Arrays are an important type because of the ubiquitous use of Cartesian coordinate systems and the huge edifice of linear algebra built on top of them. Almost all scientific and numeric computations require arrays as central data structures.

While the need for a data type of arrays is undisputed, there has always been some disagreement about exactly what arrays should represent: should the entries of an array all be of the same type (homogeneous) or might they be different (inhomogeneous); should extents be the same in each dimension (rectangular) or might they differ (ragged); are arrays of different sizes members of the same type or of different types. Different programming languages have answered these questions differently.

Arrays appeared early in languages such as Fortran, which had homogeneous, rectangular arrays but was ambivalent about how they should be typed. Arrays had to be declared with their shapes, and shapes of arguments and parameters had to agree (although some of these rules were relaxed later). Fortran even went so far as to reveal the storage allocation of arrays (by columns) at the language level. Fortran views an array as syntactic shorthand for a set of related variables for which access binding can be decided at run-time; that is an array is an umbrella for a collection of individual values.

APL takes a different view in which an array is considered more as an object in its own right and less as a collection of objects. APL operations apply to whole arrays, even though they are expressed as operations on individual elements. APL also treats arrays as a single type, avoiding mention of array indices, so that programs can apply to arrays of any size.

Mullin's *Mathematics of Arrays* (MOA) [151] is based on APL, but uses a more functional style. Its most important component is a generalised indexing function Ψ which selects partial arrays in sophisticated ways. APL operations such as reduction and prefix (scan) are properly defined as second-order functions.

More's *Array Theory* [148–150] is an equational description of nested arrays, derived from first principles. It begins from the premises that everything is an array and all functions are total on arrays. From this a complete consistent set of array identities is derived which in turn specify how to define basic operations on arrays. Array Theory is the most complete definition of an array type. Its only weakness is that there are places in the development where free choices can be made and there is no way to decide whether one choice is better or more natural than another. Array Theory has been implemented by the language Nial [111].

In functional languages, a function applied to an array is monolithic, that is it computes a result that is a new array, not an old array with a piece altered. This was for a long time seen as a deficiency of functional languages, because most existing algorithms were written in an imperative style in which changes to arrays were common. Implementing such algorithms is inefficient because of the array copying that is required. The solution suggested was to treat arrays (and other data structures) as I-structures [12], that is to return to the view of an array as an umbrella for individual values. With I-structure semantics, elements of an array are write-once variables. Attempts to read a value before it is generated cause the reading process to block. Implementing arrays this way preserves their functional semantics but it is much more efficient to implement than copying.

This problem of efficient implementation of arrays is more apparent than real. The real problem is not that arrays are inherently inefficient, but that imperative algorithms are the wrong way to describe array algorithms. In particular, they usually describe single-valued operations when it is generally better to describe operations on arrays as a whole. This view is taken, at least partly, by Haskell [107] in which array comprehensions and array accumulations are defined, by Sisal [176] in which arrays are built monolithically, although with a loop syntax, and by Fortran90 and High Performance Fortran [190], in which second-order operations are provided for array manipulation.

Two other functional views of arrays that are closely related to categorical data types are Bird's abiding arrays [31], and Jeuring's list-based arrays [112]. Bird defines arrays by analogy with join lists, n-dimensional arrays having n join operators, one per dimension, that allow arrays with the same extent in a dimension to be concatenated. The join operators must mutually distribute, a property Bird called *abiding*. Jeuring defines arrays as nested lists, with lists at each nesting level constrained to be the same size. Catamorphisms on arrays are then sets of catamorphisms on lists.

None of these views of arrays is really satisfactory, although the trends are in the right direction, that is towards high-level monolithic operations and a calculus relating them. In the rest of this chapter, we show how to construct arrays as a single categorical data type. We follow the notation and development of Banger [23].

12.1   Overview of Arrays

In fact we will build three related types, all of which represent some aspect of arrays. The conventional view of arrays is that they are pairs of shapes and contents, where the shape is a list of extents of the array in various dimensions, and the contents is a list of elements. The length of the list of elements equals the product of the elements of the shape, so that there is an element for each "hole" in the array. Thus the shape and the content list must conform. Conformance is a problem for arrays in a derivational setting, since it repeatedly introduces a proof obligation to check that the conformance condition holds. The type of arrays that we build avoids this difficulty.

We begin with *abstract arrays*. An abstract array over A is a pair, consisting of a cons list of natural numbers, and an object of some type A. There is no necessary or intuitive connection between the two components of the pair. This might seem at first to be a strange type and to have little to do with arrays, but the connection will quickly become clear.

Flat arrays are the special case of abstract arrays in which the type A is an infinite sequence of values of some underlying type. The intuition here is that the infinite sequence corresponds to the content of the flat array while the first component describes the shape in the usual way. The use of an infinite sequence as the content removes the need to check conformance; there are always "enough" elements to fill out the holes in the array. Operationally, the shape can be viewed as partitioning the infinite sequence into segments of size the product of the shapes; alternatively, only the appropriate initial segment can be considered to exist. Computation can be lazy, or backwards analysis can be used at compile time to determine how much of the sequence is actually required.

Nested arrays are instances of abstract arrays in which the type A is itself an array. A singly-nested array can be viewed as a triple, consisting of a shape vector for the outer shape, a shape vector for the element arrays, and an infinite list of contents. There are operations to create a nested array from a flat array and to flatten a nested array.

12.2 Sequences and Their Properties

The construction of flat arrays (that is arrays whose elements are not themselves arrays) takes place in the category *Type*, but we need an extra feature, the existence of a limited form of exponential. Since all exponentials exist in this category, this causes no problems. The actual properties needed are captured by this definition.

Definition 12.1 *(Extended Base Category)* The base category contains all of the objects and arrows of C together with the following:

For every object of C, an object $\vec{A}$ of infinite sequences of As.

An indexing arrow

$$\uparrow_A : \vec{A} \times \mathbb{N} \to A \tag{12.1}$$

$$\frac{f : X \times \mathbb{N} \to A}{f\uparrow : X \to \vec{A}} \tag{12.2}$$

$$\frac{g : A \to B}{\vec{g} : \vec{A} \to \vec{B}} \tag{12.3}$$

$$\frac{p : \mathbb{N} \to \mathbb{N}}{\hat{p} : \vec{A} \to \vec{A}} \tag{12.4}$$

and the following extra equations

$$u = f\uparrow \quad \equiv \quad \uparrow_A \cdot u \times id_{\mathbb{N}} = f \tag{12.5}$$

$$u = \vec{g} \quad \equiv \quad g \cdot \uparrow_A = \uparrow_B \cdot u \times id_{\mathbb{N}} \tag{12.6}$$

$$u = \hat{p} \quad \equiv \quad u \cdot f\uparrow = (f \cdot id \times p)\uparrow \tag{12.7}$$

This definition adds a limited exponential to the category: exponentials only over the type of natural numbers, and only first order. These give us infinite sequences over types that are present in C. Objects such as $\vec{A}$ correspond to arrows $\mathbb{N} \to A$, while the $\uparrow_A$ are the indexing or evaluation functions. We will write elements of the type $\vec{A}$ as

$$< a_0, a_1, \ldots >$$

From these rules we can deduce that the existence of a function

$$f : X \times \mathbb{N} \to A$$

implies the existence of a function

$$f^{\uparrow} : X \to \vec{A}$$

called a sequence generator. These functions are related in the following way: if the sequence generator is used to generate a sequence, and then the sequence is evaluated at some natural number (using $\uparrow_A$) then the result is the same as applying f directly.

Sequence maps cannot be defined in the categorical data type style because we have not introduced infinite sequences using that route, but they exist and behave in the expected way.

Definition 12.2 *(Sequence map)* If $g : A \to B$ and $\vec{A}$ is generated by $f^{\uparrow}x$ then $\vec{g} : \vec{A} \to \vec{B}$ is a sequence map, and

$$\vec{g} < a_0, a_1, \ldots > = < g\, a_0, g\, a_1, \ldots >$$

Sequence maps are more general than pointwise extensions of underlying functions, because they include functions that map sequence elements in other ways. Sequence maps that segment the elements of sequences are particularly interesting. Sequence maps compose in the obvious way.

Another interesting class of functions on sequences are those that permute sequences. For any function $p : \mathbb{N} \to \mathbb{N}$ there is a resequencing function $\hat{p} : \vec{A} \to \vec{A}$ whose effect is

$$\hat{p} < a_0, a_1, \ldots > = < a_{p0}, a_{p1}, \ldots >$$

A sequence of resequencing functions can be expressed as a single resequencing function, and the composition of a resequencing function with a sequence generator can be expressed as a single sequence generator. Furthermore, sequence maps and resequencing functions commute (in fact, resequencing functions are special cases of sequence maps). Results that give this kind of fusion are useful, as we have seen before for catamorphisms, because they allow programs to be developed naturally as a sequence of steps, but then transformed into a single step. They provide a natural optimisation strategy.

An important type of sequence operation is called *sequence compression*. It partitions a sequence into fixed size segments, and then maps a list reduction over each segment. Thus a sequence compression can be written $\oplus^{\downarrow} : \mathbb{N} \times \vec{A} \to \vec{A}$ where $\oplus : A \times A \to A$.

Another important operation is *sequence compaction* which partitions a sequence into segments of size $w \times d$, treats each segments as if it were a w-by-d matrix (so to speak) and then applies a list reduction to the columns of each "matrix". Thus a sequence compaction can be written $\oplus^\Downarrow : N \times N \times \vec{A} \to \vec{A}$ where $\oplus : A \times A \to A$. Its effect on the first w-by-d segment is to compute

$$a_0 \oplus a_d \oplus \ldots \oplus a_{(w-1) \times d}$$

and so on.

12.3 Flat Array Construction

The constructors for the type of abstract arrays, $A\square$, are

$$\sigma \; : \; A \to A\square$$
$$\rho \; : \; N \times A\square \to A\square$$

The first constructor, *scalarise*, takes an object of type A and makes it into a simple abstract array. The second constructor, *reshape*, takes an abstract array and adds an extra natural number to its shape. The endofunctor for the abstract array type is therefore

$$A\dagger^\square B = A + K_N \times B$$

Objects constructed using σ and ρ can be written using left sections of ρ as

$$(e_d\rho) \cdot \ldots \cdot (e_1\rho) \cdot \sigma$$

or as

$$([e_d, \ldots, e_1], x)$$

where we call the list of left arguments to ρ the shape, and x the content of the array. Each e_i has a natural interpretation as an extent in a dimension. Since $\dagger^\square$ is polynomial, it is clear that there is a categorical data type of abstract arrays, and all of the usual properties hold, despite the fact that abstract arrays are quite unusual.

Definition 12.3 $A\dagger^\square$-algebras are arrows of the form

$$p_1 \triangledown p_2 : A + (N \times P) \to P$$

Definition 12.4 An $A\dagger^\square$ catamorphism is an arrow $h = (\!| \, p_1, p_2 \, |\!)$ such that

$$h \cdot \sigma \;\; = \;\; p_1$$
$$h \cdot \rho \;\; = \;\; p_2 \cdot (id_N \times h)$$

As usual, catamorphisms can be calculated by replacing instances of the constructors by the corresponding component functions of the catamorphism. So applying the catamorphism $(\!| \, p_1, p_2 \, |\!)$ gives

$$(\!| \, p_1, p_2 \, |\!)([e_d, \ldots, e_1], x) = (e_d p_2) \cdot \ldots \cdot (e_1 p_2) \cdot p_1 x$$

Definition 12.5 *(Abstract Array Map)* Given an arrow $f : A \to B$, the abstract array map $f\square : A\square \to B\square$ is the catamorphism

$$f\square = (\!| \; \sigma \cdot f, \rho \;|\!)$$

Example 12.6

$$
\begin{aligned}
f\square([e_d, \ldots, e_1], x) &= f\square(e_d\rho \cdot \ldots \cdot e_1\rho \cdot \sigma x) \\
&= e_d\rho \cdot \ldots \cdot e_1\rho \cdot (\sigma \cdot f)x \\
&= ([e_d, \ldots, e_1], f\; x)
\end{aligned}
$$

Definition 12.7 *(Abstract Array Reduction)* Given an arrow $g : \mathbb{N} \times A \to A$, the abstract array reduction $g/ : A\square \to A$ is the catamorphism

$$g/ = (\!| \; id, g \;|\!)$$

Example 12.8

$$
\begin{aligned}
g/\,([e_d, \ldots, e_1], x) &= g/\, e_d\rho \cdot \ldots \cdot e_1\rho \cdot \sigma x \\
&= e_d g \cdot \ldots \cdot e_1 g \cdot id\; x
\end{aligned}
$$

Example 12.9 The content of an array can be extracted using the abstract array reduction $\hat{\pi}/ = (\!| \; id, \hat{\pi} \;|\!)$. So

$$
\begin{aligned}
\text{content}\,([e_d, \ldots, e_1], x) &= e_d\hat{\pi} \cdot \ldots \cdot e_1\hat{\pi} \cdot id\; x \\
&= x
\end{aligned}
$$

Example 12.10 The sum of an abstract array of natural numbers can be computed using a reduction with a sequence compression $+^\downarrow$. It is the reduction $+^\downarrow/$.

$$
\begin{aligned}
&+^\downarrow/\,([2,3,2], <1,2,3,4,5,6,7,8,9,10,11,12,\ldots>) \\
=\;& 2 +^\downarrow \cdot 3 +^\downarrow \cdot 2 +^\downarrow \cdot id <1,2,3,4,5,6,7,8,9,10,11,12,\ldots> \\
=\;& 2 +^\downarrow \cdot 3 +^\downarrow <3,7,11,15,19,23,\ldots> \\
=\;& 2 +^\downarrow <21,57,\ldots> \\
=\;& <78,\ldots>
\end{aligned}
$$

Abstract arrays separate structure from content in a way that can be precisely captured.

Definition 12.11 A structural catamorphism $s : A\square \to S$ is a catamorphism that can be written as

$$s = \text{struct} \cdot \text{make\_container}$$

where

$$\text{make\_container} = !_A\square$$

and *struct* is a $1\dagger^\square$ catamorphism.

make_container is a catamorphism that replaces the type A by the final object of the category, so

$$\text{make\_container } a = ([e_d, \ldots, e_1, 1])$$

which is isomorphic to the shape of the array. A $1\dagger^{\square}$ catamorphism is induced by a functor of the form $1 + (\mathbb{N}\times)$ which makes the correspondence between abstract arrays shapes and cons lists explicit.

Example 12.12 The *shape* catamorphism when applied to an abstract array $([e_d, \ldots, e_1], x)$ gives $[e_d, \ldots, e_1]$. It is

$$\text{shape} = (\!| \ K_{[]} \cdot !_A, \text{cons} \ |\!)$$

$$\begin{aligned}
&(\!| \ K_{[]} \cdot !_A, \text{cons} \ |\!)([e_d, \ldots, e_1], x) \\
= \ & e_d \text{ cons } \ldots \text{ cons } e_1 \text{ cons } K_{[]}1 \\
= \ & [e_d, \ldots, e_1]
\end{aligned}$$

Example 12.13 The number of elements in an array is computed by the catamorphism

$$\text{number\_of\_elements} = (\!| \ K_1, \times \ |\!)$$

$$\begin{aligned}
\text{number\_of\_elements}([2, 3, 2], x) &= (2\times) \cdot (3\times) \cdot (2\times) \cdot K_1 x \\
&= (2\times) \cdot 6 \\
&= 12
\end{aligned}$$

All of the discussion so far has been of results that apply to abstract arrays in general. However, we now define the following special case:

Definition 12.14 *(Flat array)* A *flat array* is an object of type $\vec{A}\square$.

Thus flat arrays are pairs of shape, a cons list of natural numbers, and content, an infinite list from some other type. Arrays viewed as pairs of shape and content in which the length of the content list is equal to the product of the shapes are formally a subtype of the type of flat arrays. It is convenient to be able to carry out program development within the larger framework of flat arrays, and only restrict programs to conforming arrays at a late stage, usually compile time.

Remark 12.15 The type of abstract arrays is separable, so all catamorphisms can be factored into the composition of an array map and an array reduction.

12.4 Evaluation of Flat Array Catamorphisms

T_A-algebras are types P with arrows

$$\begin{aligned}
p_1 &: \ \vec{A} \to P \\
p_2 &: \ \mathbb{N} \times P \to P
\end{aligned}$$

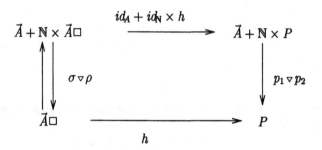

Figure 12.1: A Flat Array Catamorphism

```
eval_catamorphism(p1, p2, a)
case a of
    σ (x) : return p1 (x)
    ρ (n, x) : return p2 ( n, eval_catamorphism( p1, p2, x) )


end
```

Figure 12.2: Recursive Schema for Flat Array Catamorphisms

so that catamorphisms correspond to pairs of arrows as shown in Figure 12.1. The recursive schema for flat array catamorphisms is show in Figure 12.2. This recursive schema does not have the opportunities for parallel evaluation that have been present in all of the types we have considered up to now because there is only a single recursive call to **eval_catamorphism**. Opportunities for parallelism all occur within the component functions, p_1 and p_2. In particular, p_1 is a function from $\vec{A}$ to P and very often its result can be computed in parallel. The other component function p_2 is from $N \times P$ to P and therefore does not normally contain opportunities for parallelism unless the type P has internal structure itself.

12.5 Nested Arrays

Arrays that contain arrays as elements are called nested arrays. In this section, we show how to extend the array construction to build nested arrays.

Catamorphisms on flat arrays affect all dimensions of the array. Operations that operate only on certain dimensions cannot be expressed as catamorphisms on flat arrays, but they can be expressed as catamorphisms on nested arrays. In particular, many interesting array operations can be obtained by taking a flat array, breaking it into a nested array, mapping a flat array catamorphism over a particular level of nesting, and then flattening the array's structure again.

The abstract array construction can be applied to any type A so, in particular, it can be applied to the type $A\square$ to build a new type $A\square\square$ called a *nested array*. An element of this type looks like

$$([e'_d, \ldots, e'_1], ([e_d, \ldots, e_1], x))$$

for some x of type A. Elements of type $A\square\square$ can be built by building an element of type $A\square$ first, and then building a further structure around it. They can also be built by building the outer nesting structure first, and then mapping ρ constructors inside. In fact, any combination of these two strategies can be applied.

Catamorphisms on nested array types are arrows

$$(p_1, p_2) : A\square\square \to P$$

with $p_1 : A\square \to P$ and $p_2 : \mathsf{N} \times P \to P$. The arrow p_1 may itself be an abstract array catamorphism, and so could be written as

$$p_1 = (q_1, q_2)$$

When this happens we get the following level-factorisation theorem for nested array types.

Theorem 12.16 Given $q_1 : A \to P$, $q_2 : \mathsf{N} \times P \to P$, and $p_2 : \mathsf{N} \times P \to P$, with $p_1 = (q_1, q_2)$,

$$(p_1, p_2) = p_2/ \cdot (q_2/ \cdot q_1\square)\square$$

We next introduce the ideas of internal and external operations on nested arrays. These generalise axis-wise operations.

Definition 12.17 (*Internal Map*) Given an $f : A \to B$ the internal map is the catamorphism

$$f\square\square = ((\sigma_{B\square} \cdot f\square), \rho_{B\square})$$

Example 12.18

$$f\square\square([e'_d, \ldots, e'_1]([e_d, \ldots, e_1], x))$$
$$= e'_d\rho \cdot \ldots \cdot e'_1\rho \cdot (\sigma \cdot f\square)([e_d, \ldots, e_1], x)$$
$$= e'_d\rho \cdot \ldots e'_1\rho \cdot \sigma(e_d\rho \cdot \ldots \cdot e_1\rho \cdot \sigma \cdot f\ x)$$

The internal map applies a function f to the contents of a nested box without disturbing the structure of the box at either level.

Definition 12.19 (*External Map*) Given an $f : A\square \to B$ the external map is the catamorphism

$$f\square = ((\sigma_B \cdot f), \rho_B)$$

Example 12.20

$$f\Box([e'_d,\ldots,e'_1]([e_d,\ldots,e_1],x))$$
$$= e'_d\rho\cdot\ldots e'_1\rho\cdot\sigma\cdot f([e_d,\ldots,e_1],x)$$

The external map leaves the outer structure of the nested array unchanged but applies f to each inner array.

Definition 12.21 *(Internal Reduction)* Given a $g : \mathbb{N} \times B \to B$ the *internal reduction* is the catamorphism

$$g/\Box = (\!(\sigma_B \cdot g), \rho_B)\!)$$

Example 12.22

$$g/\Box([e'_d,\ldots,e'_1]([e_d,\ldots,e_1],x))$$
$$= e'_d\rho\cdot\ldots e'_1\rho\cdot\sigma\cdot g/([e_d,\ldots,e_1],x)$$
$$= e'_d\rho\cdot\ldots e'_1\rho\cdot\sigma\cdot e_dg\cdot\ldots\cdot e_1g\cdot id\ x$$

An internal reduction applies a reduction to the inner array of a nested structure, leaving the outer structure unchanged.

Definition 12.23 *(External Reduction)* Given an $g : \mathbb{N} \times B\Box \to B\Box$ the *external reduction* is the catamorphism

$$g/ = (\!(id, g)\!)$$

Example 12.24

$$g/([e'_d,\ldots,e'_1]([e_d,\ldots,e_1],x))$$
$$= e'_dg\cdot\ldots e'_1g\cdot id([e_d,\ldots,e_1],x)$$

The external reduction applies the reduction to the outer structure of the array, that is it is the "ordinary" reduction.

A nested array can be flattened into a flat array using $\rho/$ which removes a layer of nesting, concatenates the outer and inner shapes and leaves the content unchanged.

Example 12.25

$$\rho/\Box([e'_d,\ldots,e'_1]([e_d,\ldots,e_1],x))$$
$$= e'_d\rho\cdot\ldots e'_1\rho\cdot e_d\rho\cdot\ldots\cdot e_1\rho\cdot id\ x$$

The flattening operation plays the same kind of role as $+\!\!+/$ in the theory of lists.

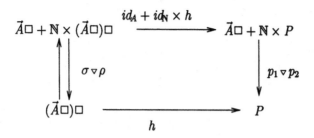

Figure 12.3: A Nested Array Catamorphism

Theorem 12.26 If $f = (\!|\ p_1, p_2\ |\!) : A\square \rightarrow B\square$ is an $A\dagger^\square$ catamorphism then

$$f \cdot \rho_{A\square}/ = (\!|\ f, p_2\ |\!)$$

Proof

$$
\begin{aligned}
&\quad f \cdot \rho/ \left([e'_d, \ldots, e'_1]([e_d, \ldots, e_1], x)\right) \\
&= (\!|\ p_1, p_2\ |\!)(e'_d\rho \cdot \ldots e'_1\rho \cdot e_d\rho \cdot \ldots \cdot e_1\rho \cdot x) \\
&= e'_d p_2 \cdot \ldots e'_1 p_2 \cdot e_d p_2 \cdot \ldots \cdot e_1 p_2 \cdot p_1 x \\
&= e'_d p_2 \cdot \ldots e'_1 p_2 \cdot (\!|\ p_1, p_2\ |\!)([e_d, \ldots, e_1], x) \\
&= (\!|\ f, p_2\ |\!)([e'_d, \ldots, e'_1]([e_d, \ldots, e_1], x))
\end{aligned}
$$

$\square$

12.6 Evaluation of Nested Array Catamorphisms

The general form of a catamorphism on a nested array is shown in Figure 12.3 where the types of the component functions are

$$
\begin{aligned}
p_1 &: \vec{A}\square \rightarrow P \\
p_2 &: \mathbf{N} \times P \rightarrow P
\end{aligned}
$$

As for flat arrays, opportunities for parallelism do not arise from the recursive schema but from parallelism within the component functions. There will always be opportunities for parallelism in the evaluation of p_1, which will often be a flat array catamorphism.

Chapter 13

Graphs

In this chapter we define the categorical data types of graphs. Graphs are ubiquitous in computation, but they are subtly difficult to work with. This is partly because there are many divergent representations for graphs and it is hard to see past the representations to the essential properties of the data type.

We follow the now familiar strategy of defining constructors and building graphs as the limit of the resulting polynomial functor.

Graphs have a long history as data structures. Several specialised graph languages have been built (see, for example, [69]), but they all manipulate graphs using operations that alter single vertices and edges, rather than the monolithic operations we have been advocating.

An important approach to manipulating graphs is *graph grammars*. Graph grammars [71] are analogues of grammars for formal languages and build graphs by giving a set of production rules. Each left hand side denotes a graph template, while each right hand side denotes a replacement. The application of a rule occurs on a subgraph that matches the left hand side of some rule. The matching subgraph is removed from the graph (really a graph form) and replaced by the right hand side of the rule. Various different conventions are used to add edges connecting the new graph to the rest of the original graph. Graph grammars are primarily used for capturing structural information about the construction and transformation of graphs. They do not directly give rise to computations on graphs.

The only other formal treatment of graphs of which I am aware is the work on *graph types* of Klarlund and Schwartzbach [121].

13.1 Building Graphs

We begin by building connected graphs with nodes from some base type A. Later we show how to extend the construction to produce other kinds of graphs.

Graphs, written $A\diamond$, have three constructors:

$$\circ \; : \; A \to A\diamond$$
$$\circ\!\!-\!\!\circ \; : \; A\diamond \times A\diamond \to A\diamond$$
$$\triangle \; : \; A\diamond \to A\diamond$$

The first constructor, $\circ$, takes a single value of the underlying type and makes it into a vertex. The second constructor, $\circ\!\!-\!\!\circ$, called *connect*, joins two graphs by an edge to makes a new graph. Unlike the simpler types we have considered so far, it is not immediately clear which vertices are used when two subgraphs are connected to make a larger one. We leave this underspecified; there are several ways of capturing this information, and the particular method does not much affect the overall structure of graph algorithms. To indicate which vertices are used both this constructor and the next one are drawn as simple straight lines connecting the two vertices. Their end points distinguish the vertices that are used to join the graphs. In any particular application of the *connect* constructor, the two vertices actually joined are available and can participate in computations. The third constructor, ⌂, called *close*, adds an extra edge to an existing graph to make a new one. Again *close* has two associated vertices, the endpoints of the added edge.

The type functor that disassembles this type into its components is

$$\mathsf{T} = \mathsf{K}_A + \mathsf{I} \times \mathsf{I} + \mathsf{I}$$

which is certainly polynomial. We define the categorical data type of graphs to be its fixed point. From the form of the endofunctor we note that the resulting data type is separable.

T_A-algebras are the codomains of triples of functions

$$
\begin{aligned}
p_1 &: & A \to P \\
p_2 &: & P \times P \to P \\
p_3 &: & P \to P
\end{aligned}
$$

They are algebraic structures whose carrier is computable from A, possessing an associative binary operation, and a related unary operation. Very often, the binary and unary operations are forms of the same operation.

The most natural way to model graphs is with vertices that are simply points, and have no associated values. In this setting, such graphs are based on **0** or **1**. It is often convenient to imagine the nodes as being from other types – for example, node-weighted graphs are modelled by choosing $A = \mathbf{N}$.

The equation arising from the initiality of the graph data type is

$$h \cdot \alpha = (p_1 \triangledown p_2 \triangledown p_3) \cdot \mathsf{T}h$$

for h any catamorphism, or expanding

$$
\begin{aligned}
h \cdot \circ &= p_1 \\
h \cdot \text{o–o} &= p_2 \cdot (h \times h) \\
h \cdot ⌂ &= p_3 \cdot h
\end{aligned}
$$

Graph maps are catamorphisms of the form

$$\text{graph map} = (\!| \circ \cdot p_1, \text{o–o}, ⌂ \,|\!)$$

with $p_1 : A \to B$. Graph reductions are catamorphisms of the form

$$\text{graph reduction} = (\!| \; id, p_2, p_3 \; |\!)$$

Because the type is separable, all catamorphisms factor into the composition of a graph map followed by a graph reduction.

We now show some simple examples of graph catamorphisms.

Example 13.1

$$\text{number of vertices} = (\!| \; K_1, +, id \; |\!)$$

To compute the number of vertices in a graph, replace each vertex by the constant 1, add the contents of vertices together whenever a $\circ\!\!-\!\!\circ$ constructor was used to build the graph, and do nothing whenever a $\triangle$ constructor was used.

Example 13.2

$$\text{number of edges} = (\!| \; K_0, p_2, p_3 \; |\!)$$

where

$$
\begin{aligned}
p_2(x, y) &= x + y + 1 \\
p_3(x) &= x + 1
\end{aligned}
$$

Example 13.3 A more complicated example is the catamorphism that replaces each node by an integer representing the number of neighbours it has in the graph. We begin by looking at this problem for lists. The list catamorphism that replaces each list element by the number of neighbours it has is

$$(\!| \; K_0, K_0, \otimes \; |\!)$$

where $\otimes$ is defined by

$$(xs \mathbin{+\!\!+} a) \otimes (b \mathbin{+\!\!+} ys) = xs \mathbin{+\!\!+} (a + 1) \mathbin{+\!\!+} (b + 1) \mathbin{+\!\!+} ys$$

For graphs the catamorphism that replaces each node by the number of its neighbours is similar. It is the catamorphism

$$\text{number of neigbours} = (\!| \; K_0, \circ\!\!-\!\!\circ \cdot p_2, \triangle \cdot p_3 \; |\!)$$

where

$$
\begin{aligned}
p_2(x, y) &= (x_{a \leftarrow a+1}, y_{b \leftarrow b+1}) \\
p_3(x) &= x_{a, b \leftarrow a+1, b+1}
\end{aligned}
$$

where a and b are the vertices joined by the constructors in each case. The result of this catamorphism is a graph with integer nodes, structured in exactly the same way as the argument graph.

Example 13.4 The catamorphism that computes the spanning tree of a graph recapitulates

```
eval_catamorphism(p1, p2, p3, g)
case g of
     ∘ a : return p1( a )
     ∘–∘ (g1, g2) : return p2 ( eval_catamorphism(p1, p2, p3, g1 ),
                                 eval_catamorphism(p1, p2, p3, g2 ))
     ⟁ (g1) : return p3 ( eval_catamorphism(p1, p2, p3, g1 ))
end
```

Figure 13.1: Evaluating a Graph Catamorphism

its construction except that no ⟁ constructors are used. It is

$$\text{spanning tree} \ = \ (\!| \ \circ, \circ\!\!-\!\!\circ, id \ |\!)$$

Catamorphisms in which the third component function is the identity are an interesting special case. Because the ⟁ constructors play no role in evaluating such catamorphisms, the ∘–∘ constructors can often be regarded as associative, which can permit more efficient implementations by dividing the graph into approximately equal-sized pieces on recursive steps.

13.2   Evaluation of Graph Catamorphisms

The CDT of graphs, unlike arrays, in one in which parallelism arises because of the recursive structure of the type definition. So the approaches outlined in earlier chapters can be used to implement graph catamorphisms.

The recursive schema for evaluating graph catamorphisms is shown in Figure 13.1. Using this schema allows the evaluation of catamorphisms whose component functions are constant time in parallel time proportional to the diameter of the graph (assuming the EREW PRAM model).

The difficult, and unsolved problem, is to implement graph catamorphisms in a way that does not depend on the topology of the graph argument. Mapping an arbitrary graph to a given machine's topology will not be possible without some dilation, that is without some edge of the graph being mapped to a long path in the topology. We have seen two strategies for doing this so far. For lists, mapping can be done so that no non-local communication is required. For trees this is not possible, since the communication requirements during tree contraction are not neatly predictable; however, a mapping so that no communication action that may arise requires traversing many links is possible. It is not known whether this second strategy can be made to work for graphs or indeed what restrictions on graphs or target topologies might make it easier.

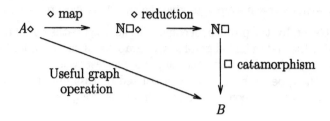

Figure 13.2: A Graph Catamorphism Using an Array Catamorphism

13.3 More Complex Catamorphisms

Many algorithms on graphs work efficiently on some representation of the graph in terms of a data structure. For example, the connectivity matrix is often used as a concrete representation of a graph. In this section we explore the catamorphisms that result from the following three-stage computation structure:

1. Use a graph map to replace each vertex of a graph by the appropriate trivial data structure for a single vertex;

2. Use a graph reduction to compute a single data structure for the whole graph (this often involves a data structure operation that is itself a *data structure catamorphism* and contains further opportunities for parallelism);

3. Use a *data structure catamorphism* to compute a property of the whole graph represented as a data structure.

This is shown in Figure 13.2 using an adjacency matrix array as the data structure.

Example 13.5 The simplest catamorphism of this kind is the one that computes the adjacency matrix of a graph. Only the first two steps are required. The map step maps each node to a 1-by-1 adjacency matrix. The reduction step then joins adjacency matrices to make larger ones, adding all-zero matrices in the off-diagonal positions, except for the two vertices that are actually joined. The result of the reduction is a single matrix for the whole graph.

The catamorphism is from a T_1-algebra to a $T_{N\square}$-algebra with

$$
\begin{aligned}
p_1(a) &= ([1,1], <1,\ldots>) \\
p_2(x,y) &= ([m+n, m+n], <x_0,\ldots>) \\
&\quad \text{where } x = ([m,m], <\ldots>), y = ([n,n], <\ldots>) \\
p_3(x) &= ([m,m], <x_0,\ldots>) \text{ with added 1s}
\end{aligned}
$$

Of course, implementing this catamorphism directly is expensive because not all of the information in the adjacency matrix is actually needed – we only need the upper triangle. In general, there is a trade-off between clarity of expression and efficiency.

Example 13.6 The adjacency matrix catamorphism can be extended by an array catamorphism, reduction with matrix multiply, to give the transitive closure catamorphism.

Example 13.7 Generally, the problem of computing shortest paths for all pairs of vertices is associated with directed and weighted graphs. Our graph construction allows only undirected and equal-weighted graphs. We build the all-pairs shortest-path computation as a graph catamorphism for the type we have so far constructed by assuming unit weights for edges. Later we show how to alter the construction to allow other weights on edges; little alteration is required.

We are required to find, for every pair of nodes v_i and v_j in G, the shortest path from v_i to v_j. The length of the path or cycle is the sum of the weights of the edges forming it. Formally, the all-pairs shortest paths problem in terms of weight matrices is stated as follows: An n-node graph G is given by an $n \times n$ weight matrix W; construct an $n \times n$ matrix D such that d_{ij} is the length of the shortest path from v_i to v_j in G for all i and j. We assume that the graph has no cycles of negative length.

The graph catamorphism has to be altered slightly so that it produces a weight matrix instead of a connectivity matrix. The difference is that nodes v_i and v_j that are not connected by an edge, have an entry 0 in a connectivity matrix but an entry ∞ in a weight matrix. The only change is in the working of the function p_2. Instead of adding two zero-filled matrices, we add matrices filled with ∞s.

The final stage is (array) reduction with matrix multiply, $MM(+, \downarrow)$. Therefore, all-pairs shortest paths is given by:

$$shortest\_paths(x) = MM(+\downarrow)/ \cdot (\!| \, p_1, p_2, p_3 \, |\!)$$

with p_1, p_2, and p_3 as above.

13.4   Construction of Other Graphs

In this section, we consider the construction of two other types of graphs: graphs with connected components and graphs with weights on edges or nodes. For constructing graphs with connected components, we need to introduce a new constructor. This constructor is like a $\circ\!\!-\!\!\circ$ constructor that takes two graphs and does not add any edge. In other words, this constructor, $\circ\!\!-\!\!\circ'$ is set union of graphs.

$$\circ\!\!-\!\!\circ' \equiv \cup : A\diamond \times A\diamond \rightarrow A\diamond$$

For example, $(\circ a) \circ\!\!-\!\!\circ' (\circ b)$ is a graph with two nodes and without any edges.

There are two kinds of weighted graphs: graphs with weights on nodes, and graphs with weights on edges. The construction of node-weighted graphs is trivial. The graph type with weights on nodes is nothing but an $N\diamond$ type which we have already considered. Therefore, these graphs have the same property as the general $A\diamond$ graphs.

We can construct edge-weighted graphs in two different ways. One of the ways is to redefine the $\circ\!\!-\!\!\circ$ and $\triangle\!\!\diamond$ constructors:

$$\circ\!\!-\!\!\circ'_A : \ A\diamond' \times A\diamond' \times N \ \rightarrow A\diamond'$$

$$\diamondsuit'_A : \qquad A\diamond' \times N \qquad \rightarrow A\diamond'$$

The disadvantage of using new constructors is that the whole algebra has to be modified to accommodate this change. This is acceptable because intuitively the type of edge-weighted graphs is different from unweighted graphs.

Using these constructors, a map operation from $A\diamond'$ to connectivity matrices is a catamorphism $(\!| \; p'_1, p'_2, p'_3 \; |\!) : (T'_A A\diamond', A\diamond') \rightarrow (T'_A N\square, N\square)$. The function p'_1 is the same as function p_1 because the $\circ$ constructor has not changed. The function p'_2 is now an arrow $N\square \times N\square \times N \rightarrow N\square$. It behaves in the same fashion as p_2 but when it finally updates the matrix, it uses the edge weight instead of 1. For example,

$$p'_2(a, b, n) = Merge4matrices(a, b, c, d); update(n)$$

where $a, b \in N\square$ and $n \in N$ and $c, d \in N\square$ are zero matrices. Similarly, the p'_3 function updates the matrix with the value n instead of 1.

Therefore a map from $A\diamond'$ to $N\square$ is the catamorphism $(\!| \; p'_1, p'_2, p'_3 \; |\!)$ of the type $A\diamond'$. The other part of the computation, that is proving that the operation is an array catamorphism, remains unchanged.

For the construction of directed graphs, we change the constructors and their properties. The $\circ\!\!-\!\!\circ$ constructor remains the same but it is no longer commutative so $x \circ\!\!-\!\!\circ y$ is not the same as $y \circ\!\!-\!\!\circ x$. This provides a direction to the $\circ\!\!-\!\!\circ$-edges. The $\diamondsuit$ constructor is also not commutative, i.e. $x\diamondsuit y$ is not the same as $y\diamondsuit x$. Similarly, we can generalise the construction to weighted directed graphs.

13.5   Molecules

The construction of graphs can also be extended to construct chemical molecules, written $Mol(A)$. The constructors need to be altered slightly. They become:

$$
\begin{array}{rcl}
\circ & : & A \rightarrow Mol(A) \\
\circ\!\!-\!\!\circ & : & Mol(A) \times Mol(A) \times \mathbb{R}^6 \rightarrow Mol(A) \\
\diamondsuit & : & Mol(A) \times \mathbb{R}^6 \rightarrow Mol(A)
\end{array}
$$

We suppose that there is a type A of atoms, on which suitable functions are defined. For example, there should be a function

$$atomic\ weight : A \rightarrow N$$

The first constructor simply takes an atom and makes it into a molecule. The second constructor joins two molecules together to make a larger one. Its third argument allows the direction of the bond to be specified as a vector. This constructor now imposes a direction on the link it creates because there must be some convention about how to interpret the vector, but it is only a convention because of the ease with which the direction of the bond can be reversed. The third constructor describes the addition of a new bond to an existing molecule.

The type described by these constructors is actually a kind of proto-molecule because the constructors do not impose constraints preventing different atoms from occupying the same physical location. This is not as bad as it seems – there are situations in which it is useful to be able to construct such proto-molecules (for example, determining minimum energy configurations of large molecules using simulated annealing, where many of the intermediate forms may not correspond to real molecules; or modelling molecules in which the bond structure does not translate neatly into covalent bonds between individual atoms). Checking whether or not a constructed object represents a genuine molecule can be expressed as a catamorphism.

Algebras for these molecules have operations:

$$
\begin{aligned}
p_1 &: A \rightarrow P \\
p_2 &: P \times P \times \mathbb{R}^6 \rightarrow P \\
p_3 &: P \times \mathbb{R}^6 \rightarrow P
\end{aligned}
$$

that is they are properties that depend on the graph structure and also on the orientation of pieces of the structure.

An obvious catamorphism computes the molecular weight of a molecule. It depends on mapping the atomic weight function we hypothesised earlier, and then reducing the resulting atomic weights additively. Note that the molecule type is separable. Thus we have

$$
\text{molecular weight} \;=\; (\!|\, id, +, id \,|\!) \cdot (\!|\, aw, id, id \,|\!)
$$

where aw is the atomic weight function. This catamorphism first replaces each atom in a molecule by a natural number representing its atomic weight. This graph structure is then reduced by adding up the atomic weights. This particular catamorphism depends only on the graph structure of molecules and could have been expressed as a graph catamorphism. However, interesting catamorphisms that use the physical structure of the molecule include:

- determining the volume occupied by a molecule (which depends on the size of the atoms it contains, but also on their relative positions);

- determining the convex hull of a molecule (which extends the volume catamorphism to record the shape of the enclosing volume);

- determining the energy of a molecule (which depends on the atoms at the end of each bond, its orientation, and its length, all of which can be computed by a catamorphism).

Chapter 14

Conclusions

The central theme of this book is that the structure of a computation on a data type reflects the structure of the data type. This is true in two senses:

- Any homomorphism on a data type is intimately related to the algebraic structure of its codomain; which can be exploited in the search for programs, and

- The evaluation of any homomorphism can follow the structure of its argument; which can be exploited in computing programs.

Structured data types and the homomorphisms on them, called catamorphisms, form a programming model for parallel computation that has many attractive properties.

There is a desperate need for a model of parallel computation that can decouple software from hardware. This decoupling occurs in two dimensions: decoupling the rate of change of parallel hardware (high) from that of parallel software (low, if it is to be economic); and decoupling the variety of parallel hardware from a single, architecture-independent version of the software.

Such a model is hard to find because the requirements are mutually in tension. A model must be opaque enough to hide target architectures and the complexity of parallel execution, while providing a semantic framework that is rich enough to allow software development. At the same time, it must be partly translucent so that the costs of programs can be visible during development, to allow intelligent choices between algorithms. Finally, it must be concrete enough to permit efficient implementation across a wide range of target architectures, and must allow for variable granularity of its basic units of computation. Finding the best balance between these conflicting requirements is a difficult task, but it is one that is crucially important to the development of general-purpose parallelism.

The categorical data type approach satisfies these requirements fairly well. Restricting programs to compositions of catamorphisms creates an abstraction that is single-threaded, hiding much of the complexity required to compute catamorphisms, architecture-independent, and in which programs can be developed by equational transformation. At the same time, a single recursive schema can be used to compute all catamorphisms on a type, providing a starting point for implementation. In common with skeleton-based approaches, the computation and communication requirements of catamorphisms are known when the type is built. Thus their potential for efficient implementation can be determined by checking how much communication they do, and particular static schedules for computing them can be determined by an implementer, independent of any application.

Categorical data types are not a perfect model for parallel computation. No doubt even better approaches will be developed. However, they are a very powerful technique, and they provide a starting place for thinking about massive parallelism for general-purpose applications.

More work needs to be done on integrating different data type constructions into a single framework and integrating CDTs with higher-level specification techniques. The other missing element is a framework for exploring implementations with the same level of formality as we use for exploring homomorphisms. Such frameworks exist only within limited environments, for example systolic arrays implemented on synchronous mesh architectures, but they need to be developed for richer computation styles.

Appendix A ——————————————————

C++ Library for Lists

```
//************************************************************************
****
//Name: eval_cat.hpp
//************************************************************************
****

template <class ANY_TYPE>

class evaluate_catamorphism: public monoid_sum<ANY_TYPE> {

ANY_TYPE init1, init2;
ANY_TYPE element_value;


public:

evaluate_catamorphism(ANY_TYPE X, ANY_TYPE Y);
ANY_TYPE eval_cat(evaluate_catamorphism &objA);
};


//************************************************************************
// Name: evaluate_catamorphism (constructor)
// Description:
// This constructor function initialises the local variables, as well as
// passing the initialisation parameters to its parent class monoid_sum.
//************************************************************************

template <class ANY_TYPE>

void evaluate_catamorphism<ANY_TYPE>::

evaluate_catamorphism(ANY_TYPE X, ANY_TYPE Y):monoid_sum<ANY_TYPE> (X,Y)
{
  // The following variables are required in eval_cat() to initialise the
```

```
   // types of list objects created at run-time.

    init1 = X;
    init2 = Y;
}


//****************************************************************************
// Name: eval_cat
// Description:
// This function evaluates catamorphisms.  It
// determines the size of the list, and calls the monoid functions
// accordingly.  It performs the following steps:
// 1 - If the list is an empty one, then call the f1() function.
// 2 - Else if the list is a singleton, then call the f2() function.
// 3 - Else the list is a long list, perform the following:
//       a - Create two new list structures; list1, and list2.
//       b - Call the split_in_two function to divide the list.
//       c - Recursively call the eval_cat function.
//       d - Free the memory allocated for each of the new list structures.
//       e - Call the f3 function of the monoid class.
//****************************************************************************
template <class ANY_TYPE>

ANY_TYPE evaluate_catamorphism<ANY_TYPE>::

eval_cat(evaluate_catamorphism<ANY_TYPE> &objA)
{
  ANY_TYPE element_copy;
  ANY_TYPE element_value1, element_value2;

  // Determine the size of the list, and call the monoid functions accordingly
  if (objA.Head->number_of_elements == 0)
      {
       return (f1());
      }
  else if (objA.Head->number_of_elements == 1)
      {
       return (f2(objA));
      }
  else
      {
// Create two list store objects to store the new split lists.

evaluate_catamorphism *list1 = new evaluate_catamorphism(init1,init2);
evaluate_catamorphism *list2 = new evaluate_catamorphism(init1,init2);
```

```
split_in_two(list1, list2, objA);

element_value1 = eval_cat(*list1);
delete list1;


element_value2 = eval_cat(*list2);
delete list2;

    return (f3(element_value1, element_value2));
    }
}
```

Appendix B

Historical Background

Chapter 2 covers desirable model properties and shows how categorical data types satisfy these properties. I developed this view of model properties during 1992 (an early survey of models using them appeared as [179]) and extended and refined it over the next two years. A preliminary version of Chapter 4 was given as a talk at the Workshop on Programming Tools for Parallel Machines at Alimini, Italy, in the summer of 1993.

Chapter 3 is based on Valiant's work which can be found in a series of papers [197, 199, 200]. The results on emulation on SIMD architectures appears in [178], although they seem to have been widely understood before that.

The construction of lists as a categorical data type in Chapter 5 follows the general presentation in Grant Malcolm's thesis [138]. An alternative presentation that emphasises the role of adjunctions in the CDT construction is due to Mike Spivey [189]. Much of the category theory on which this work depends was done in the Sixties [25]. The demonstration that lists can be efficiently implemented comes from [178].

The material on software development in Chapter 6 is a selection from a much larger range of material developed in what has become known as the Bird–Meertens formalism [17, 31–35]. The material on almost-homomorphisms (and the name) come from work by Murray Cole [55].

The development of operations to compute recurrences (Chapter 7) and the cost calculus for lists (Chapter 8) is joint work by myself and Wentong Cai during 1992, when he was a postdoctoral fellow. The material on Compound List Operations was developed by my postdoctoral fellow K.G. Kumar in 1992–93.

The general development of categorical data types described in Chapter 9 again follows the presentation of Malcolm's thesis [138], with some material from Fokkinga's thesis [78]. The presentation tries to make the technique clear even to those who are not deeply familiar with category theory. I was assisted in organising this material by thesis work of my student Colin Banger.

The development of the categorical data type of trees in Chapter 11 follows Jeremy Gibbons' thesis [83]. The extension of the standard tree contraction algorithm to handle accumulations is joint work by myself, Jeremy Gibbons, and Wentong Cai. The examples of the application of tree accumulations to structured text came from discussions with Ian Macleod and Brent Nordin.

The development of the categorical data type of arrays in Chapter 12 generally follows Colin Banger's thesis [23], although with some changes in terminology.

The development of the categorical data type of graphs in Chapter 13 is based on the Master's thesis of my student, Pawan Singh [175].

References

[1] K. Abrahamson, N. Dadoun, D.G. Kirkpatrick, and T. Przytycka. A simple parallel tree contraction algorithm. In *Proceedings of the Twenty-Fifth Allerton Conference on Communication, Control and Computing*, pages 624–633, September 1987.

[2] A. Aggarwal, A.K. Chandra, and M. Snir. Communication complexity of PRAMs. *Theoretical Computer Science*, 71:3–28, 1990.

[3] A. Aggarwal and M.-D. A. Huang. Network complexity of sorting and graph problems and simulating CRCW PRAMs by interconnection networks. In *VLSI Algorithms and Architectures*, Springer Lecture Notes in Computer Science 319, pages 339–350, June 1988.

[4] G. Agha. *Actors: A Model of Concurrent Computation in Distributed Systems*. MIT Press, 1986.

[5] G. Agha and C.J. Callsen. ActorSpace: An open distributed programming paradigm. In *Proceedings of the Fourth ACM SIGPLAN Symposium on Principles and Practice of Parallel Programming*, pages 23–32, May 1993.

[6] S. Ahuja, N. Carriero, D. Gelernter, and V. Krishnaswamy. Matching languages and hardware for parallel computation in the Linda machine. *IEEE Transactions on Computers*, 37, No.8:921–929, August 1988.

[7] M. Ajtai, J. Komlos, and E. Szemeredi. An $O(n \log n)$ sorting network. *Combinatorica*, 3:1–19, 1983.

[8] B. Alpern. Modelling parallel computations as memory hierarchies. In *Programming Models for Massively Parallel Computers*, pages 116–123, Berlin, September 1993. IEEE CS Press.

[9] F. André, O. Chéron, and J.-L. Pazat. Compiling sequential programs for distributed memory parallel computers with Pandore II. Preprint, May 1992.

[10] G.R. Andrews and R.A. Olsson. *The SR Programming Language*. Benjamin/Cummings, 1993.

[11] G.R. Andrews, R.A. Olsson, M.A. Coffin, I. Elshoff, K. Nilsen, T. Purdin, and G. Townsend. An overview of the SR language and implementation. *ACM Transactions on Programming Languages and Systems*, 10(1):51–86, January 1988.

[12] Arvind, R.S. Nikhil, and K.K. Pingali. I-structures: Data structures for parallel computing. *ACM Transactions on Programming Languages and Systems*, 11(4):598–632, 1989.

[13] R.J.R. Back. A method for refining atomicity in parallel algorithms. In *PARLE89 Parallel Architectures and Languages Europe*, Springer Lecture Notes in Computer Science 366, pages 199–216, June 1989.

[14] R.J.R. Back. Refinement calculus part II: Parallel and reactive programs. Technical Report 93, Åbo Akademi, Departments of Computer Science and Mathematics, SF-20500 Åbo, Finland, 1989.

[15] R.J.R. Back and K. Sere. Stepwise refinement of action systems. In *Mathematics of Program Construction*, Springer Lecture Notes in Computer Science 375, pages 115–138, June 1989.

[16] R.J.R. Back and K. Sere. Deriving an Occam implementation of action systems. Technical Report 99, Åbo Akademi, Departments of Computer Science and Mathematics, SF-20500 Åbo, Finland, 1990.

[17] R. Backhouse. An exploration of the Bird-Meertens Formalism. In *Proceedings of the International Summer School on Constructive Algorithmics*, Hollum, Ameland, The Netherlands, September 1989.

[18] J. Backus, J.H. Williams, E.L. Wimmers, P. Lucas, and A. Aiken. FL language manual, parts 1 and 2. Technical Report RJ7100, IBM Almaden Research Center, October 1989.

[19] F. Baiardi, M. Danelutto, M. Jazayeri, S. Pelagatti, and M. Vanneschi. Architectural models and design methodologies for general-purpose highly-parallel computers. In *IEEE CompEuro 91 – Advanced Computer Technology, Reliable Systems and Applications*, May 1991.

[20] H.E. Bal, J.G. Steiner, and A.S. Tanenbaum. Programming languages for distributed computing systems. *Computing Surveys*, 21(3):261–322, September 1989.

[21] H.E. Bal, A.S. Tanenbaum, and M.F. Kaashoek. Orca: A language for distributed processing. *SIGPLAN Notices*, 25(5):17–24, May 1990.

[22] J.P. Banâtre and D. Le Métayer. Introduction to Gamma. In J.P. Banâtre and D. Le Métayer, editors, *Research Directions in High-Level Parallel Programming Languages*, pages 197–202. Springer Lecture Notes in Computer Science 574, June 1991.

[23] C.R. Banger. *Construction of Multidimensional Arrays as Categorical Data Types*. PhD thesis, Queen's University, Kingston, Canada, 1994.

[24] D.T. Barnard, J.P. Schmeiser, and D.B. Skillicorn. Deriving associative operators for language recognition. *Bulletin of the EATCS*, 43:131–139, February 1991.

[25] M. Barr and C. Wells. *Toposes, Triples and Theories*. Grundlehren der mathematischen Wissenschaften 278. Springer-Verlag, 1984.

[26] K.E. Batcher. Sorting networks and their applications. In *Proc. of AFIPS Spring Joint Conf.*, volume 32, pages 307–314, 1968.

[27] F. Baude. *Utilisation du Paradigme Acteur pour le Calcul Parallèle*. PhD thesis, Université de Paris-Sud, 1991.

[28] F. Baude and G. Vidal-Naquet. Actors as a parallel programming model. In *Proceedings of 8th Symposium on Theoretical Aspects of Computer Science*. Springer Lecture Notes in Computer Science 480, 1991.

[29] A. Beguelin, J. Dongarra, A. Geist, R. Manchek, K. Moore, and V. Sunderam. PVM and HeNCE: Tools for heterogeneous network computing. In J.S. Kowalik and L. Grandinetti, editors, *Software for Parallel Computation*, volume 106 of *NATO ASI Series F*, pages 91–99. Springer-Verlag, 1993.

[30] A. Beguelin, J.J. Dongarra, G.A. Geist, R. Manchek, and V.S. Sunderam. PVM software system and documentation. Email to `netlib@ornl.gov`.

[31] R.S. Bird. A calculus of functions for program derivation. Oxford University Programming Research Group Monograph PRG-64, 1987.

[32] R.S. Bird. An introduction to the theory of lists. In M. Broy, editor, *Logic of Programming and Calculi of Discrete Design*, pages 3–42. Springer-Verlag, 1987.

[33] R.S. Bird. Lectures on constructive functional programming. Oxford University Programming Research Group Monograph PRG-69, 1988.

[34] R.S. Bird. Algebraic identities for program calculation. *The Computer Journal*, 32(2):122–126, February 1989.

[35] R.S. Bird, J. Gibbons, and G. Jones. Formal derivation of a pattern matching algorithm. *Science of Computer Programming*, 12:93–104, 1989.

[36] D. Bjørner and C. Jones. *The Vienna Development Method*. Springer Lecture Notes in Computer Science 61, 1978.

[37] G. Blelloch. Scans as primitive parallel operations. In *Proceedings of the International Conference on Parallel Processing*, pages 355–362, August 1987.

[38] G.E. Blelloch. *Vector Models for Data-Parallel Computing*. MIT Press, 1990.

[39] G.E. Blelloch. NESL: a nested data parallel language. Technical Report CMU-CS-92-103, School of Computer Science, Carnegie-Mellon University, January 1992.

[40] G.E. Blelloch. Programming parallel algorithms. In D.B. Johnson, F. Makedon, and P. Metaxas, editors, *Proceedings of the Dartmouth Institute for Advanced Graduate Study in Parallel Computation Symposium*, pages 11–18, June 1992.

[41] G.E. Blelloch and G.W. Sabot. Compiling collection-oriented languages onto massively-parallel computers. In *Proceedings of the 2nd Symposium on the Frontiers of Massively Parallel Computation*, pages 575–585, 1988.

[42] U. Block, F. Ferstl, and W. Gentzsch. Software tools for developing and porting parallel programs. In J.S. Kowalik and L. Grandinetti, editors, *Software for Parallel Computation*, volume 106 of *NATO ASI Series F*, pages 62–75. Springer-Verlag, 1993.

[43] S.H. Bokhari and A.D. Raza. Augmenting computer networks. In *Proceedings of the 1984 International Conference on Parallel Processing*, pages 338–345, August 1984.

[44] R.M. Burstall and J. Darlington. A transformation system for developing recursive programs. *Journal of the ACM*, 24(1):44–67, 1977.

[45] R. Butler and E. Lusk. User's guide to the p4 programming system. Technical Report ANL-92/17, Argonne National Laboratory, Mathematics and Computer Science Division, October 1992.

[46] N. Carriero and D. Gelernter. Learning from our success. In J.S. Kowalik and L. Grandinetti, editors, *Software for Parallel Computation*, volume 106 of *NATO ASI Series F*, pages 37–45. Springer-Verlag, 1993.

[47] Nicholas Carriero. Implementation of tuple space machines. Technical Report YALEU/DCS/RR-567, Dept. of Computer Science, Yale University, December 1987.

[48] Nicholas Carriero and David Gelernter. Application experience with Linda. In *ACM/SIGPLAN Symposium on Parallel Programming*, July 1988.

[49] K. M. Chandy and C. Kesselman. The derivation of compositional programs. In *Proceedings of the Joint International Conference and Symposium on Logic Programming*, pages 3–17. MIT Press, 1992.

[50] K.M. Chandy and J. Misra. *Parallel Program Design: A Foundation*. Addison-Wesley, 1988.

[51] M. Chen, Y.-I. Choo, and J. Li. Crystal: Theory and pragmatics of generating efficient parallel code. In B.K. Szymanski, editor, *Parallel Functional Languages and Compilers*, pages 255–308. ACM Press Frontier Series, 1991.

[52] A. Chin. Latency hiding for fault-tolerant PRAM computations. Technical Report PRG-TR-21-90, Programming Research Group, Oxford University, 1990.

[53] R. Cockett and T. Fukushima. About CHARITY. University of Calgary Preprint, 1991.

[54] M. Cole. *Algorithmic Skeletons: Structured Management of Parallel Computation*. Research Monographs in Parallel and Distributed Computing. Pitman, 1989.

[55] M. Cole. Parallel programming, list homomorphisms and the maximum segment sum problem. In D. Trystram, editor, *Proceedings of Parco 93*. Elsevier Series in Advances in Parallel Computing, 1993.

[56] R. Cole and U. Vishkin. Faster optimal parallel prefix sums and list ranking. *Information and Control*, 81:334–352, 1989.

[57] S. Cox, S.-Y. Huang, P. Kelly, and J. Liu. Program transformations for static process networks. In *Proceeding of a Workshop on Languages, Compilers and Run-Time Enviroments for Distributed Memory Multiprocessors, appeared as SIGPLAN Notices, Vol 28, No. 1, January 1993*, pages 60–63, September 1992.

[58] C. Creveuil. Implementation of Gamma on the Connection Machine. In J.P. Banâtre and D. Le Métayer, editors, *Research Directions in High-Level Parallel Programming Languages*, pages 219–230. Springer Lecture Notes in Computer Science 574, June 1991.

[59] P. Crooks and R.H. Perrott. Language constructs for data partitioning and distribution. Technical report, Department of Computer Science, Queen's University of Belfast, 1993.

[60] D. Culler, R. Karp, D. Patterson, A. Sahay, K.E. Schauser, E. Santos, R. Subramonian, and T. von Eicken. LogP: Toward a realistic model of parallel computation. In *ACM SIGPLAN Symposium on Principles and Practice of Parallel Programming*, May 1993.

[61] W.J. Dally, J.A.S. Fiske, J.S. Keen, R.A. Lethin, M.D. Noakes, P.R. Nuth, R.E. Davison, and G.A. Fyler. The message-driven processor. *IEEE Micro*, pages 23–39, April 1992.

[62] W.J. Dally and D.S. Wills. Universal mechanisms for concurrency. In *PARLE '89, Parallel Architectures and Languages Europe*, pages 19–33. Springer-Verlag Lecture Notes in Computer Science 365, June 1989.

[63] M. Danelutto, R. di Meglio, S. Orlando, S. Pelagatti, and M. Vanneschi. A methodology for the development and the support of massively parallel programs. *Future Generation Computer Systems*, 1992. Also appears as "The P^3L language: an introduction", Hewlett-Packard Report HPL-PSC-91-29, December 1991.

[64] M. Danelutto, R. di Meglio, S. Pelagatti, and M. Vanneschi. High level language constructs for massively parallel computing. Technical report, Hewlett Packard Pisa Science Center, HPL-PSC-90-19, 1990.

[65] M. Danelutto, S. Pelagatti, and M. Vanneschi. High level languages for easy massively parallel computing. Technical report, Hewlett Packard Pisa Science Center, HPL-PSC-91-16, 1991.

[66] J. Darlington, M. Cripps, T. Field, P.G. Harrison, and M.J. Reeve. The design and implementation of ALICE: a parallel graph reduction machine. In S.S. Thakkar, editor, *Selected Reprints on Dataflow and Reduction Architectures*. IEEE Computer Society Press, 1987.

[67] J. Darlington, A.J. Field, P.G. Harrison, P.H.J. Kelly, Q. Wu, and R.L. While. Parallel programming using skeleton functions. In *PARLE93, Parallel Architectures and Languages Europe*, June 1993.

[68] P. de la Torre and C.P. Kruskal. Towards a single model of efficient computation in real parallel machines. In *PARLE91 Parallel Architectures and Languages Europe*. Springer Lecture Notes in Computer Science, June 1991.

[69] N. Deo. *Graph Theory*. Prentice Hall, 1990.

[70] Jack J. Dongarra, Rolf Hempel, Anthony J. G. Hey, and David W. Walker. A proposal for a user-level message-passing interface in a distributed memory environment. Technical Report TM-12231, Oak Ridge National Laboratory, October 1992.

[71] H. Ehrig, H.J. Kreowski, and G. Rozenberg, editors. *Graph Grammars and Their Application to Computer Science*. Lecture Notes in Computer Science 532. Springer-Verlag, 1991.

[72] H. Ehrig and B. Mahr. *Fundamentals of Algebraic Specification I: Equations and Initial Semantics*. EATCS Monographs on Theoretical Computer Science, 1985.

[73] Express system. Available by ftp from `ftp.parasoft.com`.

[74] C. Faigle, W. Furmanski, T. Haupt, J. Niemic, M. Podgorny, and D. Simoni. MOVIE model for open systems based high performance distributed computing. In *IEEE Symposium on High Performance Distributed Computing*, September 1992.

[75] D. Feldcamp and A. Wagner. Parsec: A software development environment for performance oriented parallel programming. In S. Atkins and A. Wagner, editors, *Transputer Research and Applications 6*, pages 247–262, Amsterdam, Oxford, Washington, Tokyo, May 1993. IOS Press.

[76] J. Flower, A. Kolawa, and S. Bharadwaj. The Express way to distributed processing. *Supercomputing Review*, pages 54–55, May 1991.

[77] M.J. Flynn. Very high-speed computers. In *Proceedings of the IEEE*, volume 54, pages 1901–1909, December 1966.

[78] M.M. Fokkinga. *Law and Order in Algorithmics*. PhD thesis, Universiteit Twente, 1992.

[79] I. Foster and S. Tuecke. Parallel programming with PCN. Available by ftp from `info.mcs.anl.gov`, January 1993.

[80] P.H.B. Gardiner. Data refinement of maps. Preprint, August 1990.

[81] P.H.B. Gardiner and C. Morgan. A single complete rule for data refinement. *Formal Aspects of Computing*, 5, No.4:367–382.

[82] Alan Gibbons and Wojciech Rytter. *Efficient Parallel Algorithms*. Cambridge University Press, 1988.

[83] J. Gibbons. *Algebras for Tree Algorithms*. D.Phil. thesis, Programming Research Group, University of Oxford, 1991.

[84] J. Gibbons. Personal Communication, 1992.

[85] J. Gibbons, W. Cai, and D.B. Skillicorn. Efficient parallel algorithms for tree accumulations. *Science of Computer Programming*, to appear.

[86] J. Goguen, S. Leinwand, J. Meseguer, and T. Winkler. The Rewrite Rule Machine 1988. Oxford University Computing Laboratory, Programming Research Group, Technical Monograph PRG-76, 1989.

[87] J.A. Goguen. How to prove algebraic inductive hypotheses without induction with applications to the correctness of data type implementation. In *Proceedings of the 5th Conference on Automated Deduction*, pages 356–373. Springer Lecture Notes in Computer Science 87, July 1992.

[88] J.A. Goguen and T. Winkler. Introducing OBJ3. Technical Report SRI-CSL-88-9, Computer Science Laboratory, SRI International, August 1988.

[89] K.J. Goldman. Paralation views: Abstractions for efficient scientific computing on the Connection Machine. Technical Report MIT/LCS/TM398, M.I.T. Laboratory for Computer Science, 1989.

[90] A. Gottlieb, B. Lubachevsky, and L. Rudolph. Basic techniques for the efficient coordination of large numbers of cooperating sequential processes. *ACM Transactions of Programming Languages and Systems*, 5(2), April 1983.

[91] A.S. Grimshaw. An introduction to parallel object-oriented programming with Mentat. Technical Report 91-07, Computer Science Department, University of Virginia, April 1991.

[92] A.S. Grimshaw. The Mentat computation model: Data-driven support for object-oriented parallel processing. Technical Report 93-30, Computer Science Department, University of Virginia, May 1993.

[93] G. Hains and C. Foisy. The data-parallel categorical abstract machine. In *PARLE93, Parallel Architectures and Languages Europe*, Lecture Notes in Computer Science 694. Springer-Verlag, June 1993.

[94] T.J. Harris and M.I. Cole. The parameterized PRAM. In *International Parallel Processing Symposium*, submitted.

[95] P.J. Hatcher, A.J. LaPadula, R.R. Jones, M.J. Quinn, and R.J. Anderson. A production-quality C⋆ compiler for hypercube multicomputers. In *Third ACM SIGPLAN Symposium on Principles and Practice of Parallel Programming*, pages 73–82, April 1991.

[96] P.J. Hatcher and M.J. Quinn. *Data-Parallel Programming on MIMD Computers*. MIT Press, 1991.

[97] R. Hayes, N.C. Hutchinson, and R.D. Schlichting. Integrating Emerald into a system for mixed-language programming. *Computer Languages*, 15(2):95–108, 1990.

[98] R. Hempel. The ANL/GMD macros (PARMACS) in Fortran for portable parallel programming using the message passing programming model – Users' Guide and Reference Manual. Technical report, GMD, Postfach 1316, D-5205 Sankt Augustin 1, Germany, November 1991.

[99] R. Hempel, H.-C. Hoppe, and A. Supalov. PARMACS-6.0 library interface specification. Technical report, GMD, Postfach 1316, D-5205 Sankt Augustin 1, Germany, December 1992.

[100] J. Herath, T. Yuba, and N. Saito. Dataflow computing. In *Parallel Algorithms and Architectures*, Springer Lecture Notes in Computer Science 269, pages 25–36, May 1987.

[101] T. Heywood and S. Ranka. A practical hierarchical model of parallel computation: Binary tree and FFT graph algorithms. Technical Report SU-CIS-91-07, School of Computer and Information Science, Syracuse University, 1991.

[102] T. Heywood and S. Ranka. A practical hierarchical model of parallel computation: The model. Technical Report SU-CIS-91-06, School of Computer and Information Science, Syracuse University, 1991.

[103] T.H. Heywood. *A Practical Hierarchical Model of Parallel Computation*. PhD thesis, School of Computer and Information Science, Syracuse University, November 1991. Appears as Technical Report SU-CIS-91-39.

[104] High performance Fortran language specification. Available by ftp from `titan.rice.cs.edu`, January 1993.

[105] C.A.R. Hoare. *Communicating Sequential Processes*. Prentice-Hall International Series in Computer Science, 1985.

[106] P. Hudak. Para-functional programming in Haskell. In B.K. Szymanski, editor, *Parallel Functional Languages and Compilers*, pages 159–196. ACM Press Frontier Series, 1991.

[107] P. Hudak and J. Fasel. A gentle introduction to Haskell. *ACM SIGPLAN Notices*, 27, No.5, May 1992.

[108] R. Hummel, R. Kelly, and S. Flynn Hummel. A set-based language for prototyping parallel algorithms. In *Proceedings of the Computer Architecture for Machine Perception '91 Conference*, December 1991.

[109] S. Flynn Hummel and R. Kelly. A rationale for parallel programming with sets. *Journal of Programming Languages*, 1:187–207, 1993.

[110] K. Hwang and F.A. Briggs. *Computer Architecture and Parallel Processing*. McGraw-Hill, 1984.

[111] M.A. Jenkins. *The Q'Nial Reference Manual.* Nial Systems Ltd, Kingston, Ontario, 1985.

[112] J. Jeuring. Derivation of hierarchies of algorithms on matrices. In B. Möller, editor, *Constructing Programs from Specifications,* pages 9–32. North-Holland, 1991.

[113] G. Jones and M. Goldsmith. *Programming in Occam2.* Prentice-Hall, 1988.

[114] E. Jul, N. Levy, and N. Hutchinson. Fine-grained mobility in the Emerald system. *ACM Transactions on Computer Systems,* 6(1):109–133, 1988.

[115] K.M. Kahn and V.A. Saraswat. Actors as a special case of concurrent constraint (logic) programming. In N. Meyrowitz, editor, *OOPSLA/ECOOP 90 Conference on Object-Oriented Programming: Systems, Languages, and Applications,* pages 57–66, October 1990. Appears as SIGPLAN Notices, Vol. 25, No. 10.

[116] R.M. Karp and V. Ramachandran. Parallel algorithms for shared-memory machines. In J. van Leeuwen, editor, *Handbook of Theoretical Computer Science, Vol. A.* Elsevier Science Publishers and MIT Press, 1990.

[117] P. Kelly. *Functional Programming for Loosely-Coupled Multiprocessors.* Pitman, 1989.

[118] M.F. Kilian. Can O-O aid massively parallel programming? In D.B. Johnson, F. Makedon, and P. Metaxas, editors, *Proceedings of the Dartmouth Institute for Advanced Graduate Study in Parallel Computation Symposium,* pages 246–256, June 1992.

[119] M.F. Kilian. *Parallel Sets: An Object-Oriented Methodology for Massively Parallel Programming.* PhD thesis, Harvard University, 1992.

[120] S. King. Z and the Refinement Calculus. In *VDM'90: VDM and Z – Formal Methods in Software Development,* Springer Lecture Notes in Computer Science 428, pages 164–188, April 1990.

[121] Nils Klarlund and Michael Schwartzbach. Graph types. Preprint, 1993.

[122] D.E. Knuth. *Searching and Sorting: The Art of Computer Programming,* volume 3. Addison-Wesley, Reading, MA, 1973.

[123] Peter M. Kogge and Harold S. Stone. A parallel algorithm for the efficient solution of a general class of recurrence equations. *IEEE Transactions on Computers,* C-22(8):786–792, 1973.

[124] C.P. Kruskal, L. Rudolph, and M. Snir. A complexity theory of efficient parallel algorithms. *Theoretical Computer Science,* 71:95–132, 1990.

[125] J.T. Kuruvila. A cost calculus for parallel functional programming with nested lists. Master's thesis, Department of Computing and Information Science, Queen's University, Kingston, Canada, September 1993.

[126] R.E. Ladner and M.J. Fisher. Parallel prefix computation. *Journal of the ACM*, 27(4):831–838, 1980.

[127] J. Lambek and P.J.Scott. *Introduction to Higher Order Categorical Logic*. Cambridge Studies in Advanced Mathematics. Cambridge University Press, Cambridge, 1986.

[128] J.R. Larus, B. Richards, and G. Viswanathan. C**: A large-grain, object-oriented, data-parallel programming language. Technical Report TR1126, University of Wisconsin-Madison, November 1992.

[129] D. le Métayer. Mechanical analysis of program complexity. *Proceedings of the SIG-PLAN '85 Symposium*, pages 69–73, July 1985.

[130] T. Lehr, Z. Segall, D.F. Vrsalovic, E. Caplan, A.L. Chung, and C.E. Fineman. Visualizing performance debugging. *IEEE Computer*, 22, No.10:38–51, October 1989.

[131] C. Lengauer. Loop parallelization in the polytope model. In *CONCUR '93*, Springer Lecture Notes in Computer Science, 1993.

[132] J.M. Levesque. FORGE90 and High Performance Fortran (HPF). In J.S. Kowalik and L. Grandinetti, editors, *Software for Parallel Computation*, volume 106 of *NATO ASI Series F*, pages 111–119. Springer-Verlag, 1993.

[133] Jinke Li and Marina Chen. Compiling communication-efficient programs for massively parallel machines. *IEEE Transactions on Parallel and Distributed Systems*, 2(3):361–376, July 1991.

[134] G. Lobe, P. Lu, S. Melax, I. Parsons, J. Schaeffer, C. Smith, and D. Szafron. The Enterprise model for developing distributed applications. Technical Report 92–20, Department of Computing Science, University of Alberta, November 1992.

[135] W.W.C. Luk. Systematic serialisation of array-based architectures. *Integration, the VLSI Journal*, 14:333–360, 1993.

[136] I.A. Macleod. A query language for retrieving information from hierarchical text structures. *The Computer Journal*, 34, No.3:254–264, 1991.

[137] I.A. Macleod. Path expressions as selectors for non-linear text. Preprint, 1993.

[138] G. Malcolm. *Algebraic Data Types and Program Transformation*. PhD thesis, Rijksuniversiteit Groningen, September 1990.

[139] E.W. Mayr and R. Werchner. Optimal routing of parentheses on the hypercube. In *Proceedings of the Symposium on Parallel Architectures and Algorithms*, June 1993.

[140] W. F. McColl. An architecture independent programming model for scalable parallel computing. In J. Ferrante and A. J. G. Hey, editors, *Portability and Performance for Parallel Processors*. Wiley, 1994. To appear.

[141] W.F. McColl. General purpose parallel computing. In A.M. Gibbons and P. Spirakis, editors, *Lectures on Parallel Computation*, Cambridge International Series on Parallel Computation, pages 337–391. Cambridge University Press, Cambridge, 1993.

[142] W.F. McColl. Bulk synchronous parallel computing. In *Second Workshop on Abstract Models for Parallel Computation*. Oxford University Press, 1994.

[143] J. McGraw, S. Skedzielewski, S. Allan, R. Oldehoeft, J. Glauert, C. Kirkham, B. Noyce, and R. Thomas. Sisal: Streams and iteration in a single assignment language: Reference manual 1.2. Technical Report M-146, Rev.1, Lawrence Livermore National Laboratory, March 1985.

[144] L.G.L.T. Meertens. Algorithmics – towards programming as a mathematical activity. In *Proceedings of CWI Symposium on Mathematics and Computer Science*, pages 289–334. North-Holland, 1986.

[145] K. Mehlhorn and U. Vishkin. Randomized and deterministic simulation of PRAMs by parallel machines with restricted granularity of parallel memories. *Acta Informatica*, 21:339–374, 1984.

[146] J. Meseguer and T. Winkler. Parallel programming in Maude. In J.P. Banâtre and D. Le Métayer, editors, *Research Directions in High-Level Parallel Programming Languages*, pages 253–293. Springer Lecture Notes in Computer Science 574, June 1991.

[147] R. Miller. Personal Communication, 1993.

[148] T. More. The nested rectangular array as a model of data. In *Proceedings of APL 79, APL Quote Quad, 4*, 1979.

[149] T. More. Notes on the diagrams, logic, and operations of array theory. Technical Report G230-2137, IBM Cambridge Scientific Center, 1981.

[150] T. More. On the development of array theory. Technical report, IBM Cambridge Scientific Center, 1986.

[151] L.M.R. Mullin. *A Mathematics of Arrays*. PhD thesis, Syracuse University, December 1988.

[152] L. Mussat. Parallel programming with bags. In J.P. Banâtre and D. Le Métayer, editors, *Research Directions in High-Level Parallel Programming Languages*, pages 203–218. Springer Lecture Notes in Computer Science 574, June 1991.

[153] M.O. Noakes and W.J. Dally. System design of the J-Machine. In *Proceedings of the Sixth MIT Conference on Advanced Research in VLSI*, pages 179–194. MIT Press, 1990.

[154] C. Pancake. Graphical support for parallel debugging. In J.S. Kowalik and L. Grandinetti, editors, *Software for Parallel Computation*, volume 106 of *NATO ASI Series F*, pages 216–230. Springer-Verlag, 1993.

[155] G. Papachrysantou. Higher level forms for parallel computation in solid modelling. M.Sc Project Report, Department of Computing, Imperial College of Science, Technology, and Medicine, London, September 1992.

[156] Ronald Peierls and Graham Campbell. ALMS - programming tools for coupling application codes in a network environment. In *Proceedings of the Heterogeneous Network-Based Concurrent Computing Workshop*, Tallahassee, FL, October 1991. Supercomputing Computations Research Institute, Florida State University. Proceedings available via anonymous ftp from `ftp.scri.fsu.edu` in directory `pub/parallel-workshop.91`.

[157] S.L. Peyton-Jones, C. Clack, and N. Harris. GRIP – a parallel graph reduction machine. Technical report, Department of Computer Science, University of London, 1987.

[158] B.C. Pierce. *A Taste of Category Theory for Computer Scientists*. MIT Press, 1991.

[159] F.P. Preparata and J. Vuillemin. The cube-connected cycles: A versatile network for parallel computation. In *Proceedings of 20th Annual IEEE Symp. on Foundations of Computer Science*, 1979.

[160] M.J. Quinn and P.J. Hatcher. Data-parallel programming on multicomputers. *IEEE Software*, pages 69–76, September 1990.

[161] F.A. Rahbi and G.A. Manson. Experiments with a transputer-based parallel graph reduction machine. *Concurrency Practice and Experience*, to appear.

[162] A.G. Ranade. *Fluent Parallel Computation*. PhD thesis, Yale University, 1989.

[163] P. Roe. Derivation of efficient data parallel programs. Technical report, Queensland University of Technology, December 1993.

[164] G.-C. Roman and K.C. Cox. A declarative approach to visualizing concurrent computations. *IEEE Computer*, 22, No.10:25–36, October 1989.

[165] G.-C. Roman and K.C. Cox. A taxonomy of program visualization systems. *IEEE Computer*, pages 11–25, December 1993.

[166] G.-C. Roman, H.C. Cunningham, and A. Ehlers. A shared dataspace language supporting large-scale concurrency. In *Proceedings of the 8th International Conference on Distributed Computing Systems*, pages 265–272, June 1988.

[167] G. Sabot. *The Paralation Model: Architecture-Independent Parallel Programming*. MIT Press, 1989.

[168] D. Sands. Complexity analysis for a higher-order language. Technical report, Department of Computing, Imperial College, Technical Report 88/14, London, December 1988.

[169] D. Sands. *Calculi for Time Analysis of Functional Programs*. PhD thesis, Imperial College, London, September 1990.

[170] V.A. Saraswat and M. Rinard. Concurrent constraint programming. In *Proceedings of the 17th Symposium on Principles of Programming Languages*, pages 232–245, 1990.

[171] M. Sheeran. μFP, a language for VLSI design. In *Conference Record of the 1984 ACM Symposium on Lisp and Functional Programming*, pages 104–112, August 1984.

[172] M. Sheeran and G. Jones. Relations + higher order functions = hardware descriptions. In *Compeuro 1987*, January 1987.

[173] T.J. Sheffler. *Match and Move, an Approach to Data Parallel Computing*. PhD thesis, Carnegie-Mellon, October 1992. Appears as Report CMU-CS-92-203.

[174] T.J. Sheffler. Writing parallel programs with Match and Move. In *Second Workshop on Abstract Models for Parallel Computation*. Oxford University Press, 1994.

[175] P. Singh. Graphs as a categorical data type. Master's thesis, Computing and Information Science, Queen's University, Kingston, Canada, 1993.

[176] S.K. Skedzielewski. Sisal. In B.K. Szymanski, editor, *Parallel Functional Languages and Compilers*, pages 105–158. ACM Press Frontier Series, 1991.

[177] D.B. Skillicorn. A taxonomy for computer architectures. *IEEE Computer*, 21:46–57, November 1988.

[178] D.B. Skillicorn. Architecture-independent parallel computation. *IEEE Computer*, 23(12):38–51, December 1990.

[179] D.B. Skillicorn. Models for practical parallel computation. *International Journal of Parallel Programming*, 20(2):133–158, April 1991. Actually appeared in 1992.

[180] D.B. Skillicorn. Deriving parallel programs from specifications using cost information. *Science of Computer Programming*, 20, No.3:205–213, June 1993.

[181] D.B. Skillicorn. Categorical data types. In *Second Workshop on Abstract Models for Parallel Computation*, Oxford University Press, 1994.

[182] D.R. Smith. KIDS: A semiautomatic program development system. *IEEE Transactions on Software Engineering*, 16, No.9:1024–1043, September 1990.

[183] D.R. Smith. KIDS – a knowledge-based software development system. In *Automating Software Design*. AAAI Press, 1991.

[184] D.R. Smith. Structure and design of global search algorithms. *Acta Informatica*, to appear.

[185] D.R. Smith and M.R. Lowry. Algorithm theories and design tactics. In *Mathematics of Program Construction*, pages 379–398. Springer-Verlag Lecture Notes in Computer Science 375, June 1989.

[186] M.B. Smyth and G.D. Plotkin. The category-theoretic solution of recursive domain equations. *SIAM Journal of Computing*, 11(4):761–783, 1982.

[187] D. Spencer. *Categorical Programming with Functorial Strength*. PhD thesis, Oregon Graduate Institute of Science and Technology, January 1993.

[188] J.M. Spivey. *Understanding Z: A Specification Language and its Formal Semantics*. Cambridge University Press, 1988.

[189] J.M. Spivey. A categorical approach to the theory of lists. In *Mathematics of Program Construction*, pages 399–408. Springer-Verlag Lecture Notes in Computer Science 375, June 1989.

[190] G.L. Steele Jr. High Performance Fortran: Status report. In *Proceeding of a Workshop on Languages, Compilers and Run-Time Enviroments for Distributed Memory Multiprocessors, appeared as SIGPLAN Notices, Vol 28, No. 1, January 1993*, pages 1–4, September 1992.

[191] D. Szafron, J. Schaeffer, P.S. Wong, E. Chan, P. Lu, and C. Smith. Enterprise: An interactive graphical programming environment for distributed software. Available by ftp from `cs.ualberta.ca`, 1991.

[192] B.K. Szymanski. EPL – parallel programming with recurrent equations. In B.K. Szymanski, editor, *Parallel Functional Languages and Compilers*, pages 51–104. ACM Press Frontier Series, 1991.

[193] P. Thanisch, M.G. Norman, C. Boeres, and S. Pelagatti. Exponential processor requirements for optimal schedules in architectures with locality. In *Proceedings of a Workshop on Bulk Synchronous Parallelism*, London, December 1993.

[194] C.-W. Tseng. *An Optimizing Fortran D Compiler for MIMD Distributed-Memory Machines*. PhD thesis, Rice University, January 1993. Also Rice COMP TR-93-199.

[195] L.H. Turcotte. A survey of software environments for exploiting networked computing resources. Technical report, Mississippi State University, June 1993.

[196] R. Vaidyanathan, C.R.P. Hartmann, and P.K. Varshney. PRAMs with variable memory word-size.

[197] L.G. Valiant. Optimally universal parallel computers. *Phil. Trans. Royal Society Lond. Series A*, 326:373–376, 1988.

[198] L.G. Valiant. Bulk synchronous parallel computers. Technical Report TR-08-89, Computer Science, Harvard University, 1989.

[199] L.G. Valiant. A bridging model for parallel computation. *Communications of the ACM*, 33(8):103–111, August 1990.

[200] L.G. Valiant. General purpose parallel architectures. In J. van Leeuwen, editor, *Handbook of Theoretical Computer Science, Vol. A*. Elsevier Science Publishers and MIT Press, 1990.

[201] D.S. Wills. Pi: A parallel architecture interface for multi-model execution. Technical Report AI-TR-1245, MIT Artificial Intelligence Laboratory, 1990.

[202] Allan Yang and Young-il Choo. Parallel-program transformation using a metalanguage. In *Proceedings of the Third ACM SIGPLAN Symposium on Principles and Practice of Parallel Programming*, 1991.

[203] Allan Yang and Young-il Choo. Formal derivation of an efficient parallel Gauss-Seidel method on a mesh of processors. In *Proceedings of the 6th International Parallel Processing Symposium*. IEEE Computer Society Press, March 1992.

[204] Allan Yang and Young-il Choo. Metalinguistic features for formal parallel-program transformation. In *Proceedings of the 4th IEEE International Conference on Computer Languages*. IEEE Computer Society Press, April 1992.

[205] S. Ericsson Zenith. The axiomatic characterization of Ease. In *Linda-Like Systems and their Implementation*, pages 143–152. Edinburgh Parallel Computing Centre, TR91-13, 1991.

[206] S. Ericsson Zenith. A rationale for programming with Ease. In J.P. Banâtre and D. Le Métayer, editors, *Research Directions in High-Level Parallel Programming Languages*, pages 147–156. Springer Lecture Notes in Computer Science 574, June 1991.

[207] S. Ericsson Zenith. Ease: the model and its implementation. In *Proceeding of a Workshop on Languages, Compilers and Run-Time Enviroments for Distributed Memory Multiprocessors, appeared as SIGPLAN Notices, Vol 28, No. 1, January 1993*, page 87, September 1992.

[208] Steven Ericsson Zenith. Programming with Ease. Centre de Recherche en Informatique, École Nationale Supérieure des Mines de Paris, September 20, 1991.

Index

Abiding arrays, 152
Abstract array map, 155
Abstract array reduction, 156
Abstract arrays, 152
Abstract data types, 11
Abstract machine, 27
Accumulations
    trees, 137
Action systems, 30
Active messages, 36
Actors, 35
ActorSpace, 35
Adjacency matrix, 167
Algorithmic skeletons, 42
All-pairs shortest path, 168
Almost-homomorphisms, 72
ALMS, 33
APL, 151
Arbitrary computation structures, 29
Architecture classes, 6
Architecture independence, 1, 8, 13
    lists, 62
Architecture-specific, 37
Array algebras, 155
Array catamorphism, 155
Array Theory, 44, 151
Arrays, 151
Attribute grammars, 148

Bags, 131
Bifunctor, 118
Bird-Meertens formalism, 59
Bitonic sorting, 85
BSP, 25
Bulk Synchronous Parallelism, 25, 39, 90

C**, 45, 59
Calculational software development, 10
Caliban, 32
Catamorphism, 53, 121, 171

evaluation, 54
Categorical data types, 3, 11, 45, 171
    general construction, 115
Category, 49, 116
Chemical molecules, 169
CLOs, 79
Communication, 9
Commutative idempotent monoids, 133
Composition of costs, 89, 91
Compositional C++, 33
Compound List Operations, 79
Concurrent constraint programming, 34
Concurrent rewriting, 31
Cons lists, 120
Constructors, 115
    arrays, 155
    bags, 131
    finite sets, 133
    general, 119
    graphs, 163
    lists, 51, 129
    trees, 135
Coordination languages, 32
Coproducts, 50, 117
Correctness-preserving transformation, 69
Cost calculus, 69, 89
    lists, 63
Cost measures, 10, 13
Cross-references, 148
Crystal, 45, 65
Cube-connected-cycles, 18

Data refinement, 68
Data reification, 68
Dataflow, 34
Dataflow architectures, 6
Dataparallel C, 44
Debuggers, 7
Decomposition, 9

Derivational software development, 10
Diameter, 17
Dimension collapsing, 64
Directed graphs, 169
Distributed-memory MIMD, 6
   $p \log p$ interconnect, 15, 16, 22
   sparse interconnect, 15, 16, 23
Documentation, 69
Documents
   structural properties, 144
Downwards accumulation, 139, 140, 148,
   149
DPML, 44

Ease, 33
Edge-weighted graphs, 168
Efficiency, 20
Efficiently implementable, 11, 14
   lists, 63
Emerald, 35
Endofunctor, 50, 115
Enterprise, 43
EPL, 36
Express, 38
Extended base category, 153
External map, 159
External reduction, 160

Factorisation, 124, 144
   arrays, 157
   bags, 132
   finite sets, 134
   graphs, 165
   lists, 57, 130
   trees, 136
Fast Fourier Transform, 81
Fault tolerance, 4
FFT, 81
Filter, 60
   on text, 149
Finite sets, 133
Firing rule, 34
Fixed point, 120
Flat arrays, 152, 157
Fortran, 151

Fortran-D, 44
Fortran90, 152
FP, 81
Free bag monoid, 132
Free list monoid, 53, 129
Functor, 50, 117

Gamma, 44, 134
Generalised map, 123
Generalised prefix, 61, 137
Generalised reduction, 124
GL, 40
Granularity, 10, 13
   lists, 63
Graph grammars, 163
Graph reduction, 29
Graph types, 163
Graphical User Interfaces, 7
Graphs, 163
   directed, 169
   edge-weighted, 168
   node-weighted, 168
   with connected components, 168

Haskell, 29, 152
Hierarchical PRAM, 41
High Performance Fortran, 44, 152
Homomorphism, 1, 171
HPF, 44, 152
HPRAM, 41

I-structures, 152
Implementation equation, 97
   inits, 99
   list map, 97
   list reduction, 97
   prefix, 101
   recur-prefix, 105
   recur-reduce, 104
Inefficiency, 21, 24, 25
Initial object, 53
Inits, 98
Injective function, 60
Intellectual abstractness, 9, 13
Interleaving, 30
Internal map, 159

Internal reduction, 160

J-language, 36

KIDS, 43

Level-factorisation, 159
Linda, 32
Linear recurrences, 75
List map, 59, 94
List reduction, 59, 94
List-based arrays, 152
Locality, 26
logP, 40

Map as functor, 58
Map catamorphisms, 57
Mapping, 9
Match and move, 44
Mathematics of Arrays, 44, 151
Maude, 31
Maximum segment sum, 110
Memory hashing, 21
Memory latency, 15
Memory-mapped communication, 7, 33
Mentat, 36, 59
Message Passing Interface, 38
Model of parallel computation, 3, 8, 171
Model properties, 8
Monoid, 53, 130
Movie, 36
MPI, 38
μFP, 81
Multiprefix, 44
Multisets, 131
Multithreaded architectures, 6
Multithreading, 7, 41

NESL, 44
Nested arrays, 153, 158
Nial, 44, 151
Node-weighted graphs, 168

OBJ, 31
Occam, 38
Orca, 37

P^3L, 43
p4, 37
Pandore II, 44
Parafunctional programming, 32
Paralations, 44
Parallel SETL, 44
Parallel sets, 44
Parallel slackness, 22
Parallelising assistants, 7
Parallelism
    benefits, 4
    drawbacks, 5
    state of the art, 6
Parmacs, 38
Parsec, 43
Path catamorphisms, 140
Path expressions, 149
Paths, 140
PCN, 33
Permutations, 79
Pi, 37
Pisa parallel programming language, 43
PMI, 37
Polymorphic construction, 122
Polynomial functor, 51, 117
PRAM, 18
PRAM model, 39, 90
Prefix, 61, 100
    non-constant-space, 102
Process nets, 34
Processing element, 16
Products, 50, 117
Program annotation, 32
Promotion, 122
PVM, 37

Queries on structured text, 149

Recur-prefix, 77, 105
Recur-reduce, 76, 104
Recursive schema, 1, 54, 63, 65
Regular language, 146
    recognition, 147
Relationships between T-algebras, 125
Resequencing function, 154

Restricted computation structure, 39
Reusing derivation, 69
Rose trees, 143
Ruby, 81

Scan, 61
Scan model, 44
Scan vector model, 44
SDL, 33
Separable functor, 125
Separable types, 57
Sequence compaction, 154
Sequence compression, 154
Sequence map, 154
Shape vector, 95
Shared-memory MIMD, 6, 15, 21
SIMD architecture, 15, 18, 24
Single Program, Multiple Data, 6
Sisal, 35, 152
Skeletons, 42
Software development, 1
Software development methodology, 9, 13,
    65, 67
  lists, 62
Software lifetimes, 7
Sorting, 85
SPMD, 6
SR, 37
Standard topology, 62
String search, 146
Structural catamorphism, 156
Structured text, 143
  queries, 149
Synchronisation, 9
Systolic arrays, 45

T-algebra, 52
T-algebras, 115
  arrays, 155
  bags, 132
  finite sets, 133
  general, 118
  graphs, 164
  lists, 52, 129
  trees, 135

T-homomorphism, 118
Transformation assistant, 69
Transformational derivation, 69
Tree contraction, 141, 144
    conditions on, 142
Tree map, 136, 141
Tree reduction, 136, 141
Trees, 135
Tuple space, 7, 32

UNITY, 30
Upwards accumulation, 139, 148

VDM, 67
Visualisation tools, 7
Volume of communication, 25, 28

Work, 19

YPRAM, 41

Z, 67